CHARLES DICKENS
A Biography from New Sources

Charles Dickens
A newly discovered portrait
In the possession of Charles J. Sawyer

CHARLES DICKENS

A Biography
from New Sources

by
RALPH STRAUS

GROSSET & DUNLAP
PUBLISHERS   NEW YORK

Copyright, 1928, by
RALPH STRAUS
All rights reserved including that of translation into foreign languages, including the Scandinavian

Printed in the United States of America

To
ARTHUR WAUGH
An old friend and colleague, who, without resembling Mr. Pickwick in personal appearance so closely as some of his admirers choose to think, shares all that great man's most lovable characteristics

Contents

I	*"A Very Queer Small Boy"*	1
II	*"The Deed"*	16
III	*Search for a Profession, With an Interlude for Romance*	36
IV	*On the Eve of Fame*	72
V	*Pickwick*	93
VI	*A More Serious Note, and Some Quarrels*	122
VII	*Master Humphrey's Clock*	152
VIII	*The First American Visit*	167
IX	*Disappointments*	190
X	*Distractions*	206
XI	*High Tension*	229
XII	*Breaking-Point*	249
XIII	*Professional Reader*	278
XIV	*The Second American Visit*	304
XV	*"From These Garish Lights. . . ."*	323

Illustrations

Charles Dickens
  From a newly discovered portrait   *Frontispiece*

An unpublished letter of Dickens
  mentioning his family troubles   Facing Page   178

The earliest copy of "A Christmas
  Carol"   "   "   200

The first page of an unpublished
  manuscript by Charles Dickens   "   "   264

Charles Dickens reading to his
  daughters   "   "   298

A photograph of Dickens taken in
  1869 and hitherto unpublished   "   "   308

Charles Dickens's Last Reading,
  1870   "   "   320

Dickens and Disraeli, 1870   "   "   334

Introduction

Here, in some sort of outline, is the life, as I see it, of Charles Dickens.

You will be aware of the fact that this is not the first attempt of the kind to be made. There are Lives of Dickens of all sorts and sizes. There are ceremonious giants of Lives and light-hearted midgets of Lives, Lives more or less built up from Dickens's own books, and Lives manufactured to prove some pet theory of the writer. There are Lives written for children and for literary students and even for those harmless and sometimes most useful folk, the book-collectors. As if all these were not enough, Dickens's life has been broken up into small pieces, and Lives have been written about every one of the fragments. Moreover, there are critical books into which biographical matter must be brought; collections of letters; a whole library of "personal recollections"; a bewildering array of explanatory theses which contradict one another in the most cheerful way; and a magazine, now in its twenty-fourth year, which pays quarterly homage in a manner which would probably have delighted (as it would assuredly have astonished) Dickens himself.

Of these Lives one stands out from the rest. "The Life of Charles Dickens" by John Forster has been called all sorts of harsh names, but it is a very great book. Its author, that stubborn and masterful but very loyal old man, has been blamed on various grounds. It is said that he was too fond of writing about John Forster. It is said that he shows you an idealized Dickens.

It is said that he is too ready to rely on the letters addressed to himself. Undoubtedly the work has its faults. It is not always accurate, there are serious omissions in spite of its inordinate length, and not all of Dickens's friends are quite fairly treated. It must be remembered, however, that he wrote his book in circumstances of peculiar difficulty. Dickens had but recently died; his widow and several of his children were alive. It was necessary to be extremely discreet. He *was* discreet, but did not escape criticism on that score.

Nevertheless he wrote a book of absorbing interest, which nobody else could have written, and if you would understand its true greatness you have only to glance at its successors—for the most part the dullest and flattest compilations. Take, for instance, Kitton's "Life," issued at the beginning of the century. Kitton adored Dickens, and his knowledge of his hero was encyclopedic, yet he could do nothing better than sift Forster and the "Letters of Charles Dickens," coolly reprinting whole sentences from these works as his own. This was all the more inexcusable as in his day new facts had come to light, and hundreds of unpublished letters—some very important indeed—must have passed through his hands.

But I fancy that Kitton, like most "loyal Dickensians," was a little afraid of the truth. Ever since the days when "Pickwick" had come to delight half the civilized world, there had been in existence a sort of legend about Dickens. He had come to stand for all that was most solidly respectable in this most solidly respectable country. He had come to be placed apart from the rest of hard-working humanity. And so, everything that tended to show him as an ordinary man with the ordinary man's faults must not be printed. The blue pencil must be applied to every letter which touched upon "private" matters, before it was published.

It was tacitly agreed that Dickens's various domestic worries were of no public importance. For years, indeed, this policy of silence persisted, and I suppose it was natural enough. Besides, there was plenty to be said about his books, which continued to sell in their hundreds of thousands. By consequence you had, in place of new Lives, queer semibiographical works written by men more eager to describe the bed in which Mr. Pickwick was supposed to have slept when he visited Rochester or the "originals" from whom Sam Weller or Skimpole or Mr. Pumblechook had been taken, than to give you the real story of Dickens's life.

Yet at the same time real biographical work was being done—by the book-collectors! For, rather queerly perhaps, Dickens alone among modern "best sellers" began to be "collected." Enormous sums were paid for his first editions. His letters, which in the eighties and nineties could have been bought for a few shillings apiece, became the most valuable property. His presentation copies came to fetch three-figure sums. America in particular took a hand in the business, and began to print letters and papers that had not been blue-penciled in the old way. And so it happens that the man who would attempt a life of Dickens today has at his disposal a mass of new material which, though it may not enable him to give a wholly new Dickens to the world, at least allows him to tell a story rather different from that commonly accepted.

There are incidents in Dickens's life which even now need not be told, and I dare say that I, too, have been rather more discreet than I need have been. This, I hasten to say, does not mean that Dickens himself was ever guilty of any action whatsoever which could not be told in detail today: it means only that in my opinion there should be clearly marked limits in any biographical work. I have read, for instance, a great number of unpublished family letters, from which I have not thought fit to quote. On the other hand I have not hesitated to make use of such information as they contained if it helps in any way to make clearer the character of Dickens himself.

Incidentally, I have little enough to say of his books. Gissing and Chesterton, it seems to me, have said all that it is necessary to say on the matter. And I confess that I care not a straw to know that the Bull and Three Cows at Appleby Minima was the actual inn where somebody in one of the novels once dined. I can find no amusement in the Droodian epilogues. Only where there is a useful autobiographical note to be found do I quote from the books. To me Dickens is far more interesting than any of his characters. It has often been said that a number of these characters were "exaggerated," and perhaps that is the best word to apply to their author. As I have endeavored to show, he lived a sort of "exaggerated" novel himself.

A word more before I make my acknowledgments. In the pages that follow there is nothing to show you when I am quoting from passages that have been printed before and when from unpublished material. A personal, and probably irrational, dislike for the footnote must be my only excuse. Also there are passages in my book, more especially in the earlier chapters, which might seem to be purely imaginative. I can only say that in all cases they have been built up most carefully from the materials placed at my disposal, and I do not believe that I have strained the truth in any one instance. . . .

Many people have been exceedingly kind. I wish

particularly to thank Mr. W. K. Bixby, the well-known American collector, for permission to make any use I please of such letters and documents in his possession as have already been privately printed. I desire to thank Mr. F. J. Harvey Darton, Mr. S. M. Ellis, Ainsworth's biographer, Mr. Cecil Palmer, most genial of publishers, and my fellow directors of the firm of Chapman & Hall for their advice and help. The officials of the Dickens Fellowship will, I hope, accept my warmest thanks for their courteous assistance at the Dickens house in Doughty Street. Most of all, however, am I indebted to my friend Mr. Charles J. Sawyer, of Grafton Street, who not only placed the whole of his private Dickens collection at my disposal—and it must be easily the finest in England—but provided me with all but one of my illustrations.

I think it right to add a very short list of such printed authorities as I have found most useful.

The two editions of Forster's "Life" most necessary to be consulted are the Memorial Edition (Chapman & Hall, 1913) and the new edition (Cecil Palmer, 1928) edited and annotated by Mr. J. W. T. Ley, well-known for his "Dickens Circle." "The Letters of Charles Dickens," of course, must be mentioned, though it is well to remember that the blue pencil was in constant use during the preparation of this work. Mr. Robert Langton's "Childhood and Youth of Dickens" (1891) was a pioneer work, and I have made free use of Mr. William J. Carlton's excellent "Charles Dickens: Shorthand Writer" (Palmer, 1926). For the romance with Maria Beadnell, the two volumes of letters issued by the Bibliophile Society of Boston have been consulted. Mr. W. Glyde Wilkins's "Dickens in America" (Chapman & Hall, 1911) and Mr. Edward F. Payne's "Dickens Days in Boston" (Houghton Mifflin, 1927) are trustworthy guides. Mr. S. J. Adair Fitz-Gerald's "Dickens and the Drama" and Mr. George Dolby's "Charles Dickens as I Knew Him" have also been of considerable assistance.

R. S.

think that he cared very much for the work, and I am convinced that he considered himself to be scandalously ill-paid. For Mr. Dickens, you are to understand, had ideas about life. He had ideas about his own importance in the general scheme of affairs. He saw himself even at this time, as a Figure: naturally gay, although sometimes tragic, but always a Figure. ... As a young gentleman of breeding and culture—was he not a government servant?—a careful deportment was essential to his well-being. In his rooms there must be books, and his table must be spread for his friends at stated and regular intervals. In particular there must be wine: decently mellow. With such things, indeed, life could be the most attractive affair.

Unfortunately, he found, there were occasions when you were expected to direct your attention to the absurdest trifles. Money, for instance, and a bundle of vague attributes which others besides his mother termed "one's responsibilities." In a well-ordered world, of course, Providence would have arranged for everybody of any parts to possess a respectably large fortune, but for some strange reason Providence had neglected to place Mr. Dickens in any such delectable position. It was very annoying. It was so annoying that Mr. Dickens was obliged to devise some means whereby this inexplicable mistake could be satisfactorily ignored. He fell into the regrettable habit of behaving as though that respectably large fortune were actually his.

That at this time he had certain moderate "expectations" can hardly be doubted, but these must always have been viewed in the rosiest light, and as a result there came what he himself invariably called "moments of difficulty." There are charming, Skimpolish creatures who seem able to convince themselves that an

I.O.U. legibly signed is the fullest and most honorable discharge of a debt. Mr. Dickens never deceived himself to that extent, but I would hazard a guess that he looked on these moments of difficulty with a sort of amused wonder that anybody except himself could seriously be annoyed at their steady recurrence. He was annoyed himself, because their arrival meant last-moment appeals, which are always a nuisance. But why he should be *blamed* because some wretched tradesman, who would naturally be paid in due course, suddenly and indecently had recourse to the law passed his comprehension.

Nevertheless the time came when others besides his mother disapproved, and at moments of extreme difficulty he was obliged to adopt a drastic measure of self-defense. This took the form of a quiet "disappearance." Whither he went or how he existed at such times, we do not know, but disappear he would and only return to his family when some friend or relation had done what was necessary. It says much for his personal charm that such help was almost invariably forthcoming.

You are not greatly surprised to hear that he married at twenty-three on a salary of little more than £80 a year. Amongst his fellow clerks was one Thomas Barrow, a relation of Sir John Barrow, the Arctic explorer. Thomas Barrow had several brothers and sisters. Mr. Dickens fell in love with Elizabeth Barrow, and in June, 1809, married her in the church which still stands opposite to Somerset House. It is quite possible that the wedding was hurried on—Elizabeth at the time was a minor—because the bridegroom had heard that he was about to be "detached." He was ordered, as it happened to "proceed" to Portsmouth, there to attend to the important task of paying off the various men-of-war: a pleasantly adventurous change, to be sure, after four years spent at a desk in the Strand.

In any case the young couple left London at once, and found a neat little house for themselves in Portsea. You may still see this house with its square patch of front garden, much as it always was, though the Mile End Terrace of Georgian times has become the Commercial Road of today, and there is little risk of its being pulled down in the near future, for it was here that Charles Dickens was born.

The rent was £35 a year: not an extravagant sum, it is true, even for those days, but rather more, perhaps, than most young men whose salary obstinately refused to rise much above £85 would have cared to pay. Appearances, however, must be kept up—in Portsmouth no less than elsewhere. Besides, there were those expectations, and possibly a small allowance from Mrs. Dickens or even from her shadowy husband, and I dare say a little help now and then from the Barrows. . . .

They lived in the neat little house for three years, and the neighbors came to the conclusion that Mr. Dickens was not only the pleasantest of companions, but a man of the most generous instincts. Clearly an acquisition to Portsea. Unfortunately the time came when the family found it convenient to move into rather less pleasant quarters in Hawke Street near by. It was the first of many such moves brought about by the disturbed state of the exchequer. As most married people will tell you, small children can be unbelievably expensive; and by this time Mr. Dickens was the proud father of two: Frances, called Fanny, born in 1810, and Charles John Huffam, who had made his first appearance at midnight on a Friday—February 7, 1812.

[2]

The Portsmouth job came to an end. It had lasted five years. Mr. Dickens was summoned back to London, and was no doubt very glad to return. Lodgings were found in Norfolk (now Cleveland) Street near to the Middlesex Hospital, and work was resumed at Somerset House. They were evidently satisfied with him, for in a little while his salary was materially increased—to £200. This was additionally lucky as there was also a steady increase in the family. Another boy had followed Charles and died in the Hawke Street days: now in London a girl, Letitia, was born, and Charles was no longer the baby.

Then, for the second time, Mr. Dickens heard that he was to be "detached." And so, probably at the end of 1816 or in the spring of the following year, we find the family, now pleasantly prosperous, taking the coach into Kent, and within a few months settled in another neat little house, No. 2, Ordnance Terrace, Chatham.

There followed four happy years, marred only by the death of one of two other babies. The little household came to include Mrs. Dickens's widowed sister Mary Allen, invariably known as Aunt Fanny, an old woman as general servant, and a juvenile nurse with a passion for telling the bloodthirstiest stories to look after the children. This nurse's name, you learn, not without some sort of thrill, was Mary Weller, and she may have been a daughter of the Thomas Weller who at this time was keeping the Granby Head in the High Street. The family next door—Stroughill by name—became friendly, the old lady at No. 5 took to petting the children, and Mr. Dickens, as became a responsible government official and a Figure, entertained in a genteel way.

A Very Queer Small Boy

And it was here that the small Charles began to "take notice." . . .

It is not always realized how vivid are a child's early impressions, and it is even seldomer understood how important and lasting those impressions may be. In Dickens's case they must have been even more vivid and lasting than is usual. All his life he retained memories of these Chatham days, and although a little embroidery must unconsciously have been added, in general they were singularly accurate. We must suppose him to have been a quaint little fellow, very lively except when he was ill, as was often the case, very ready to make friends, extraordinarily observant, and full of droll fancies. Old for his age but not introspective.

In after years his nurse recalled his good looks, his "open disposition," and his unwillingness to quarrel. (Unfortunately she had nothing to say of the one terrible fight—I suspect with a butcher's boy—in which he is known to have indulged.) The "spasms" from which he suffered so regularly—they seem to have been attacks of giddiness, sometimes accompanied with great pain—debarred him from indulging in outdoor romps, but there are exciting games to be played on the nursery floor which entail no physical exertion, and I can imagine the miraculous voyages and foolhardy explorations which he safely accomplished either alone or with Fanny and the Stroughill boy—very strong and handsome and heroic—to help him.

It is not only the embryo writer who in his earliest years will invent a whole wondrous world for his playground. Even the most "ordinary" child will discover astounding monsters disguised as tables and chairs, and find caves filled with treasure beneath the shabbiest rug. Similarly, the least imaginative girl will conduct

long and highly didactic conversations with her doll
or even with a wholly imaginary friend. But in the
case of a romantically minded little creature like
Charles, so often forced to take only a spectator's part,
what marvels of pretense must not have been devised!

When, moreover, these queerly imaginative games
took a more definitely theatrical turn, as I feel sure they
did, Mr. Dickens must have come to the conclusion
that he was the father of a very remarkable person indeed. This, he doubtless considered, was only what
might have been expected, but even so—what a pleasant reflection! How many other parents could exhibit
to their friends such an accomplished son? His own
friends must certainly be shown the little prodigy. And
so it happened that Master Charles was initiated into
the delights of "showing off" at a dangerously early
age. We hear of the dining-room table being used as
a primitive stage, upon which the boy would be invited
to sing and recite.

We hear of very youthful performances given with
the athletic Stroughill from next door and the athletic
Stroughill's small sister, the beautiful Miss Lucy with
golden hair and a blue sash. And as the years pass,
and Mrs. Dickens—"a dear, good mother," according
to Mary Weller, though possibly not too firm with her
children—succeeds without much difficulty in teaching her small son his letters, the songs and the recitals
become rather more elaborate ("The Voice of the Slug-
gard," by the way, remains a warm favorite.) By and
by a magic lantern is brought in. Little plays are "made
up." Fanny puts her small hands to the keys of the
piano, and produces remarkably good tunes. And Lucy
Stroughill acts the heroine and becomes Charles's
first sweetheart.

Mr. Dickens is charmed, of course, more especially

A Very Queer Small Boy

when his son assumes one of his more comical rôles. The parties at No. 2, Ordnance Terrace become more formal, and incidentally more expensive; but that does not matter, for the government understands the worth of one of her servants at any rate, and has increased his salary to £300.

So, too, there come visits to the Rochester Theatre, and when the stage-struck Charles is eight years old, he sees no less a celebrity than Joseph Grimaldi, the greatest of all the clowns. So, too, he goes to picnics, and is allowed to cruise with his father aboard the navy pay yacht, and is shown the ugly old ship called the Hulks, where curious folk called convicts live, and watches the rope-makers at work in the yard, and attends the great military reviews, and finds life very good indeed. Once there comes a great fire, and then his father sits down at his desk and writes out a full account of it, which goes up to London by the mailcoach and returns actually printed in the Times.

And, naturally, there are parties away from home. He goes to the Stroughills, where Lucy seems able to have a birthday whenever she wants, and where her athletic brother George is now known as Struggles. He goes to the jolliest old inn called the Mitre, where live new friends of his, Miss and Master Tribe; and here he and Fanny are loudly applauded when they mount the dining-room table to join in a duet, and Miss Tribe is also "loved to distraction." He goes to the Ordnance Hospital, where a jolly Dr. Lamert lives with his son James, and both of them are tremendously keen on theatrical entertainments. (Once, indeed, there is a performance in the hospital itself.) The surgeon and Aunt Fanny are particularly good friends, but so are he and James, who is allowed to take him to the theater.

Also he goes for walks with his father, and, as we

are told by the Uncommercial Traveller himself, one of them is an especial favorite. It is the one which takes them alongside the river toward Gravesend. On the way they come to a hill—the very hill where Sir John Falstaff robbed the travelers and ran away. It is called Gad's Hill, and here there is a house which is a kind of fairy palace. It is the only house in all the world which this "very queer small boy"—I use the Uncommercial Traveller's words—would like for his own. So much he confesses to his father. Mr. Dickens, amused, no doubt, at such enthusiasm, decides that this is one of those occasions which calls for the expression of some sound moral precept. He assumes a pontifical aspect. "If you were to be very persevering," says he, and nods his head sagely, "and were to work very hard, you might some day come to live in it."

He was not usually a very good prophet, but for once at any rate his words came true.

[3]

Young Charles was happy enough in those days, and never happier than when he could steal upstairs into a little room which none of the grown-ups ever seemed to use. Here he had discovered a small library of the most splendidly exciting books. Tales of adventure and discovery; "Don Quixote" and "Robinson Crusoe"; the stories of Smollett and Fielding; "Tales of the Genii" and the "Arabian Nights": he would read every one of them again and again. And in his queer vivid way he would tumble somehow *into* these books, sharing their heroes' adventures, even becoming some particular favorite himself. He would *be* Tom Jones, or, rather, his own childish idea of that amiable fellow, and the story would act itself round about him. He would read of some daring exploit amongst pirates; and straightway the little upstairs room and Fanny and the family would fade away, and he was on the desert island which the pirates had made their headquarters.

Nobody, as you know, really enjoys a novel without more or less identifying himself with one or other of the characters; but few readers can ever have lost themselves so completely in the printed page as did this small boy. And here one may begin to understand just what his own books were to mean to him in later days; they were as real to him as anything in actual life. So much, of course, is common knowledge; so much he himself would freely admit; but it is not always realized what a great part this mingling of fancy and fact was to play in his own life. If he put himself into his books, he also allowed his books to become part of himself. In a sense he may be said to have been living a Dickens novel all his days.

There are men who are wholly unlike their books. Dickens, on the contrary, saw himself always as a character in a book or a play that he might have written— not necessarily its hero, but at least a protagonist in the story—and, as it seems to me, it is only after accepting this assumption that the real drama of his life can be appreciated in the right way. Moreover, it was in the little room upstairs in the Chatham house that this drama—and it was a very strange drama indeed—began to be staged by himself. As yet he had only himself for an audience, but that made little difference to the play. The footlights were there, if only dimly lighted, and never were they to be wholly extinguished throughout his life.

Soon enough, indeed, there was to be a tangible foretaste of what was to come. Mr. Dickens's remarkable son was not satisfied to sing and recite on a table or perform some gory drama with his young friends: he must needs write a play himself. I have not read "Misnar, Sultan of India," but it seems to have been a most tragic affair. Royal folk were probably slaughtered very neatly with sticks, beautiful sultanas must have languished in dungeons, and I hope that Mrs. Dickens provided enough red ink to make a decent show of blood. Here, however, we have Master Dickens appearing as his own dramatist, and no doubt his father's guests thoroughly enjoyed themselves.

Unfortunately it was Mr. Dickens's good-natured desire to play host on such occasions that helped appreciably to bring him to disaster. It is a curious phenomenon—the ease with which money disappears. Unknown laws seem to regulate its withdrawal from your pocket and with no reference whatever to the state of your exchequer. In his own opinion, I suppose, there never was a less extravagant and more careful person than John Dickens. Did he live in a large mansion and keep butlers and footmen? He did not. Did he spend his leisure hours at the gambling-tables or in other questionable pursuits? Everybody knew that he was the pattern of respectability. Was he constantly taking coach up to London, there to mix with the fashionable crowd? No. He was a hard-working official, in receipt of a fair salary and in the additionally pleasant position of having "expectations." Then why should he find himself compelled to move out of the neat little house in Ordnance Terrace, and crowd his family and himself into a cottage in St. Mary's Place, which really had no claims to gentility at all? Why should such things happen to him and not to his friends? There seemed to be no adequate reply.

So, however, it happened. The family removed to

A Very Queer Small Boy 13

"The Brook," as the cottage was called, and remained there for nearly two years. True, they were now nearer to the pay office, and Mary Weller's services could still be retained, but—what a difference from Ordnance Terrace. How tiresome to be obliged to forgo those cheerful parties and home-made entertainments! Yet it had to be done, more especially as the time had now come when Fanny and Charles must really be sent to school. Luckily the son of Mr. Giles, the minister of a Baptist chapel next door, kept a small preparatory school, which was not too expensive, and to this establishment Fanny and Charles were accordingly sent, thus becoming enrolled amongst Giles's Cats, in contradistinction to pupils at the three other local schools of the kind, known respectively as Baker's Bulldogs, Newroad Scrubbers and Troy Town Rats.

Mr. Giles himself seems to have been an admirable tutor. He was an Oxford man—in itself a fact not without interest, for at that time few men in his position had taken a university degree—and he realized soon enough with what an exceptional boy he had to deal. "The dangerous kind of wandering intelligence," as Forster calls it, would have to receive very careful guidance. Intimate acquaintance with a dozen old novels and a passion for the stage were hardly the best foundations for the sort of education which it was his business to provide. Yet he must have treated the boy with tact and consideration, and the extra lessons which he arranged for the evenings—I cannot think that he was paid for them—took on that wise informality which can mean so much to a sensitive child.

The two became friends, and in after years the author of "Pickwick Papers" did not forget what he owed to his amiable teacher. It was Mr. Giles, by the way, who sent to "the inimitable Boz"—the oft-repeated epithet was his—a silver snuff-box to mark his appreciation of his old pupil's work; and with the disapproval that might be expected of him, Forster relates how at school the master taught the small Charles to take snuff. He even names the particular brand. It is not a matter of much importance, but one is amused to be told that in after years Mr. Giles's sister, who at this time was living with her brother and saw Dickens every day, indignantly denied the whole story. For myself, I confess that I like to imagine the boy playing at being grown-up in this not very heinous way and appreciating all the more on that account the wise words of his tutor.

So you are to see him in these days, a good-looking boy with very bright eyes and fair curly hair worn rather long. You are to figure him thoroughly enjoying his holidays, though no longer able to give many parties at home and still liable to the giddy attacks which circumscribe his activities abroad. Already, however, he is a great walker—in the neat dark clothes and the white beaver hat upon which Mr. Giles insists—and his powers of observation are not growing less.

He is indeed looking about him as few boys of his age ever did. Nothing seems to escape him or be forgotten, whether it be a boy home from a Yorkshire school, which is so different in every way from his own, or the curiously unpleasant noises that old Mr. Giles makes in chapel. He does not like this chapel overmuch—and here, I think, Mr. Dickens agrees with him—but his mother has lately taken to going there and insists on his regular attendance. And as he looks about him, it may be that he comes to see people and things not quite as they really are, but, more excitingly, as he would have them be. The stage in the Rochester Theatre is a wonderful place, but there is another, much larger stage outside. . . .

Chatham, too, comes to stand definitely for home. For himself, he is not in the least shy, laughs very loudly even when the joke is a poor one, has not given up his comic songs, rereads his books and in his own room nurses curious dreams which concern a very glorious but as yet vague career for himself.

Incidentally he welcomes another little brother, and accompanies his parents to church when Aunt Fanny marries her surgeon and goes off with him to Ireland. Aunt Fanny is assuredly missed; but young Lamert, now a Sandhurst cadet, comes to live at "The Brook" in the vacations, and at this time "Cousin James" shares with Sister Fanny the first place in his affections.

In this way the months pass until another summons comes from Somerset House, and it is then that the strange drama really begins.

Chapter II

"THE DEED"

[1]

THE drama was beginning, but for a few months the boy may have remained in ignorance of its unhappy significance for himself. He did not accompany the family to London, but stayed on in Chatham during the winter, presumably at Mr. Giles's house. This was probably the schoolmaster's own suggestion. Unlike his pupil he must have been fully aware of the distinct change for the worse which Mr. Dickens's affairs were taking at this time.

There were debts, of course, though how and where contracted I do not know, and some kind of arrangement—to be known henceforth as the "Deed"—was made. The Barrows may have advanced money for this purpose, and Charles's godfather, Christopher Huffam, then "Rigger to His Majesty's Navy" and fairly prosperous, may have helped. But I cannot help thinking that the change may have been in great part due to the recall itself. Local creditors who had allowed their claims to stand over while Mr. Dickens remained at the yard would naturally become insistent when the news came of his impending departure.

His position was certainly serious, and it may even be that Somerset House was not ignorant of the state of affairs and was becoming uneasy. It is known that there was some sort of sale when "The Brook" was given up—the young shipwright who was to marry Mary Weller bought the best set of chairs—and it was to no fashionable address that the family went when it arrived, with James Lamert and a "workhouse girl," in London.

Perhaps, however, the eleven-year-old boy knew that all was not well, even before he was sent for, apparently to attend the funeral of one of the younger children in London. He may even then have heard of that mysterious "Deed," and read into it vague horrors, and tried to imagine what it would mean to himself. . . . What, one wonders, did he think of his family at this time? With Fanny he had always been the best of friends, and few of his secret aspirations were hidden from her, but between his parents and himself there must, I think, have been some sort of vague barrier.

True, his mother had taught him his letters, but he never seems to have given her his confidence, and I doubt very much whether she ever really understood her son. True, his father was almost as keen as himself on theatrical entertainments, and could be the most delightful companion on a walk. There were no "rows" with him, there was no unkindness—on the contrary, in times of sickness he would be the most devoted of nurses—but was he *quite* like other fathers? Was he particularly interested in his children? Was there not generally something aloof about him, as though he belonged by rights to a world very different from that in which he found himself? I think the boy must have puzzled himself not a little, and wondered why it was so much easier to get on with Mr. Giles or some other less intimate friend.

But, whatever his feelings may have been, a real

crisis came when, sometime in the early spring of 1823, he bade good-by to Mr. Giles, and took his seat in the London coach. That journey was never forgotten. He was the only inside passenger, and, as he tells us himself, never "lost the smell of damp straw in which I was packed—like game—and forwarded carriage paid, to the Cross Keys, Wood Street, Cheapside." He ate his sandwiches without enjoyment, and it rained all the while, and he "thought life sloppier than I expected to find it."

Afterwards he realized well enough what he was losing on that mournful day, but even then he must have felt vaguely unhappy. He was leaving, perhaps forever, "the birthplace of his fancy," as he called it, and his friends, and the theater—and for what? A small boy packed off for the first time to boarding-school may be miserable enough, but at least he can look forward to the holidays. The small boy in the coach had no notion of what was in store for him, except that he was not going "home."

Yet he was no less observant than usual on that lonely run along Kentish roads. "Old Chumley," the driver of the coach, was suspiciously like an unlucky widower who at a later date was to be known the world over as Mr. Weller, Senior; and the coach itself was afterwards to be commandeered for the worthy purpose of taking Mr. Pickwick and his friends to a Rochester inn.

And, in London, to what sort of place was he taken? Well, it was a poor little house in a struggling suburb: not nearly so squalid as some of the biographers seem to have thought, but a mean enough cottage for those who had known the comforts of Ordnance Terrace. Bayham Street, Camden Town, was not genteel—a washerwoman was living next door—and it had seen better days; but it was not the broken-down, dirt-encrusted slum of a place which Forster's description conjures up in one's mind. London had not then become the sooty Colossus that it is today, and Camden Town with its green fields and its shady walks still retained a countrified air.

If, however, the wretchedness of this new abode has been exaggerated, nobody has made too much of the financial troubles of its tenant. Mr. Dickens, indeed, was in a very bad way, and not all the "expectations" in the world could do very much for him. His salary remained at its highest level, but the "Deed" was swallowing most of it up. It was no longer a question of foregoing cheerful parties; it was a question of finding food and clothes for five or six children. And yet it was just at this time that he seems to have first exhibited those ridiculous qualities which were to give him immortality as Wilkins Micawber. You are forced to the conclusion that he closed his eyes to stern fact altogether, and decided to stand wholly aloof from family worries. He had signed the "Deed": that was surely enough. If, perchance, at moments of difficulty not all its provisions were being kept to the letter, his creditors would doubtless understand that even with the best will in the world a gentleman was not always in a position to carry out his intentions.

As for the tradesmen who were apparently making some ridiculous fuss about their bills, they must be told —presumably by Mrs. Dickens—that they would be paid in good time. That, surely, was the obvious procedure. He was a government official himself, engaged on important work and not to be worried by mere trifles of that kind.

As for his parental responsibilities, naturally a father would take the greatest interest in his children, and he did take the greatest interest in his own, particularly in Charles, whose comic songs were remarkably good; but he was a man who must be allowed to do things in his own way. At the moment it was not his intention to send Charles to school: the boy was old for his age, and could be of great assistance to his mother in the house. Many boys of his age, indeed, were probably earning large sums of money. And Charles *had* been to school. Very well then. They must not expect impossibilities from him. In due course any little inconvenience there might be would settle itself. . . .

So I can hear him declaiming. Afterwards Dickens chose to speak only of the more gracious side of his father, but at the time he felt bitter enough. "He appeared," he told Forster once, "to have utterly lost at this time the idea of educating me at all, and to have utterly put away from him the notion that I had any claim upon him in this regard, whatever. So I degenerated into cleaning his boots of a morning, and my own; and making myself useful in the work of the little house."

"As I thought," he declared on another occasion, "in the little back garret in Bayham Street, of all I had lost in losing Chatham, what would I have given, if I had had anything to give, to have been sent back to any other school, to have been taught something somewhere!" It is not every youngster who speaks of school in this way, but Dickens was an exceptional boy, and although he was inclined at times to allow, unconsciously, his imagination to color the truth, I believe that here he was accurately describing what he had felt. Of course he was bitter. I do not insist on his good opinion of himself; but he knew well enough that he was no ordinary boy—Mr. Giles must have admitted so much—and yet, just when it was most important for him to concentrate on his lessons, there were no lessons to be had. Surely any other father would have arranged something, in spite of all the "Deeds" in the world? He was thinking only of himself, of course, but most boys do. Moreover, Fanny had been accepted as a scholar at the Royal Academy of Music, and if Fanny could be taught music . . .

Nevertheless, there were compensations for this unhappy neglect. There might be few new friends to make, no birthday parties to enjoy, no teacher to take Mr. Giles's place; Fanny might be away at her academy; but James Lamert was still with them, now waiting for his commission, and together they built a toy theater, on the stage of which the old farces and dramas could be played puppet-wise for the younger children.

Mr. Huffam, too, occasionally invited the boy to his house, and would call for one of those comic songs, and express himself highly delighted when it had been willingly rendered. There was also Thomas Barrow, his uncle, who was soon to sever all relations with his brother-in-law; and on one occasion, as Forster relates, while Uncle Tom was in lodgings in Gerrard Street after an accident, the landlady, a bookseller's widow, lent the boy some books. The story goes that amongst them was George Colman's "Broad Grins," which impressed him so much by its description of Covent Garden "that he stole down to the market by himself to compare it with the book"—the first of many such metropolitan explorations.

It was while this uncle was still confined to his room and eager to receive visits from his small nephew that the boy himself was struck down. A bad attack of fever kept him for some time in bed, and when he recovered, it was to learn of an amazing resolution of his mother's. Suddenly she had decided to take matters into her own not very skilful hands. If her husband could look on and do nothing to save them from ruin, it behooved her to play head of the family. She proposed, she said, to turn her abilities as a teacher to professional use. She announced her intention to establish a school for girls. Her family and friends would help her, she thought, and Mr. Huffam, in particular, would be in a favorable position with his East Indian "connection" to send her pupils.

It was a brave but ludicrous resolve, and from the beginning the whole scheme was foredoomed to failure. What did she know of girls' schools? What madness induced her to lease a fairly large house before the promise of a single pupil had been obtained? Yet such a house was taken in Gower Street North—then rather more fashionable than it is today—a large brass plate was affixed to the front door, circulars were printed, and sometime in October or November, 1823, the family moved in.

What Mr. Dickens thought of it all does not appear. Doubtless he approved of any scheme which might assist him to keep his creditors fairly content, and he must have welcomed a move into a neighborhood appreciably more genteel than Camden Town. But it availed him nothing at all. Mr. Huffam chose this moment of all others to go bankrupt, and his valuable "connection" dissolved into nothing. No neighbors seemed to have daughters of a teachable age, and nobody offered to help. James Lamert, tired of waiting for his commission, had gone into business, and left them. The Barrows did nothing.

"I left," recounts Dickens, "at a great many other doors, a great many circulars calling attention to the merits of the establishment. Yet nobody ever came to school, nor do I recollect that anybody ever proposed to come, or that the least preparation was made to receive anybody. . . . But I do know," he adds, "that we got on very badly with the butcher and baker; that very often we had not too much for dinner; and that at last my father was arrested."

This was in February, 1824. You can imagine the general consternation. You can imagine the boy's feelings. A fine birthday celebration! Mrs. Dickens must have rushed wildly to her family, but the Barrows had had enough of John Dickens. Afterwards, his family became well accustomed to such arrests, but at this time they must have felt themselves helpless and hopeless and wholly disgraced. Only Mr. Dickens himself remained calm and tragically aloof. If they chose to take his liberty from him, so be it. He would know how to suffer in dignified silence. . . . According to custom they took him to one of the sponging-houses before carrying him off to the Marshalsea prison, and he managed to bring down the curtain with a very good line. His last words to his son before the prison gates closed between them might have graced the best Drury Lane drama. The sun, he said, was set upon him forever.

Always a Figure . . .

[2]

There followed for the twelve-year-old boy a time of utter misery and despair. Now, it seemed to him, there could be no more schooling, no chance of preparing himself for that distinguished career, no possibility of escape from the meanest poverty and degradation. His father was in prison: not a criminal, it is true, but apparently unable or unwilling to suggest any plans except those which concerned his own personal comfort.

His distracted mother was in the Gower Street house with three or four children clamoring for food. I cannot be certain, but I imagine that Thomas Barrow had already severed all relations with his brother-in-law. What then was to be done? To whom should they apply for assistance, when every friend and acquaintance had turned himself into a creditor crying out for blood? There was nobody except the second-hand furniture dealer or the pawnbroker.

There is a passage in Dickens's story "The Haunted Man" which tells of a pitiful little sale of household goods, and it would seem to be not too far from the truth. "My own little bed was so superciliously looked upon by a power unknown to me, hazily called 'The Trade,' that a brass coal-scuttle, a toasting-jack, and a bird-cage were obliged to be put with it to make a Lot of it, and then it went for a song—so I heard mentioned, and I wondered what song—and thought what a dismal song it must be to sing."

In "David Copperfield," too, you may read of these wretched days in some detail. Almost daily visits to the pawnbroker, who seems to have realized that his small client was no ordinary boy; frequent walks along the Hampstead Road to a stall, where a bookseller, who was generally drunk, came gradually to possess the whole of the much-prized little library of books; regular hours to be spent with his father in the Marshalsea prison: you can imagine the ghastly routine. The day came at last when there were only two rooms in the Gower Street house which were not wholly bare.

It was then that James Lamert came forward with a suggestion. In conjunction with a cousin of his, he had established a bootblacking business which, with the help of an "original" recipe, was endeavoring to rival the then well-known Warren's Blacking. He proposed that Charles should make himself generally useful in the warehouse, where at certain hours it might also be possible to superintend his interrupted studies. A small wage would be paid: six or seven shillings a week.

Lamert, of course, meant to be kind. He had always been fond of the boy, and probably believed that he was doing him and his family a good turn, as indeed in a sense he was; but to Dickens himself it ever remained "an evil hour" when his parents thankfully accepted the proposal and sent their son to the warehouse in Hungerford Stairs. Only once in later years did he speak of these days, and then it was due to the merest chance that he steeled himself to write out a fragment of autobiography for Forster.

He was, indeed, stunned and horrified. That after all his dreams of success, of becoming a learned man, of owning that wonderful house on Gad's Hill, he should find himself a warehouse drudge, expected to mix on terms of equality with men and boys of the commonest sort! That he should be forced to undertake the most menial jobs! It seemed to him not only the end of all joy in life, but a very real disgrace. . . .

You may read his own account of the sad business in Forster's "Life," and perhaps ask yourself whether it is not a little too highly colored. Would a boy, you wonder, even an exceptional and rather egotistical boy like Dickens, suffer so much because he spent a few months pasting labels on to bottles? Well, there were times when the adult Dickens would play with an idea, particularly if it happened to be painful, until he was incapable of looking at it, judicially, from the outside, but I am inclined to think that there was no exaggeration in what he told Forster of these bootblacking days. I think that he must have worked himself up into a state of passionate self-pity, when it was impossible for him to think of the boy Charles Dickens except as a pariah, utterly and entirely degraded.

It is often assumed that the mental sufferings of children cannot be really acute. It is a comfortable belief—for the grown-ups—but it is wholly false. A boy of twelve is quite as capable of going through hell as is his father, and the fact that the hells need not be quite the same makes no difference. Moreover, with young Dickens there were good reasons for his "secret agony of soul" as he called it. He was a delicate, sensitive boy, accustomed to live in a polite little world of his own; now he was forced to work on his bottles at a window through which all the world might look. The time was to come when he can almost be said to have lived for the limelight, but he was no longer labeling bottles. . . .

Again, although there may have been no actual bullying in the warehouse, there were rough words and difficult moments. They called him "the little gentleman," but the phrase was not quite so polite as it sounds. It conveyed some sort of contemptuous abuse. Above all, however, was the feeling of complete and undeserved neglect. He felt that even as things were, something might have been done for him. But neither his parents nor anybody else—Cousin James, after all, could find no time for teaching—seemed to care twopence about him. They saw nothing objectionable in his work with the labels.

"It is wonderful to me," he wrote in explanation to Forster, "that even after my descent into the poor little drudge I had been since we came to London, no one had compassion enough on me—a child of singular abilities, quick, eager, delicate, and soon hurt, bodily or mentally"—the words sound a little curious, but they were true—"to suggest that something might have

been spared, as certainly it might have been, to place
me at any common school. Our friends, I take it, were
tired out. No one made any sign. My father and mother
were quite satisfied. They could not have been more
so, if I had been twenty years of age, distinguished at
a grammar school, and going to Cambridge."

There you have the real explanation of his bitterness
and shame. His parents were satisfied. They knew him
so slightly that they could banish him to the warehouse
for the sake of a few shillings a week and remain
wholly unaware of any "secret agony of soul" or indeed
anything like it. And when on one occasion he was
taken to Tenterden Street and saw his sister receive a
prize for her musical studies, he felt that his humilia-
tion was complete.

Yet, even so, there were certain small compensations.
The work under James Lamert might be uncongenial,
the boy might be brooding at all hours over his unfortunate lot, but the smell of bootblacking, singularly
vile though it be, was doing nothing to blunt those keen
powers of observation which were to help him so much
in the future. He was not being "taught," but he was
giving himself the education that is most worth having.

He might, of course, have run away, as David Copperfield did; but apart from the fact that there was no
Betsy Trotwood to go to, there was grit in the boy:
he hated and loathed the work, but he came to take
a pride in its performance. Moreover, that weekly six
shillings, miserably inadequate as it was, allowed him
some sort of independence. He could buy his own
meager dinners, or a Saturday journal of the more
thrilling kind. (The Terrific Register, you hear, was
his favorite.) He could give himself "treats" now and
then: an extra "feed" or a glass of superior ale. He
could wander abroad when his work was done, and

weave strange stories for himself. In addition, his warehouse companions were not all of them suspicious and aloof. One boy was even indirectly connected with the stage, for a sister of his was known to have appeared at Drury Lane, and here at any rate was one interest in common.

Once, too, when one of the old attacks came on during work, Bob Fagin, the youth who had first taught him the correct way of applying the paste and knotting the string, made up a bed of straw in a corner, filled blacking-bottles with hot water to assuage the pain, and nursed him tenderly throughout the day. It is a little odd, by the way, to find the name of such a good Samaritan afterwards used for a villainous Jew.

Meanwhile Mr. Dickens was still playing the tragedian in an upstairs room in the Marshalsea prison. He was not exactly its father, like Mr. Dorrit, but as a civil servant in a responsible position—his salary, by the way, does not seem to have been stopped—he was naturally a Figure; and I can imagine the deference paid him by the shabby unfortunates doomed to live and die in the prison. Indeed, he was soon chosen chairman of the little committee which conducted the affairs of the Common Room.

Every Sunday morning his two eldest children would come to see him, and then there would be talk of a new "Deed." But hard cash was required for any composition, and the money from Somerset House was needed for his immediate requirements. And so, at the end of the spring quarter, when the white elephant in Gower Street could be given up, Mrs. Dickens came with her family to live with her lord in prison.

It was a wise move. In the Marshalsea, you were permitted to do more or less as you chose. Except for the loss of freedom, you could be as comfortable there as in your own house. As a matter of fact the family were probably more comfortable in that upstairs room in the prison than they had been since Chatham days. The little workhouse girl waited upon them, coming in when the gates opened, from a lodging near by. And for a short while Charles himself seems to have lived there with them, for in his own account of Fagin's kindness, he relates what pains he was at to keep the secret of his abode. Fagin, it appears, had refused to allow him to go home alone, and insisted on accompanying him to his door-step.

"I was too proud," wrote Dickens, "to let him know about the prison; and after making several efforts to get rid of him, to all of which Bob Fagin in his goodness was deaf, shook hands with him on the steps of a house near Southwark Bridge on the Surrey side, making believe that I lived there. As a finishing piece of reality, in case of his looking back, I knocked at the door, I recollect, and asked, when the woman opened it, if that was Mr. Robert Fagin's house."

Very soon, however, accommodation was found for him in Camden Town, where an old friend of the family, a Mrs. Roylance, who had seen better days, "took in" children. She was not too unlike the Mrs. Pipchin who afterwards came to be very well known. Here, it seems, he was even unhappier than he had been in Gower Street. There was a "miserable blank," and "one Sunday night I remonstrated with my father on this head, so pathetically and with so many tears, that his kind nature gave way. He began to think that it was not quite right. I do believe he had never thought so before, or thought about it. It was the first remonstrance I had ever made about my lot, and perhaps it opened a little more than I intended."

Perhaps it did. Perhaps it caused an astonished Mr.

Dickens to realize that children could have their worries as well as hard-working and much misunderstood civil servants. At the moment, however, he was hardly in a position to do very much. But he did arrange for the boy to leave Mrs. Roylance, and a lodging was found for him in Lant Street, Borough, where Bob Sawyer was to have such trouble with his landlady. Here at least he was near to his parents, and rather more independent. He would slip into the prison for his meals, and if the gates were not yet open when he arrived, and the little servant was waiting, as she often was, he would pass the time telling her "quite astonishing fictions" about the buildings in sight.

And then, on a sudden and at a time when the boy had abandoned all hope that this sort of existence could ever be ended, there came very real help. At long last one at any rate of those old "expectations" had materialized. "A relative" died, and left a fair sum to John Dickens. We are not told who this relative was. It may have been the old lady up in Chester or even her shadowy husband, though he, I suspect, had been dead for some years. Nor do we know precisely how large the sum of money was; but part of it was immediately paid into court, and Mr. Dickens was free.

I can figure him as he prepared to cast himself for a less tragic rôle and searched for a suitable gesture to mark his departure. He found it in the composition and display of a solemn petition to the king for a bounty to the prisoners to drink his Majesty's health on his forthcoming birthday. The prisoners filed into the upstairs room, to sign their names and be favored with a few last words. It was so notable a ceremony that one of the oldest inhabitants had actually washed himself for the occasion: so important that Mr. Dickens's son was given a half-holiday in order to be present.

"I would rather have seen it," he declared, "than the best play ever acted." Well, that is hardly to be wondered at. With the "Deed" satisfactorily finished and done with, what might not happen? They would surely take him away from Hungerford Stairs.

You would have thought that they would, and yet for some little time no such move was made or even suggested. The family went to live in Somers Town. The blacking business removed to the neighborhood of Covent Garden, and the boy went with it.

"The establishment was larger now," he wrote, "and we had one or two new boys. Bob Fagin and I had attained to great dexterity in tying up the pots. I forget how many we could do in five minutes. We worked, for the light's sake, near the second window as you come from Bedford Street; and we were so brisk at it that the people used to stop and look in. Sometimes there would be quite a little crowd there. I saw my father coming in at the door one day when we were very busy, and I wondered how he could bear it." How, indeed, could he? Yet no word was said, and every day the boy would walk down to the warehouse with his dinner "in a small basin tied up in a handkerchief" like any laborer's son.

Yet there must have been rising in Mr. Dickens's curious mind a suspicion that he was not doing all that he should for his son. Perhaps he was only now fully aware that James Lamert was not playing "teacher" as he had promised to do. Perhaps with the remains of the legacy still safely banked, the older ideas were asserting themselves. He was hardly a man to have a son pasting labels in a warehouse. He would have to see Lamert about it. Lamert had not behaved well. He was angry with Lamert, very angry indeed. He wrote a letter to say so.

Charles delivered it by hand, and was astonished to hear his cousin attack his father in the most violent manner. At the end of which he was told that in view of the insults the letter contained, he would have to go. And "with a relief so strange," he relates, "that it was like oppression, I went home."

We shall never know the contents of that letter, but there can be little doubt that it was intended to have the result that it did. Mr. Dickens for once in his life was thoroughly roused. The boy should be sent to school. And not even his wife's unexpected opposition turned him from his purpose. She, no doubt, was thinking only of the pennies when she went next day to the warehouse and persuaded James Lamert to take the boy back. But he did not go back, and he found it difficult ever to forgive his mother for what she had done. "I do not write resentfully or angrily: for I know how all these things have worked together to make me what I am: but I never afterwards forgot, I never shall forget, I never can forget, that my mother was warm for my being sent back."

Poor Mrs. Nickleby-Dickens! . . .

[3]

"There was a school in the Hampstead road kept by Mr. Jones, a Welshman, to whom my father dispatched me to ask for a card of terms. The boys were at dinner, and Mr. Jones was carving for them with a pair of holland sleeves on, when I acquitted myself of this commission. He came out, and gave me what I wanted; and hoped I should become his pupil. I did. At seven o'clock one morning, very soon afterwards, I went as day scholar to Mr. Jones's establishment, which was in Mornington Place, and had its schoolroom sliced away by the Birmingham Railway, when that change came about. The schoolroom, however, was not threatened by directors or civil engineers then, and there was a board over the door graced with the words WELLINGTON HOUSE ACADEMY."

There you have the plain facts in Dickens's own words, but what must his feelings have been when he found himself once again amongst boys of his own standing! What a glorious new freedom was this which kept him tied to a desk for long hours together! What a delightful joke that Mr. Jones, according to common report, was really an ignoramus, whose sole accomplishment was his prowess with cane or birch! He was at school, and nothing else mattered.

Yet you are not to suppose that this new happy Charles immediately transformed himself into a grimly keen student. He did nothing of the kind. So far as mere scholarship went, he was the ordinary boy, bright and attentive, but no schoolboy genius. To say truth, it was not a particularly good school, and young Dickens was not particularly successful with his form-work. But he was liked by his fellows, and the warehouse had left no unseemly mark. It is possible to build up a rough vignette of the school from his writings and from the various recollections of old schoolfellows, delighted, but amazed, to find that they had once sat in form or played with the author of "Pickwick Papers."

The schoolroom itself was a separate building, long and narrow and containing three rows of desks. The playground was large. One at any rate of the ushers was a man of many parts. He taught English and mathematics and the flute, took charge of the stationery and mended the pens, acted as Mr. Jones's secretary and made out the bills, and was invariably sent to call upon parents when their boys were ill because of his "gentlemanly" manners. There was a fat little man who taught dancing, and a Latin master with the curious habit of putting small onions in his ears in the fond hope of overcoming his deafness. There was a man of all work who hid a kind heart under a very gruff manner, and was not unlike Phil Squod in "Bleak House."

A few boarders were taken, amongst them some girls from the East Indies under Mrs. Jones's particular care, but the majority of the pupils were day boys, and they seem to have been a good-natured lot. With a few of them Dickens made particular friends. A boy named Daniel Tobin was his especial favorite, and their friendship continued for some years. With one of the boarders called Bowden, a "newspaper" was edited, and lent round on payment of the usual slate-pencil or marble.

Another, by name Thomas, was in later years able to give Forster more definite details. He remembered Dickens as a boy who had held his head unusually high, and thought there had been "an air of smartness" about him. "His week-day dress of jacket and trousers . . . were what is called pepper-and-salt; and instead of the frill that most boys of his age wore then, he had a turn-down collar, so that he looked less youthful in consequence."

Thus early, then, Master Charles was showing sartorial fancies of his own.

Another contemporary, Henry Danson, remembered him as a handsome, curly-headed boy very willing to take part in any mischief that was going. Of more interest is his recollection of the stories that young Dickens would write and circulate amongst his chosen friends. And of course there were theatricals on every possible occasion. "We mounted small theaters," records Danson, "and got up very gorgeous scenery to illustrate 'The Miller and His Men' and 'Cherry and Fair Star.' I remember the present Mr. Beverley, the scene-painter, assisted us in this. Dickens was always a leader at these plays, which were occasionally presented with much solemnity before an audience of boys, and in the presence of the ushers. My brother, assisted by Dickens, got up 'The Miller and His Men,' in a very gorgeous form. Master Beverley constructed the mill for us in such a way that it could tumble to pieces with the assistance of crackers. At one representation the fireworks in the last scene, ending with the destruction of the mill, were so very real that the police interfered, and knocked violently on the doors."

A Mr. Walsh also remembered a play being performed in the back kitchen at Tobin's house. This, he thought, had never been written out or rehearsed; there was a rough plot settled beforehand, but the actors made up their speeches as they went along.

For two years Dickens stayed on at Wellington House, and I think that they must have been very happy days. He might still be looking on Chatham with regret, and the warehouse remained the nightmare that it was always to be, but the old dreams had returned, and with them his belief in himself.

Chapter III

SEARCH FOR A PROFESSION, WITH AN INTERLUDE FOR ROMANCE

[1]

THERE came the question of a career, and for the youngster fresh from a Hampstead academy, not, apparently, too brilliant a scholar, and by no means convinced that one profession more than any other would prove to his liking, the choice was bound by one consideration alone. Mr. Dickens, that is to say, was not in a position to spend further sums on preparing his son to earn a living. There was no new crisis in his affairs, but he could hardly be expected, in view of the fact that he was no longer employed at Somerset House, but only in receipt of a small pension, and in view of his very large family—there was shortly to be yet another addition—to do very much— Well, Charles would perfectly understand. He had been given a good schooling at considerable sacrifice, and he must earn his living at once. But—how and where?

I can imagine the family discussions. Mr. Dickens himself, assuming some solemnity of demeanor—so much is clearly expected of him—gives tongue to a few admirably sounding phrases, which mean very little, but possibly hint that young men with the proper determination may go far without too much parental interference. It is unfortunate that his own knowledge of the professions is so slight. He is of the opinion, however, that numerous openings will suggest themselves. Amiable, but not very helpful.

The boy, growing ever more conscious of those vague ambitions stirring within him, and perhaps not unmindful of certain exciting theatrical performances at school, feels, as most of us do at his age, that in a well-ordered world all considerations of finance should be a matter solely for parents. But by this time he has a fairly shrewd idea what sort of man his father is, and knows that he must depend on himself. Very well then, he will take any chance that offers itself. Upon which, I fancy, Mrs. Dickens murmurs the name of her family. . . .

There were, of course, friends and relations to be consulted, even though Thomas Barrow had cut himself off and James Lamert was no longer on cousinly terms. Mr. Huffam was hardly in a position to be of much use; but what of the others? Mr. Dickens in his pleasantly careless way made inquiries. He sought out his friends. One of these, Forster records, asked where the boy had been educated. "Why, indeed, sir—ha! ha!"—he was told, "he may be said to have educated himself": a fairly truthful if not too judicious reply.

Definite help in the end was forthcoming from a gentleman who happened to be lodging at a Berners Street boarding-house kept by an aunt of Mrs. Dickens. This was Mr. Edward Blackmore, junior partner in the firm of Ellis & Blackmore, solicitors in Gray's Inn. He suggested the law, then as now considered to be the most respectable of professions. Surely, however, there were premiums to be paid? There certainly were. But in the legal as in other professions there are grades, the lowest of which knows nothing of premiums; and, as millionaires are fond of telling their children, it is a fine thing to begin at the bottom and work yourself up.

Whereupon young Dickens entered the law—at the bottom.

Presumably Mr. Blackmore had no immediate vacancy in his own office, for the boy seems to have spent a few months in the Chancery Lane office of another solicitor—Mr. Charles Molloy, afterwards to be one of his own legal advisers—where one of the clerks was the Thomas Mitton who had been at school with two of his brothers and was to remain his friend for so many years. In May, 1827, however, he went to Ellis & Blackmore, and his career as a man of the world had begun.

He was little more than the office boy, but what of that? Here was no blacking warehouse where he pasted labels on bottles. In a lawyer's office he was a junior clerk, who could consort on terms of something like equality with his immediate seniors, who could assume the dress proper to professional youth, and who away from Gray's Inn was more or less his own master. Now, too, he could be gloriously contemptuous toward the unfortunates still condemned to construe in school, and do adventurous things wholly impossible a few months before.

His duties, it is true, cannot have been wildly exciting—wills to be registered, processes served, the petty-cash book to be kept—but without doubt he was seeing life. He "didn't much like it," he told Wilkie Collins years later; but there were queer little incidents in the office which stamped themselves on his mind—Mr. Blackmore found some of them recorded in the earlier books—and I have no doubt that the boy himself was fairly happy and only waiting for his chance.

He stayed with the firm for a year and a half, and the chance did not come. His salary was raised from ten shillings to thirteen-and-six and even to fifteen shillings; but this was not too extravagant a sum for a youngster keen to get as much out of life as he could, who, incidentally, was spending many of his evenings at the theater. So much was only to be expected; but it did so happen that one of his fellow clerks, Potter by name, was as keen on the stage as himself, and these two, with a possible Tobin in occasional attendance, seem to have had the merriest, if not always the soberest, times.

You will find a picture of them, not, I dare say, too highly colored, in Boz's sketch "Making a Night of It," where Mr. Potter is mentioned by name. He and Mr. Robert Smithers are "thick-and-thin" pals, and their adventures with mild Havannahs and Scotch whisky are certainly breezy. In the description of Smithers, moreover, may be found a useful autobiographical note: "There was a spice of romance," wrote Boz, "in Mr. Smithers's disposition, a ray of poetry, a gleam of misery, a sort of consciousness of he didn't exactly know what—which stood out in fine relief against the off-hand dashing amateur-pickpocket sort of manner, which distinguished Mr. Potter in an eminent degree."

There may have been a gleam of misery now and then, for the chance showed no signs of coming, and it was rather too soon for much satisfactory romance (except on the stage), but in general there was plenty of fun to be had, and fun of a kind that was to stand him in very good stead. With Potter he came to know London as few other youngsters can ever have known it. They were not satisfied to visit only the fashionable haunts—incidentally to worship at Macready's shrine

—but sallied forth to Sadlers Wells and queer suburban halls, to take their fill of riotous melodrama. It was even said that they actually appeared more than once on the professional stage, and this may be so. At the time old Thomas Dibdin was managing Sadlers Wells, but he was not too prosperous and would welcome amateurs for "walking on" parts. On the other hand, it seems equally likely that the parts which, as Mr. Blackmore was afterwards told, were so frequently being played by his junior clerks, belonged to the private theatricals once again a popular pastime in the Dickens household.

These theatricals were highly important. Indeed, no fair estimate of Dickens's character can be formed without detailed consideration of their nature. All his life he retained a boyish delight in their preparation and performance. He adored the theater and theatrical folk, and what is often called the actor's temperament was certainly his. In all probability he could have risen high on the professional stage. Already his friends knew what a good mimic he was, and already, I fancy, he was quite willing to "act" outside a theater. Certainly the great success of his public readings was largely due to this talent for acting, brought to perfection, be it noted, only after the most careful rehearsals.

It was on the amateur stage, moreover, and at this early date, that he first showed that degree of concentration upon, and almost tyrannical enthusiasm for, the work in hand, which in later years was to carry him away to the heights. It was he who, as a matter of course, was stage-manager and producer at all the performances. It was he who superintended all those troublesome jobs behind the scenes of the existence of which a well-behaved audience is expected to remain in complete ignorance, and not even Sir William Gilbert himself was a sterner taskmaster than he at rehearsals.

There is, however—or should be—one figure in the making and presenting of plays even more important than the official producer. The dramatist himself, I am aware, is not always given a free hand; his existence may even be ignored altogether. But it can happen that the author or adapter is his own producer, and this was almost certainly the case with young Dickens.

The day of Indian tragedies was over, but in their place had come entertainments possibly better suited to postprandial audiences squeezed into parlors temporarily deprived of their usual contents. How many farces and dramas were written or adapted at this time by the author of "Misnar" we do not know, but one at least has survived. "The Stratagems of Rozanza: a Venetian Comedietta" by C. J. H. Dickens exists in manuscript (apparently in the handwriting of his mother) and was doubtless produced sometime in 1828 either at Hampstead or at the house in the Polygon, Somers Town, to which in this year the family seems to have gone. It has been pointed out that this comedietta is a translation of a play of Goldoni's, and what precisely was Dickens's share in giving it an English dress is not known. I imagine that he had discovered some translation or other, and altered it to suit his own purpose. Its first line, I feel, should be quoted. "Long live the bottle!" sings Monsieur le Blau. "Long live mirth!" In which admirable sentiments, so it seems to me, you have much of the real Dickens, already by no means averse to the good things of life, enjoying nothing so much as a joke—a hearty, likable, good-looking youngster, very full of the proverbial beans.

But there was that meager fifteen shilling, and there were those vague ambitions. Mr. Blackmore had certainly given him a start, but was the law precisely the career for an adapter of comedies with a ray of poetry about him? Would it ever lead to anything much, without that unobtainable premium? Was there no other opening rather more to his taste?

I can imagine further family discussions, in which, peradventure, Mr. Dickens now assumes a more helpful rôle, for he, very creditably indeed, has adopted a new profession which is adding appreciably to his income. That old contribution sent from Chatham to the Times has not been forgotten, and its writer is now regularly working for a London newspaper of the most respectable kind. Yes, he is a reporter on the Morning Herald. It is a position of dignity. It brings him into contact with prominent people. Moreover, his is a profession with plums, unmistakable plums, for the really good man. Uncle Edward Barrow, also a newspaper reporter, will assuredly bear him out. And is not Uncle John Barrow, already connected with more than one newspaper, about to launch a new venture—the Mirror of Parliament—which is to rival Hansard itself? True, only the most expert shorthand-writer can hope for a seat in the parliamentary gallery, but once there, to what heights can he not reach?

Now at what exact date Dickens came to the decision that a suitable new opening had really presented itself I cannot be certain, but whether the investigation of those dashes and dots began in the evenings while he was still at Gray's Inn, or whether his father's easier circumstances at the moment allowed him from the beginning to give his whole time to their conquest, he set to work in no half-hearted spirit.

I gather from victims that the study of shorthand remains to this day amongst civilization's ghastliest inflictions, and Dickens himself found it no simple matter.

He gives an amusing account of his difficulties in "David Copperfield." He had purchased a copy of Gurney's "Brachygraphy"—a half-guinea book—and was soon in the depths of its sinister secrets. There came a time when "unaccountable consequences" resulted from "marks like flies' legs," and an equally unhappy day when there "appeared a procession of new horrors called arbitrary characters," which, once they had become fixed in his mind, drove everything else from it. He even dreamed of the wretched things. But he was not to be beaten, and if the parliamentary plum was still far out of his reach, he was soon in a position to put his new craft to some purpose. In 1829 he was regularly practicing as a reporter in the law courts and probably at Bow Street and the Old Bailey as well.

And it was at this time that he became aware, very naturally and properly, of the most powerful spur as yet known to man. He fell desperately and madly in love.

[2]

You are to see him just now working very hard, but you are also to watch him in the hours of relaxation. The theaters had lost none of their fascination, and private theatricals were in constant preparation. Fanny Dickens had left the academy, and was teaching, but there was a piano for her at home. The little parties which had been such a success in Chatham days were renewed, new friends were coming to the house—there had been another removal to a more convenient quarter —and young Dickens, with his good looks, his lively chatter, and his powers as an entertainer, naturally received many invitations. Amongst these new friends was a certain Henry Kolle, a bank clerk at this time but afterwards in business as a quilt-printer, and towards the end of 1829 or at the beginning of the following year Kolle introduced him to a family called Beadnell.

The Beadnells were well-to-do middle-class folk who lived in Lombard Street over, or next door to, a bank. Two brothers, John and George, shared the house. John was the manager of the bank, and his brother was afterwards to occupy the same satisfactory position. George, moreover, was married, and had three daughters, Margaret, Anne, and Maria.

Margaret was engaged to a young tea-merchant called Lloyd. Anne was about to follow her example and proposed, with her parents' consent, to become Mrs. Kolle. And Maria, nineteen, a little dark beauty with eyebrows which showed a tendency to meet over a presumably pert little nose, well aware of her own attractions, and very ready for a little flirtation, does not seem to have disguised her preference for this new and most personable acquaintance, who in spite of a certain shy reserve—the "shame" of the bootblacking days could not be entirely forgotten—kept everybody in such excellent spirits and was subtly different from all the other young men who were being brought to the house.

As for the young man himself, he was swept into a maelstrom. His "Dora" had appeared, and straightway there could be but one great purpose in his life. He must carve out a career for himself which would enable him to support a wife in the comfortable Beadnellian manner.

He was only eighteen, but, as everybody knows, that is the magical age for a first romance. And of course never before had young man conceived a grander, more stupendous or more amazing passion; never had there been born a lovelier, more wondrous—indeed, miraculous—creature than the youngest Miss Beadnell. It was all inconceivably splendid. Never by any possibility could this supreme passion grow less, even in the slightest degree. It would remain at white heat all the days of his life. It was probably the most marvelous phenomenon in the world's entire history. He was in love, and she—well, she at least was very willing that he should love her.

You do not need to be told that there was no official engagement. In the respectable Beadnellian world all kinds of material considerations must be taken into account before parental consent may be graciously accorded to young folk desiring to marry. . . . The good folk of Lombard Street find themselves discussing this young Mr. Dickens. Maria and he? But he is barely eighteen. Absurd! And his social position? Well, they do not wish to be unkind, but— And then his prospects: decidedly poor. A shorthand reporter in the law courts; apparently, too, a gay spark who thinks nothing of wasting the few shillings he does earn at the theater. But of course it is a mere boy-and-girl affair, which will last at most a few months. No need to be unduly alarmed: dear Maria is a sensible girl.

They were soon to understand that it was no ordinary flirtation. They were soon to realize that Henry Kolle's young friend could hardly be treated in the usual casual manner. There was something about him that was unfamiliar to them and even a little alarming: a fieriness that was uncomfortable and an outlook not wholly to be approved. It might be well, after all, to take some little precautions. For a while, however, nothing was done. Dickens seems to have been a welcome guest for more than a year.

At this time he had "worked up a connection" with some of the proctors in that queer survival known as

Doctors' Commons—"a little out of the way place," David Copperfield records, "where they administer what is called ecclesiastical law and play all kinds of tricks with obsolete old monsters of Acts of Parliament" —and had an office, or part of an office, within its precincts, in Bell-yard. The work must have been extraordinarily dull, though one or two cases were sufficiently comic to provide him a few years later with good material for a sketch, but it was all part of his resolution to become the admitted master of his craft; and with the image of the adorable Maria forever before him, he lost no opportunity of widening the scope of his studies. At the earliest allowable moment—the day after his eighteenth birthday—he applied for and obtained a ticket of admission to the reading-room of the British Museum, and with the impatient zeal which characterized every one of his future undertakings, set out to consolidate his position, and, to use his own words, "fight his way out of poverty and obscurity."

As it happens there has survived a set of verses written by Dickens about this time for the Beadnells, which allows us an intimate peep at the family. "The Bill of Fare" was probably composed in the autumn of 1831. It describes a gay party in Lombard Street, and ends with a series of premature epitaphs of those who are present. Besides the Beadnells themselves there are the Moules from Lower Clapton—father, mother, a military-minded Joe devoted to gold lace, and two daughters, one of whom sits by herself in a corner and is not altogether unlike the Miss Podsnap of later days. There are the Porter Leighs, also from Clapton, with a daughter, Mary Anne, a great friend of Maria's and destined to play no small part in her unlucky romance. There is Dr. Beetham, a provocative creature chiefly remarkable for the uncommon precautions he takes against catching cold, and there is Mr. Francis M'Namara renowned for his wonderful waistcoats. Kolle is there, and Mr. Lloyd, now married to Margaret, and of course Dickens himself—

> ". . . a young Summer Cabbage, without any heart;
> Not that he's *heartless,* but because, as folks say,
> He lost his, twelve months ago from last May."

"The Bill of Fare" was intended to amuse, but it was also intended, I fancy, to impress, and amongst the epitaphs will be found a few shrewd thrusts. Dickens might still be invited to the Lombard Street parties, but difficulties were arising. His financial position was hardly improving, and a little pressure, I suspect, was already being brought to bear on Maria. On the family itself, of course, nothing but praise was bestowed. Mr. Beadnell is

> "beyond contradiction,
> An excellent man, and a good politician."

Mrs. Beadnell is tactfully thanked for what she has done to put Dickens at his ease in polite society. Anne is "a truly delightful and sweet-tempered girl," whose favorite author is naturally *Colley* Cibber.

Maria of necessity is treated in a more serious vein, and it is interesting to find her lover writing lines which he could have recited as the truth twenty years later:

> "The impression that Memory engraves in my heart
> Is all I have left, and with that I ne'er part."

She has, by the way, her little dog, liver-colored and white, "who would eat mutton-chops if you cut off the fat"; and so at this early stage Jip makes his appearance in literature. Towards the Leighs, however, a hostility is shown which cannot altogether be hidden. Mary Anne in particular is chosen out for attack. Her liking for scandal is not omitted, and there is a veiled accusation of interference in his affairs:

> "The greatest tormentor that I e'er knew;
> On every flirtation she kept a sharp eye."

But most interesting of all is the epitaph on himself, for it hints at that excitable impatience with those who were in disagreement with him which in later years so often led to misunderstandings and even to serious trouble:

> "Last, here's Charles Dickens who's now gone for ever;
> It's clear that he thought himself very clever;
> To all his friends' faults—it almost makes me weep,
> He was wide awake—to his own fast asleep.
>
> "His faults,—and they were not in number few,
> As all his acquaintance extremely well knew,
> Emanated,—to speak of him in good part
> I think rather more from the head than the heart."

Difficulties were arising, but so far they had not been very dreadful. Maria Beadnell seems to have been capricious and exacting, but there is no reason to suppose that at this time she was not as genuinely in love as her shallow little soul would allow her to be. She can have had no inkling of the kind of career that was to be his, and it may be that even at this time she had no real intention of ever marrying into so "uncertain" a family as his; but I like to think that in the portrait of Dora Spenlow there was not too much exaggeration.

As for Dickens himself, he must have been waiting with what patience he could summon for such an improvement in his fortunes as would bring the Beadnells to reason. And I can imagine his shock when the news came that the youngest Miss Beadnell was to be sent to Paris to complete her education. She was twenty at the time, but no matter. To Paris she must go, in which city of politeness, presumably, she would have ample opportunity to forget this slightly dangerous young man who, for all his amusing verses and sparkling ways, seemed unlikely to go, financially speaking, very far.

So the lovers parted. No doubt they swore eternal devotion and promised to count the days until they should meet again. No doubt many cunning arrangements were made whereby letters could be dispatched and delivered without parental detection. Dickens may have persuaded himself that now was the time to show the world that he was no ordinary person. It is certain that he worked as never before. You remember how Traddles, dear good man, spent long hours nobly declaiming to Betsey Trotwood and Mr. Dick, the while David took down in his note-book every word that was uttered; and friends like Tom Mitton and Tobin were now helping Dickens in much the same way.

Some sort of parliamentary damson, indeed, seems to have been put into his hands even before the break with the Beadnells, for there is evidence to prove that he was receiving occasional employment on a newspaper called the Sun. But his income remained obstinately small, and the legal cases in Doctors' Commons were becoming drearier each week, and once again he began to doubt whether he had made a wise choice.

Quite seriously, he thought of the professional stage. No one can have known better than he the great difference between amateur and professional behind the footlights, but his theatrical studies were being both extensive and peculiar.

"I went to some theatre every night," he told Forster once, when he was recalling these days, "with a very few exceptions, for at least three years: really studying the bills first, and going to where there was the best acting: and always to see Mathews whenever he played. I practised immensely (even such things as walking in and out, and sitting down in a chair): often four, five, six hours a day: shut up in my own room, or walking about in the fields. I prescribed to myself, too, a sort of Hamiltonian system for learning parts: and learnt a great number." He did more, however, than merely practice. From one of his letters, which seems to have escaped the notice of all the biographers, we find that for some time he was taking regular lessons from Robert Keeley, the well-known actor who, with his wife, was afterwards to appear in so many of the dramatizations of Dickens's novels. And in that queer, vivid way of his he probably saw himself making a triumphant début in public, astonishing all London, earning an ambassadorial salary, and laying the laurels of a new Garrick at Somebody's feet in the Lombard Street house.

He took his decision, and only Fanny was let into the secret. Sometime in February or March, 1832, a letter was sent to George Bartley, a well-known comedian who was then Mathews's stage-manager at Covent Garden Theatre. It set forth what the writer believed that he could do, and asked for a trial. "There must have been something in my letter," he told Forster, "that struck the authorities, for Bartley wrote to me almost immediately to say that they were busy getting up 'The Hunchback' (so they were), but that they would communicate with me again, in a fortnight. Punctual to the time another letter came, with an appointment to do anything of Mathews's I pleased, before him and Charles Kemble, on a certain day at the theatre."

The day came; Fanny had promised to go with her brother to play his songs; but a bad cold and a swollen face caused him to ask for a postponement. He would renew his application, he said, next season.

That application was never renewed, for almost immediately another opening presented itself. At the same time, however, there came further troubles at home. Mr. Dickens had manfully adopted a new profession, but its practice had not led him into less extravagant ways. Always keen to play host to his friends, he would give them the best of good dinners and the most gracious of wines. There might no longer be any "expectations," but had he not two clever children who were already contributing, as clever children should, to the family's expenses? And was not Charles's income bound to increase very materially in the near future? Who could doubt it? In due course, too, those other boys of his would be delighted to see that their father was not worried with paltry affairs of the purse. And—really, if a hard-working gentleman like himself, who at forty-five had settled down to new and most tiring, in fact exhaustive and brain-racking work, could not spend a few shillings now and then on a decent bottle of wine to be shared with his family and friends, what was the world coming to? . . .

Unfortunately the wine merchant had none too good an opinion of his financial standing, and after all polite attempts to get his account settled had failed, he had recourse to the law. For the second time Mr. Dickens was arrested. His son, very busy himself at the time, wrote to Tom Mitton, then qualified as a solicitor, imploring him to see what could be done.

Some arrangement seems to have been made, largely,

no doubt, at Dickens's own cost, for he was to be desperately hard up for a considerable time, and for a while all was well. But there were other tradesmen whose bills remained unpaid, and now it was that at "moments of difficulty" Mr. Dickens found it convenient to "disappear" until such times as his son and that nice Thomas Mitton had put matters right. An ignoble business, I am afraid; but there have always been many John Dickenses about. I dare say he could have argued with some reason that he was not spending money selfishly on himself; I dare say he believed that he was free from all blame; but that even now he was taking shameful advantage of his eldest son, there can be no doubt whatever.

How often he "disappeared" I do not know, but the family became well accustomed to the proceeding. "I own," wrote Dickens to Mitton on one such occasion, "that at present his absence does not give me any great uneasiness, knowing how apt he is to get out of the way when anything goes wrong." How apt! delightful word! You are not surprised to hear Dickens speaking of the truant as "the prodigal father." But Mr. Dickens knew what he was doing. He knew that Charles would arrange something or other. Had he not always declared that Charles was an exceptional boy? And it is certainly the fact that this time his eldest son never refused his help, even when he was almost penniless himself and forced to ask Mitton for a loan of a shilling or two as he wanted "to give the governor some money."

When one remembers, moreover, that at this time he was straining every nerve—I can think of no more accurate words—to make himself financially secure, it will be realized how well he was behaving. And in later years, when he was accused of being a mere money-grubber, it is not to be forgotten that there were half a dozen John Dickenses forever hanging on with a very tight grip to his coat-tails. There were times, of course, when he could not restrain his anger—he could write, for instance, of his father's "damnable shadow"—times when in a fury he allowed himself to take a course that was most injudicious; but for his "prodigal father" he ever retained a warm affection. There is no unlovely touch, as you will have noticed, in Wilkins Micawber. . . .

Meanwhile there was the new opening, and within a short while he had made his "great splash," as he called it, and found the finest parliamentary plums within his grasp. A new evening journal had just made its appearance—the first number had appeared on March 5, 1832—and Dickens was offered and accepted a position on its staff. This paper was the True Sun. Its editor was Samuel Blanchard, and it had for its dramatic critic a young enthusiast from Newcastle whose name was John Forster. Moreover, within a very few months while he was still on the True Sun, room was found for him on the reporting staff of his uncle's paper, the Mirror of Parliament, which had for some time been employing his father.

It is to Forster that we owe the single anecdote which relates to Dickens's journalistic activities at this time. There was a general strike of reporters on the True Sun, he records, "and I well remember noticing at this dread time, on the staircase of the magnificent mansion we were lodged in, a young man of my own age whose keen animation of look would have arrested attention anywhere, and whose name upon enquiry I then for the first time heard. It was coupled with the fact which gave it interest even then, that 'young Dickens' had been spokesman for the recalcitrant reporters, and conducted their case triumphantly."

And so at last we find Dickens perched uncomfortably in a "preposterous pen" of a gallery, but in parliament and well capable of dealing with even the most "difficult" speaker. It was the old House of Commons—the fire did not occur until October, 1834—and room could be found for the newspaper men only at the back of the Strangers' Gallery. Notes had to be taken with the book on one's knee; and with a hundred visitors or more sitting in front of one and probably mumbling in that discreetly low tone which is as maddening to the involuntary listener as a veritable shout, it can have been no easy task to produce a faithful record of the proceedings below.

Now the ordinary young man, you would think, finding himself in such distinguished company—and there were men of distinction in the back row of the gallery as well as within the bar of the House—would be conscious of a certain degree of awe. Here was a great historical occasion—the first session of a reformed parliament, brought together after such a change in the constitution as the country had not witnessed for nearly a century and a half. There was no dearth of great figures. There were Lord John Russell and Palmerston and Sir Robert Peel. There were Cobbett and O'Connell and Stanley. In the Upper House Lord Grey, the prime minister, faced Wellington himself.

But it does not seem that Dickens at twenty was greatly impressed. On the contrary, he found nothing exhilarating in the spectacle of these rather quarrelsome old gentlemen who went to such lengths to wrap up their meaning in a polite mass of verbiage. He deplored the waste of time, and symbolized his feelings in an acute dislike of the shape of the prime minister's head.

And, indeed, to him who had already passed through such a varied experience, there must have seemed to be an air of unreality over things. Or perhaps it was that the common human affairs, which meant so much to himself, were so rarely considered worthy of comment. "Away with this bauble!" he may have felt inclined to cry out, and I, for one, am not surprised to learn that, when a few years later and at the height of his fame Dickens was invited to stand for parliament, he refused. I admit that in his letters declining the invitation he was careful to point out that financial considerations alone were dictating his refusal, but I cannot believe that he ever seriously considered the proposal. If he had, nothing would have kept him out of the Commons.

He came to look on himself as a Radical, though he was by no means such an out-and-out Radical as he liked to think, but, luckily for his fame, he found a more efficacious method than any speeches in parliament to lead public attention in the direction he wanted. But, whatever his own feelings may have been about the proceedings which it was his duty to record, he was doing his work so remarkably well that in a short while he was very generally considered to be the most efficient reporter in the House.

His salary, moreover, was good—fifteen guineas at least each week during the session. It was not a fortune, of course, for sessions in those days were short, and nobody knows how much of it had to be given up to his father; but surely a career was now shaping itself. Surely in a little time he would be definitely out of Queer Street and sufficiently prosperous to satisfy the demands even of a bank manager and his wife?

[3]

We come to the sad affair of the jilting, if jilting it is to be called.

Unfortunately such of Dickens's letters of this period as survive are not very numerous, and as often as not they are undated. Forster has practically nothing to say of the matter, and even the most careful researches since his day fail to provide too clear-cut a picture. About the two main facts, however, there is no question at all. The Maria Beadnell who returned from Paris— probably at the end of this year—was no longer the affectionate creature who had enjoyed all the excitements of a secret understanding, and young Dickens was told plainly enough that his presence would no longer be welcome in the Lombard Street house.

Imagine his feelings! The very chance for which he had been waiting so long had come, and he had made the most of it. But everything had been done for her—or so he chose to think—and for her alone. She was forever in his thoughts, and it needed only a sight of her to complete his triumphant success. And now she was home, and he was not permitted to see her!

Even more dreadful, she apparently expressed no particular desire to see him. Yet how could this be? She was his. All those letters of hers which were so carefully treasured, those little gifts of hers which he examined so lovingly every day—no, he could not believe it. There must be some horrible mistake. Her family or that interfering Miss Leigh—he had always disliked her in spite of her apparent liking for himself—had put Maria against him. Well, Henry Kolle must make matters right. Luckily Kolle's own suit was progressing, and in a month or two his engagement to Anne would probably be announced.

The two men had remained good enough friends. When Dickens took advantage of the parliamentary vacations to steal away for some country air and learn how to sit a horse, Kolle would be invited to join him. We hear of one such invitation to Fulham, where "an 'oss" was to be provided for him, whose appearance was such that "you would think (with the exception of dog's meat) there was no earthly purpose to which he could be applied." It was Kolle, too, who was given the particular reason why his friend found it inconvenient to retain the lodgings he had taken in Cecil Street: there was too much water in the hashes. And it was only Kolle who could help him in this present trouble. Accordingly, a letter was sent asking him to hand to Maria a written proposal of marriage. Kolle agreed to act as messenger whenever he might be required, and the letter was duly delivered.

Neither this letter nor the curiously indefinite reply which it seems to have called forth survives. His declaration, however, led to the much-desired meeting. It was not a success. Maria was cold and reproachful. I think I understand the attitude she appears to have adopted. Away from Dickens, life was very pleasant and easy. She had no particular desire for the responsibilities of marriage, more especially with a man younger than herself, who was hardly in a position to give her the luxuries to which she was accustomed. She liked and admired him, and in his presence perhaps was not always sure of herself; but he was too headstrong, too uncomfortably intense, a man who asked for so much more than she could give. To be courted and admired, even to be loved—in a genteel way—was clearly her right, but with Charles you never quite knew where you were.

She must have known, of course, that he had done nothing to incur her displeasure; she must have realized that she was not behaving very well herself; and so, in the manner of other young women in a similarly awkward situation, she found her best defense in attack. I do not know in what way the attack was begun, nor whether Miss Leigh's name was made use of from the beginning, but whatever it was, poor Dickens found himself somehow in the wrong. It is a very old story. . . .

There came other meetings, and more poignant letters from the hard-worked parliamentary reporter, none of which does discredit to his memory. He appealed to Anne, but Anne frankly admitted that she could not understand the state of her sister's affections. Kolle continued to take letters to Lombard Street, and Fanny's good offices seem to have been requisitioned; misunderstanding only followed misunderstanding. The accusation that Dickens had told "some garbled story" of his relations with Maria to Mary Anne Leigh was now being continually repeated, and his denials were as continually being disbelieved.

I confess I do not know what exactly to make of Miss Leigh. She may have been in love with Dickens herself; she may have been genuinely anxious to help a friend of hers; she may have been Maria's chief accomplice in a very cruel game. But most probably she was a born mischief-maker, ever on the lookout for a few harmless words which could be embroidered and transformed into the most maliciously indiscreet story. I do not doubt that Dickens in his distress had spoken of Maria to her old friend—what more natural? But that he had ever taken her into his full confidence —even after she had assured him, as he is goaded to admit in one of his letters, that Maria "had made her a confidante of all that had ever passed between us without reserve"—he stedfastly denied. This, however, was the weapon upon which Maria herself came to rely, and it was Mary Anne Leigh in whom the wretched wrangles continued to center. Moreover, it was due to her "duplicity and disgusting falsehoods" —I quote Dickens again—that he was temporarily estranged from his sister.

The time came when further suspense was not to be borne. On March 18, he wrote to his "Dora" a letter that marked the beginning of the end. "Your own feelings," he told her, "will enable you to imagine far better than any attempt of mine to describe the painful struggle it has cost me to make up my mind to adopt the course which I now take ... Our meetings of late have been little more than so many displays of heartless indifference on the one hand, while on the other they have never failed to prove a fertile source of wretchedness and misery; and seeing, as I cannot fail to do, that I have engaged in a pursuit which has long since been worse than hopeless and a further perseverance in which can only expose me to deserved ridicule, I have made up my mind to return the little present I received from you some time since (which I have always prized, as I still do, far beyond anything I ever possessed) and the other early mementoes of our past correspondence, which I am sure it must be gratifying to you to receive, as after our recent relative situations they are certainly better adapted for your custody than mine."

He spoke of his "utter desolation and wretchedness," but could not bring himself to see how he had ever acted otherwise than "fairly, intelligently and honourably." He repeated his denial of having made any "mock confidante to whom to entrust a garbled story for my own purposes," and concluded with a perhaps too conventionally expressed hope for the happiness of his "first and last love."

It is possible that this was a rather more abrupt move than any that Maria was contemplating at the moment. Nothing will convince me that these recurring "scenes" were wholly disagreeable to her. She returned his letter —though not without keeping a copy!— with a reply which only renewed his wretched uncertainty. There came further meetings, and more letters passed through the faithful Kolle's hands. But the breach showed no signs of closing. Dickens was being disillusioned, though he could not immediately bring himself to the point of breaking away. "I have no hopes to express," he wrote, and the tragic vein may be excused, "no wishes to communicate . . . I have borne more from you than I do believe any creature breathing ever bore from a woman before." Nevertheless he did make one further effort to show that his own conduct had been blameless, in the course of which he administered a sharp rebuke to Miss Leigh. It did nothing to help on his cause.

As it happened, some grand theatricals had been arranged to take place in the new house which Mr. Dickens, presumably in one of his less involved "moments," had taken in Bentinck Street. The date chosen was April 27. Kolle had been given a part in the opera of "Clari, or the Maid of Milan," ever popular since its first production in London ten years before, and containing the song "Home, Sweet Home,"—and had, incidentally, received a reprimand from the worried stage-manager for not attending rehearsals. But he had a good enough excuse, for his engagement had been announced, and the wedding was fixed for May.

The theatricals duly took place—the playbill is still

to be seen—and both Maria and Mary Anne Leigh were amongst the audience. I can imagine the agonies of that evening. Here she was, actually under his father's roof, but just one amongst many guests. She did not come peeping behind the scenes, eager and anxious for his success—though I fancy that Miss Leigh did—but sat in her seat, politely aloof. And he was obliged to pretend that he was his ordinary cheerful and bustling self. But your great comedian will run onto the stage with a laugh, and crack his jokes, even though his heart may be thumping and there are tears at the back of his eyes; and Dickens, I think, must have steeled himself, and gone through the four different parts for which he had cast himself, without a tremor. She should see what he could do. I dare say he had never acted so well before. . . .

As ill luck would have it, however, Miss Leigh chose this evening to throw herself in Dickens's way, and, as he was forced subsequently to explain to Maria, "after we went upstairs I could not get rid of her." Maria became more distant than ever, and her distracted lover, realizing that after Kolle's marriage he would be without a messenger, determined to pocket his pride for the last time and made his final appeal.

He was anxious to write, he told her, "knowing that the opportunity of addressing you through Kolle—now my only means of communicating with you—will shortly be lost." She had asked to see Mary Anne Leigh's reply to his letter of protest, but of course she would be shown it if ever it came. There followed a passage which few will read wholly unmoved: "I have come to the unqualified determination that I will allow no feeling of pride, no haughty dislike to making a reconciliation, to prevent my expressing it without reserve. . . . I will only openly and at once say that there is nothing I have more at heart, nothing I more sincerely and earnestly desire, than to be reconciled to you. ... All that any one can do to raise himself by his own exertions and unceasing assiduity I have done, and will do. I have no guide by which to ascertain your present feelings, and I have, God knows, no means of influencing them in my favour. I have never loved and I never can love any human creature breathing but yourself. We have had many differences, and we have lately been entirely separated. Absence, however, has not altered my feelings in the slightest degree, and the love I now tender you is as pure and as lasting as at any period of our former correspondence."

He begged for a definite answer, and once again Maria was cold and reproachful.

Whereupon Dickens, to use his own words, went his way. ...

It may be that he placed exaggerated importance on the part, whatever it really was, that Mary Anne Leigh had chosen to play. It is a fact that he was at all times easily moved to a mood of extremes, and it may be that the mixture of hurt vanity and unduly sensitive pride which was to project him in later years into so many unnecessary quarrels, had already made its appearance. Throughout his life, you will find, he was to take himself and his own affairs with a solemnity not always accorded to the affairs of other people. At theirs, he could laugh; at his own, seldom or never.

I do not, of course, suggest that a young man in love is expected to see anything comic in the spectacle of his own impending dismissal, but I do believe that his misery was enormously accentuated by this queer inability to look at himself in what I may call the Dickensian manner. "I would much rather mismanage my own affairs," he wrote to Miss Leigh, "than have them ably conducted by the officious interference of any one." The words were to remain true all his life. Unfortunately the word "officious" became almost unduly elastic. There were even times when the semisacred Forster himself drove Dickens almost to desperation.

It is nothing that within two or three years he was married. The agony of these last few months left its mark, and it was a mark that was to be reflected in more than one of his books. He had "nursed his love," as one of his biographers says, "till it became infatuation," but that was his way. Many men find their Doras and are dismissed; few are so wholly at the mercy of their emotions as was Dickens. There was much of David Copperfield within him, but there was also a trace of the unfortunate Bradley Headstone. Yet the Fates had not been too cruel. What sort of a life would have been his, had "Dora" married her love and refused, as I feel certain she would have refused, to die at the appointed hour?

Years later, and, as we shall see, at another time of emotional distress, he was to meet Maria again. Then, perhaps, we may legitimately smile.

[4]

The career, however, was shaping.

There may have come a little extra reserve; there did come a decision to live henceforth away from his family; above all there was a grim determination to show the world, which included Lombard Street, that there were very great things to be done. For a while he seems to have had serious thoughts of reading for the bar—years later he did enter his name as a student at the Middle Temple—but already they were discovering that "young Dickens" was as expert at his present job as any of his seniors, and wisely he stayed where he was.

Then in June of this year, at a time when he may have been reporting Gladstone's maiden speech in the House, his uncle John Barrow took the first step toward securing his promotion. The Mirror of Parliament could afford to pay its staff well, but it was being published only during the sessions. A more regular position was sought: a position, moreover, which, it was to be hoped, would not limit him to the same dreary succession of late nights at Westminster. Something more adventurous and unusual was wanted. On the dailies, it seemed a good reporter might hope for an almost kaleidoscopic existence.

The choice of newspaper was not very wide, but there was a certain range. The one colleague with whom he had made especial friends, Thomas Beard, was on the Morning Herald. John Barrow himself worked for the Times. Dickens seems to have expressed a preference for the Whig Morning Chronicle. Unfortunately there was no immediate vacancy on this journal, and for another two sessions he was obliged to remain on the Mirror.

Powerful influences, however, were at work on his behalf. John Barrow had introduced him to that curiously unreliable but remarkable critic, John Payne Collier, at that time on the Chronicle, and Collier was favorably impressed and promised his help. But it was Joseph Parkes who was really responsible for any definite engagement. Parkes was one of those people behind the political scenes who can wield the power of a cabinet minister and be hardly known to the public. At this time he was what would now be called chief agent to the Whig party.

The Chronicle had recently changed hands, and was not in too flourishing a state. In John Black it had an excellent man for its editor but it was in need of new blood, and Parkes was called in to help in its reorganization. Incidentally, he seems to have insisted on a more bellicose policy, and relations with some of the Tory organs became strained—a matter not altogether without interest to the readers of "Pickwick." The story goes that Parkes engaged Thomas Beard amongst others, and asked him to recommend a colleague. Beard had no hesitation in naming Dickens, and the thing was done.

This must have been sometime in the summer of 1834. Dickens was given a weekly salary of five guineas, and seems to have celebrated the occasion by laying in a stock of smart clothes. From this time, indeed, we must figure him as more than a bit of a dandy, and to his last days he retained an affection for bright color and unconventional cut which would be astonishing were it not for that love of theatrical display from which, even as a boy, he was never wholly free. Payne Collier remarks on the change in his appearance at this time. He mentions "a new hat and a very handsome blue cloak, with black velvet facings, the corner of which he threw over his shoulders *à l'espagnol.*" Well, well, he must have made a fine figure.

It was still of course one of his duties to listen to the parliamentary debates. Like Copperfield, he continued to record predictions that never came to pass, professions that were never fulfilled, and explanations that were only meant to mystify. But in the vacations there came opportunities for more interesting work. So we may accompany him with Beard to Edinburgh and attend the great banquet given to Lord Grey on his retirement from office.

It was to be a function of the highest importance, and the newspapers had made the most elaborate arrangements. The representatives of the Chronicle went north by sea and arrived in good time to review the preparations. Accounts of the various proceedings were sent post-haste to London, and the authorship of one of them at any rate—it is an amusing description of a guest's impatience at the banquet—cannot be in doubt.

The guest in question, one gathers, saw no reason to wait for the arrival of Lord Grey and his friends, and "appeared to think that the best thing he could do would be to eat his dinner, while there was anything to eat. He accordingly laid about him with right goodwill, the example was contageous, and the clatter of knives and forks became general. Whereupon several gentlemen, who were not hungry, cried out 'Shame!' and looked very indignant; and several gentlemen who were hungry cried 'Shame!' too, eating, nevertheless, all the while as fast as they possibly could. In this dilemma, one of the stewards mounted a bench, and feelingly represented to the delinquents the enormity of their conduct, imploring them for decency's sake, to defer the process of mastication until the arrival of Earl Grey. This address was loudly cheered, but totally unheeded; and this is, perhaps, one of the few instances on record of a dinner having been virtually concluded before it began."

Good stuff, surely! And if a touch of exaggeration and caricature had already made its appearance, it was a novel touch, which the world was very ready to welcome. One wonders, indeed, how many other reporters in those solemn days would have been daring enough to garnish their solid fare with so frolicsome a sauce.

The Edinburgh outing was but the first of many delectably unusual affairs which came Dickens's way.

There were all sorts of adventures in all sorts of places. Tom Beard was often his companion, but sometime he set out alone. We know of one such expedition in a gig into Essex and Norfolk; and "I have a presentiment," he wrote gaily to Henry Austin, one of his little band of amateur actors who was to become his brother-in-law, "I shall run over a child before I reach Chelmsford, my first stage."

There is detailed news, too, of a tour in the west. Lord John Russell had joined the ministry of the Whigs, and was conducting his campaign down in Devon. It was necessary for Dickens to make the most careful plans, so that no item of news should be lost and Mr. Black up in London should receive all dispatches at the earliest possible moment.

Your reporter at this time must have had an uncomfortable time. Telephones, motorcars, reserved seats for the press—these were luxuries undreamed of. You sat where you could and hoped for the best. If there was an out-of-doors meeting, and the rain was turning your note-book to pulp, it was only a lucky chance that provided two colleagues temporarily at leisure and willing to protect it, umbrella-wise, with a kerchief. This actually happened to Dickens in Exeter. And there was no lack of incident on the road.

"I have had to charge," he was writing two or three years later, "for half a dozen break-downs in half a dozen times as many miles. I have had to charge for the damage of a great-coat from the drippings of a blazing wax candle, in writing through the smallest hours of the night in a swift-flying carriage and pair. I have had to charge for all sorts of breakages fifty times on a journey. . . . I have charged for broken hats, broken luggage, broken chaises, broken harness—everything but a broken head—which is the only thing," he added in his whimsical way, "they would have grumbled to pay for."

His work, moreover, was being highly appreciated in London, as much for the reports themselves as for the careful manner whereby they reached their destination. And you are not surprised to be told that the time came soon enough when John Black was telling his staff that this very junior reporter must be kept in reserve for great occasions. "Any fool," he is supposed to have said, "can pass judgment, more or less just or unjust, on a book or a play—but 'Boz' can do better things."

"Boz?"

[5]

Something else had happened, something so thrillingly important to Dickens that the memory of its excitements never faded. You will remember that there had been youthful dramas; there had been comediettas and playlets; and in more recent years the private theatricals in his father's house had generally included a program of the most varied kind. On the night when "Clari" had been the most ambitious item, there was also an Introductory Prologue for which, I dare say, the stage-manager was wholly responsible; and in the same year a burlesque entitled "The O'Thello," written by Dickens, had also been produced. In a note-book, too, were rough sketches of people and things seen, scribbled down more or less for the fun of the thing. But nothing of his own composition had been printed, for the simple reason that it had never been submitted for publication. In the autumn of 1833, however, he had written, or revised, a short sketch of a comical nature, and this he posted off "with fear and trembling" to the old-established Monthly Magazine.

There is not an author who does not remember with pleasure the astonishing thrill of seeing himself for the first time in print. It is an experience like none other in the world. He will stare at the thing, in secret of course, and wonder how a bit of himself has come to be there on the page. He will read and reread it until the words mean nothing at all, and then will be suddenly afraid lest somebody should discover what he is doing and laugh at him for his enormous conceit. Dickens, as a reporter, was well accustomed to find in the newspaper printed work for which he had been responsible, but when he learned that the Monthly Magazine for December was to contain something of his which had nothing to do with his professional duties, something, it is true, unheralded and unsigned, but wholly his own, he experienced an entirely novel sensation, and behaved, I am glad to say, in the usual way. He bought a copy of this magazine, casually, at a bookshop in the Strand, and no doubt wondered what the man who sold it him would have said had he divulged the authorship of the only contribution of any importance.

And here you find one of those curious coincidences in real life to which Dickens was so fond of drawing attention and of which he made such frequent—some people would say too frequent—use in his books. In those days, you must understand, the publishing business had not yet been generally divorced from that of bookselling—even today certain booksellers continue to publish new books—and, as it happened, the Strand shop was the very one from which many of Dickens's most famous works were to be issued. Moreover, the man who sold him the magazine was one of the partners in the already existing firm of Chapman & Hall who were, within a year or two, to commission "Pickwick." . . . It was a great moment.

"I walked down to Westminster Hall," Dickens tells us, "and turned into it for half an hour, because my eyes were so dimmed with joy and pride that they could not bear the street, and were not fit to be seen there." Well, Dickens was always partial to tears, but on this occasion they may be forgiven. Already, perhaps, he realized that he had found his right work. It was a very modest beginning, and few outside his immediate circle of friends might learn who had written the sketch, but—he was an author.

To be candid, "A Dinner at Poplar Walk," which was afterwards rechristened "Mr. Minns and His Cousin," was not much of a thing, but its writer was in print, and, more important, the editor of the magazine was asking for more. True, he did not offer to pay, but what of that? The young man had found a way to put his various experiences to good account, and the new kind of writing was far more to his taste than any newspaper reporting.

Hitherto he had been limited by actual facts, but in this new work there was nothing to prevent him from embroidering such facts in any way that he liked. It was as if he were once again in the little upstairs room in Chatham, able at will to project himself into a delightful world of his own. Now, however, an audience was to be imported there with him, and amongst that audience, I imagine, he had every intention of seeing that Miss Beadnell was included.

He wrote to Kolle "to beg Mrs. K.'s criticism of a little paper of mine (the first of a series) in the Monthly (not the New Monthly Magazine) of this month." He had no copy to send, but doubtless Kolle would not mind spending a half-crown on such an occasion or object to showing the magazine to his sister-in-law. He added that his hand was shaking so badly with nervousness that he doubted his words would be legible.

There was no mention of Maria in this letter, but

one may read between the lines. Most certainly she must be told of the great things that were afoot, and I have not the least doubt that when, a month or two later, he asked to be allowed to stand godfather to the first Kolle child and wrote to excuse himself from calling in person, the proffered excuse was not meant to be hidden from her. He was full of work just then, but there was also some agreeable relaxation. Pleasure, he wrote, "in the shape of a very nice pair of black eyes" called him to Norwood, and of course such a call could not be disobeyed. We do not know who owned the black eyes, but it is pleasant to hear of their appearance on the scene at this time, and I hope that Miss Beadnell heard about them. . . .

The series of sketches was duly continued, and in August, 1834, a curious name was for the first time attached to them. "Boz" was a contradiction of Boses, itself a nasal emendation of Moses, which happened to be Dickens's nickname for his youngest and favorite brother Augustus, now seven years old. "Boz" was therefore "a very familiar household word," and the new writer chose it for his pen-name. The sketches themselves were appreciated, by nobody more than John Black, and gained for their author no little reputation. But after eight or nine had appeared, the very natural question of remuneration arose. Unfortunately the Monthly Magazine showed no sign of increasing its circulation to any marked extent. It had come into the hands of a visionary called Holland, who was running it principally as a mouthpiece for his own ideas on social reform, and it had to contend with wealthier and better-edited rivals. Dickens, now convinced that he really could write, asked for payment. The proprietor was afraid that he was not in a position to pay anything except his printer's bill.

So "Boz" said good-by, and made other arrangements.

Chapter IV

On the Eve of Fame

[1]

We may conveniently take a very brief glimpse at the literary world of these days of the thirties.

A distinguished critic, Mr. J. B. Priestley, has expressed the opinion that this was "the period of high spirits, or, if you will, the period of plentiful spirits and high jinks." Evidence in proof of this assertion is certainly not lacking. Ever since Pierce Egan's Life in London had entertained the town in the early twenties, there had been a succession of boisterous, rollicking stories and sketches which had much to tell of eating and drinking and the good things of life, and left "romance" to look after itself.

Sport, too, was now receiving attention from those who were not necessarily accomplished sportsmen themselves. There was an ever-increasing library of sporting books, and Bell's Life in London, begun in 1824, had opened a new era in journalistic experiment. And so, while William IV was sitting, a little uncouthly, on his not too popular throne, you had a whole series of jovial publications, produced, as Mr. Priestley slyly suggests, "between bottle and bottle, as it were," in which woolly-headed lieutenants or sportive squires with the help of a great deal of strong liquor would manage to play hero in some sort of fantastic panorama.

There was fun to be found, it seemed, in the unlikeliest quarters, and stories to be built up from the most unexpected material. The proletarian mother-in-law had not yet been permanently placed in the stocks, but the foreigner's head and wrists already fitted neatly enough into the holes in the pillory-frame. To add to the fun of the thing, a new sort of illustrator had presented himself: not the caricaturist as we know him today, but a painstaking artist ready with just that touch of ironical exaggeration which the frolicsome text was demanding.

So you had comic annuals and sketch-books, with new Toms and Jerrys playing Corinthian and poking inquisitive noses into unexplored corners. So you had Surtees inventing Mr. Jorrocks and describing his "Jaunts and Jollities" in the New Sporting Magazine. You had Theodore Hook, that incomparable, if dangerous, buffoon, surprising fashionable London by the smartness of his cabriolet, but also by his sprightly novels. A city clergyman called Barham was projecting his "Ingoldsby Legends," and he was not the only one of his cloth who found pleasure in composing witty verses and wittier speeches. Thomas Hood was but one of many to find humor more profitable than pathos.

On the stage, too, you could find much the same thing, for although Macready reigned like a king, with an intimate knowledge of and insistence upon regal etiquette, it was the roguish farce or the harlequinade, the burlesque or the festive comedietta, which filled most of the theaters. Greville might complain of the stagnation of the political world, the "hungry forties" might be somewhere in the offing, but when Dickens sat down at his desk to write the "Sketches by Boz," the reading world at any rate was very ready to welcome all the high jinks that it could get.

At the same time, of course, there was no dearth of more solid fare. Never perhaps had the learned reviews been more solemn, nor their editors more solemnly set in their lines. True, a lighter note was allowed to creep in now and then, and soon a new kind of journal was to become popular; but, at the moment, you were expected to be properly academic. In 1834 Carlyle, then at work on his "French Revolution," had been able to print his "Sartor Resartus" in Fraser's Magazine, but the Edinburgh Review did not approve of him altogether, and in general there was heavy thunder about.

Macaulay had made his name as an essayist as well as a politician, and was now to be found in that Holland House circle which, in its own view, at any rate, was highly important. Hazlitt and Coleridge were dead, but Landor, leaving his "Imaginary Conversations" for a while, was busy with critical work. Leigh Hunt was editing a weekly, and occasionally apologizing for the non-appearance of its leading article, due, rather delightfully, to the demands made on his time by a new poem. There was a polite little group about old Samuel Rogers, and two young poets, Tennyson and Browning, had already interested the critics.

Amongst the novelists, I suppose, Edward Bulwer, not yet Lytton, was the most popular. At the beginning of 1835, when he published "Rienzi," his earlier stories were being reissued in more than one form, but he had a rival in Harrison Ainsworth, whose "Rookwood," with a whitewashed Turpin for its hero, continued to delight a not too critical public. Captain Marryat, busily quarreling with Nathaniel P. Willis, the American writer who was then in Europe as correspondent for a newspaper, had lost none of the popularity that had been his since the appearance of that admirable story "The King's Own." He was to publish four or five new books about this time, including "Mr. Midshipman Easy." Mrs. Trollope, Anthony's astonishing mother, now fairly launched on her long literary career, which had begun in a blaze two years back with the publication of "Domestic Manners of the Americans," was receiving much attention for a book upon Paris and a new novel. The younger Disraeli, not content with fiction, was writing the "Runnymede Letters," and Thackeray in relinquishing a minor editorial post was also minded to relinquish his pen.

Incidentally, the publishers had devised a new method of bringing their books to a wide public. The three-volume novel had come to stay—at any rate until the nineties—but editions were necessarily small. You could hardly expect many people to pay thirty-one shillings and sixpence for a novel which they might not wish to keep on their shelves, and as yet the circulating libraries were not too enterprising. (Mr. Mudie did not begin to lend books until 1840.)

At this time, however, a first issue of a new book in monthly, paper-backed "parts," sold generally at a shilling, was meeting with considerable success, and this is a matter of more than merely bibliographical interest. For it often happened—many times in Dickens's case—that part of a novel would be in print a whole year before the last chapters were written: a serious handicap, it seems to me, to most writers, however strictly they may be able to keep to their original plan. No matter: these monthly "parts" became popular, and it was not only novels which appeared in this way. Even the Encyclopædia Britannica could be purchased in this form at six shillings the part.

As for the publishing houses, few except Murray's in Albemarle Street were of any long standing. Henry Colburn had a good business in Marlborough Street, and for some time had been in loose partnership with Richard Bentley, of whom I shall have something to say in a little while; but at this time they were separating, and Dickens was only once to have dealings with Colburn, although the publisher's widow, who was so surprisingly to marry John Forster, became his very good friend. In the Strand, as we have seen, Chapman & Hall had made a beginning, but as yet they were not very well known.

Probably the most enterprising of the younger men was John Macrone of St. James's Square. His rash speculations ultimately brought him to grief, but at this time he was flourishing, and his advertisements filled columns in the newspapers. He had secured Ainsworth and Willis amongst others, and was prepared to give new men a chance. And to him fell the honor of issuing Dickens's first book.

[2]

That first book, however, was some time in the making. Work on the Morning Chronicle did not grow less, and funds remained low. Mr. Dickens was having his "moments" again, and his son had decided that he must have a home for himself. Humble chambers had been found in Furnival's Inn—they cost about twelve shillings a week—and it was here in Holborn that the majority of the sketches were written. But to whom were they to be sent after the editor of the Monthly Magazine had confessed his inability to pay for them? Fortunately for the hard-worked reporter, he was not forced to post off his work to strange editors, for there were men on the staff of his own paper who admired the work and saw no reason why it should not be printed in their own columns.

As it happened, too, it was just at this time that the proprietors of the Morning Chronicle were projecting a new evening paper, and had appointed as its editor a musical Scotsman whose name was George Hogarth. Mr. Hogarth suggested to Dickens that a sketch would go very well into the first number of the new paper that was due to appear on January 31, 1835. Dickens agreed to write what was wanted but, not unnaturally, hinted at the desirability of some financial return.

In the middle of that month he wrote to the new editor, and in view of what was to happen in little more than a year, his words have a curious sound. He hoped, he said, that he would not be considered to be "unreasonably or improperly trespassing," if he asked for "*some* additional remuneration (of course, of no great amount)" for supplying a series of articles on the lines of those which had already been printed. He did not wish to be misunderstood, but *if* the new series "would be considered of use to the new paper," and if the proprietors thought it "fair and reasonable" to pay for work which was outside his ordinary duties as a reporter, would Mr. Hogarth support his claim? Mr. Hogarth did support his claim, and two extra guineas were added at once to his weekly salary.

Seven guineas a week! It was not a vast sum, but it came at a time when Mr. Dickens was learning to "disappear" on the slightest provocation, and when the family in Bentinck Street would be left more or less "in the air." And for that sum the Chronicle, in both morning and evening dress, received, during the year, twenty original sketches. Undoubtedly they were popular contributions. There was a quaintness about them, and a freshness of outlook. The touches of satire were divertingly novel, and the people to whom you were introduced were ordinary folk of the kind you were constantly meeting, without, however, realizing that there was anything of particular interest about them. The extra two guineas, indeed, were being fully earned, and I fancy that when the series suddenly, although only temporarily, came to an end in August, it was either because their author, now more sure of himself, asked for a further increase in his salary, or because other offers were being made for his work.

A new editor, James Grant, had succeeded Holland on the Monthly Magazine, and in later years he was ruefully recalling the fact that in answer to his invitation Dickens had offered at this time to write for him at half a guinea a page. Unfortunately even that modest sum had been beyond the magazine's purse. Another old parliamentary colleague and admirer, however, Vincent Dowling by name was now editing Bell's Life in London; and twelve further sketches appeared in that journal under the signature, curiously enough, of "Tibbs." But, whatever may have been the reason for these contributions being sent "outside," Dickens's personal relations with George Hogarth remained cordial, and sometimes in the summer of 1835 he became engaged to one of his daughters.

So Maria Beadnell had been entirely forgotten? By no means; but Dickens's naturally buoyant spirits had responded to the kindnesses shown him by the Hogarth family. At a time when there was so often trouble in Bentinck Street, where Mrs. Dickens, I am afraid, was doing little to make matters easier for her husband or children, the Hogarths' house in Chelsea soon came to be another such comfortable oasis as Dickens had once found in Lombard Street.

George Hogarth himself seems to have been an amiable man, self-made but educated in the Scottish way, who had begun his career in the law and come into contact with Sir Walter Scott. He had married the daughter of Burns's friend, George Thomson, and had numerous children, including four daughters. Of these the two eldest were Catherine, who was now twenty, and Mary, who was almost sixteen; and I can picture to myself their guest's enormous relief when he found himself once again surrounded by young people who appreciated and understood him and were allowing the last bitter memories of Lombard Street to fade from his mind.

There must have come wonderful days when he would rush round to Chelsea to be made a fuss of and generally mothered. There were practical jokes, too, which were thoroughly enjoyed. Mrs. Hogarth remembered one such occasion when the family were sitting quietly in their drawing-room. "Suddenly a young man"—I quote Dickens's daughter's account—"dressed as a sailor, jumped in at the window, danced a hornpipe, whistling the tune, jumped out again, and a few minutes afterwards Charles Dickens walked gravely in at the door, as if nothing had happened, shook hands all round, and then, at the sight of their puzzled faces, burst into a roar of laughter."

The joke, indeed, was typical of his new joyous mood. He knew now what it was in him to do: he could write, and at any moment might be widely acclaimed. In Bentinck Street there would be an air of unrest and petty squabbling; but here in Chelsea were two beautiful sisters, ready to talk of the exciting things of life, eager to hear of his adventures on the road, applauding those amusing recitals of his, enjoying the sketches that he had written. . . .

In a little while they were filling his thoughts. In

a little while he was falling in love. With Catherine, you ask? I wonder. In a way, I suppose, he was in love with them both, but few who read his letters or study his books will doubt that it was Mary who had stolen his heart. She, however, was little more than a child, and manlike he wanted to marry. And so in his romantic way he made of her a youthful goddess to be worshiped very humbly from below, and chose Catherine for his mate.

The Hogarths seem to have ordered no objection, and the engagement was made known to their friends. It only remained for "Boz" to make a litte more money, and this was forthcoming in a very few months. The sketches had not yet obtained a wide circle of readers. Not many people knew, or cared very much, who "Boz" might be. There were those, however, in a position to judge, who had recognized the merits of this new and engaging writer, and at least one man of importance in the literary world took the trouble to find out who he was, and offered his help. You may imagine the young reporter's pleasure when a letter arrived from no less a person than Harrison Ainsworth, whose "Rookwood" still continued to hold first place in Macrone's list, and was certainly the most popular romance of the day.

This letter was the beginning of a warm friendship which, although it did not last very long, was of the greatest importance to the young Dickens, for, apart from his literary position, Ainsworth knew something of the publishing business from the inside and was able to offer the right kind of advice. A book, he considered, could be made of the sketches, and Macrone, he thought, would be willing to publish it.

He introduced Dickens to the publisher and also to

his own illustrator, the equally well-known George Cruikshank. Macrone was willing to risk his money, only asking for a few additional sketches to make enough material for two half-guinea volumes, Cruikshank was engaged to provide what in the advertisements were called "improvements," and early in the new year the two volumes of "Sketches by Boz" in their dark green cloth duly made their appearance. A sum of money was advanced—apparently £150—and the proud author, though still faithful to Furnival's Inn, moved into one of its more spacious suites.

This, however, was not all. Somebody else of importance was interested in the "Sketches," and before the two volumes had been bound, another firm of publishers had come forward with a very different commission. One Wednesday morning there came to Furnival's Inn a partner in this firm—the man, as it happened, who had sold Dickens his copy of the Monthly Magazine two years ago. This Mr. Hall wished him to "write and edit" a new monthly publication for which Robert Seymour, a well-known sporting artist, was doing the plates. It was the sort of thing, he thought, that "Boz" would do very well: something jovial and sprightly and clubbish, with a background of sport such as would suit Mr. Seymour's particular vein. Fourteen pounds a month was suggested as suitable remuneration, and—would Mr. Dickens mind giving the firm a definite answer by Friday morning? . . .

Dickens wrote off in haste to Catherine Hogarth. The work, he thought, would be "no joke," but the emolument was "too tempting to resist." Whereupon the now very busy and moderately successful young man "thought of Mr. Pickwick."

[3]

How is one expected to relate clearly and with any sobriety the amazing events of the next eighteen months? In the whole history of letters nobody had ever been called on to occupy the position into which this newspaper reporter—almost on a sudden—was to be thrust. Mr. Pickwick naturally insists on a separate chapter devoted to himself and his friends; and this fact in itself lends complication to the business. It was he (with considerable help from his personal servant) who by the end of this—to Dickens—most marvelous year had carried the name of Boz over the civilized world; but his appearance on the scene gave rise to no immediate furore, and for a little while his creator cannot have anticipated the astounding and unheard-of reception that was to be accorded to his work.

As a matter of fact there were many irons in the fire when on the last day of March, the first number of "Pickwick" appeared, and at one curious moment shortly afterwards it seemed not impossible that the young reporter—and you are to remember that he was still on the staff of the Morning Chronicle at seven guineas a week—who could compose such sprightly sketches about "everyday people," would meet with his greatest success as a writer, on the stage.

What, you wonder, was he thinking about things in the earlier part of this year? Well, there can have been little enough time to think of anything except his forthcoming marriage and the sudden rush of new and most fascinating work; but he must have enjoyed the success of his first book, coming as it did after so many years of drudgery and disappointment—at a time, too, when he was proposing to shoulder a new responsibility. I can imagine with what ill-concealed anxiety he searched the newspapers for reviews. These in general were kind. Chamber's Edinburgh Journal in particular was encouraging, and was of the opinion that unless Boz were to "fall off very miserably in his subsequent efforts" he could "scarcely fail to become a successful popular author." Fall off very miserably, forsooth! Why, he had not begun to show them what he could do! And when Macrone announced his intention of printing a second edition of the "Sketches," their author must have hugged the delicious possibility of his being freed very soon from all financial worry.

Undoubtedly the book was a success, and four editions were called for within the year. People talked about it, and wanted to know who Boz might be. The newspapers coolly printed whole sketches in their columns, but if this was good "copy" for them, it was better advertisement for the author. In the House of Commons the member for Reading, Thomas Talfourd, whose "Ion" had been recently staged by Macready and whose efforts to amend the miserable copyright laws of the day had endeared him to Dickens, must have been delighted, and undoubtedly introduced the young man to many of his political and theatrical friends. Ainsworth, of course, was equally pleased, and may have suggested to Macrone the advisability of securing a novel from so uncommon a writer. Yes, it must have been a time of excitement, and not only for Boz and the Hogarths and Tom Beard, already chosen to be best man. Mr. Dickens, you may be sure, found every satisfaction in the prospect of further agreeable "expectations" from a relative. . . .

It was on April 2 that the wedding took place, at St. Luke's Church, Chelsea, where Charles Kingsley's father was rector. A modest little function, it was, with only the two families and Tom Beard at the breakfast. Mr. Dickens made a speech in his best manner, and no doubt there was a copy of a thin publication bound in green paper, somewhere about—perhaps in his hands—as he spoke. The bride, we are told, "was dressed in the simplest and neatest manner, and looked better perhaps than if she had been enabled to aim at something more." There was not, indeed, too much money at the moment for fine dresses or elaborate feasts, and, as it was, only the willingness of "Pickwick's" publishers to advance the sum due for the first two numbers—a meager twenty-nine pounds—allowed the ceremony to take place when it did.

Almost from the day of the marriage Dickens plunged into that one long spell of feverish activity which was to end only on the day before his death. There came holidays of a sort and unrestful periods when nothing in particular was being done, but in general there was to be a self-inflicted sentence of more than thirty years' hard labor. A short honeymoon was spent in the village of Chalk, not far from his beloved Chatham; but even at that time there was a great deal of work to be done, and on his return to London, there was not only work but fresh worries as well.

He came to be indirectly involved in a tragic affair that seemed likely to interfere very seriously indeed, if not actually put an end to, all Pickwickian activities. There was also the business of finding a new house—it had been arranged that Mary Hogarth should come to live with them—and this meant a further drain on his purse, for he was unable to be rid of the chambers in Furnival's Inn, and for some time was obliged to pay double rent. Mr. Dickens too, in the excitement of seeing his son the author of a successful book, was having more unfortunate "moments," and seems to have found Bentinck Street too much for his purse: more than once, in the next year, he was obliged to move house.

The "Sketches," however, were still selling, and in April or May, Macrone was definitely offering terms for another book. The success of "Rookwood" seems to have suggested the desirability of an historical novel, and Dickens, full of Pickwick though his mind must have been, was ready enough to undertake a commission which promised so much larger a financial return than the "Pickwick Papers" seemed at the moment likely to produce.

We know the exact terms that Macrone offered, and although he was never to receive the book, the figures are interesting as suggesting the sort of profit he was making out of the "Sketches." Dickens wrote to him at the beginning of May, accepting the offer of two hundred pounds to be paid on delivery of a new manuscript to be called "Gabriel Vardon, the Locksmith of London." That sum, however, was only payment for a first edition of a thousand copies, and if further editions were required, profits were to be equally divided.

It was a rash business on Dickens's part, for he had mentioned the last day of November as the date on which he hoped to have the book ready, but he is not really to be blamed. It was Ainsworth who was behind this agreement, Ainsworth who knew that a bigger man than himself had begun work, Ainsworth who was urging him on. To a Dickens, moreover, in the first glorious realization of his own powers, nothing seemed impossible. A thousand entrancing ideas were dancing within him; he had only to sit down at his desk, and they would be crystallized out on the paper.

His letter to Macrone, which was unknown to Forster, is not unimportant, for it bears definite relation to the first of those business squabbles which were to mean so much not only to Dickens but also to his work. At the time, of course, he had every intention of sending "Gabriel Vardon" to Macrone before the end of the year; but he never did send the book, because other work was overwhelming him, and so there was trouble.

Here perhaps you have the first appearance of a curious trait in Dickens's character. It was not exactly conceit, as the word is ordinarily used, and it was not precisely undue self-confidence. It was, rather, an almost ingenuous inability to understand that he could possibly be mistaken about himself. He had discovered that he could project himself into worlds of his own creation as easily as in the old Chatham days he had projected himself into the worlds of Tom Jones and Roderick Random and the rest. With a pen in his hand there seemed to him to be no limit to these worlds that could be conjured up at will. When, moreover, in later years there came an ever-increasing restlessness, which at moments seems almost to have touched hysteria, it must have been largely due to the fact that he still refused to believe that there could be any mistake.

Most novelists will tell you that their best work appears to be writing itself, and there will be no pose in their words. They will also admit that at times there is not a single word to be written that is really in place. They do not deceive themselves, and hide their disappointments as best they can. Dickens, I cannot help thinking, always saw himself in the first flush of glorious creation, when everything was writing itself, and could only fight those other moments, whose existence he refused to admit, by putting away reality from him—with the usual result: an almost unbearable strain. . . . At this time, however, the strain was slender enough, and when a third publisher came forward with proposals, you are not surprised to learn that they were not rejected.

Richard Bentley wished to bring out a new monthly magazine, and wanted an editor who would be chief contributor as well. Would Boz accept an editorial fee of twenty pounds a month, and provide a serial story, to appear in an early number? Editors as a rule are not young men of twenty-four, but people were just then waking up to the unusual qualities of "Pickwick," and Mr. Bentley was a shrewd man. He made his offer in good time, before Boz had been swept away to the heights, and in August Dickens accepted it, as I dare say he would have accepted anything else of a similar nature that had been suggested to him.

This, however, was not enough. Macrone, not perhaps too happy about "Gabriel Vardon," was talking of another volume of "Sketches," and the Morning Chronicle was very willing to print them in its columns. And so in the autumn you had this astonishingly prolific young man not only writing "Pickwick," but also making plans for his new magazine, evolving "Oliver Twist," the serial story which it was to contain, and writing a new series of "Sketches." But even this was not all, for in this very same year you find Boz the author of the most successful farce of the season and a collaborator in the musical piece that followed it at the same theater.

Now in later years Dickens did not care to be reminded of this theatrical work, and for the best of reasons. His farce and his comedietta were poor enough things, written in haste and because they were asked for; but I cannot think that he was justified in saying, as he did, that they had been written "as a sort of practical joke." Very naturally he was keen to see something of his performed on that London stage which had held him fascinated for so many years, and an opportunity had now presented itself.

At the end of the previous year a new theater, the St. James's, had been built. It belonged to John Braham, a peculiar man who had enjoyed enormous success as an operatic singer and married a woman who seems to have believed that her true vocation was to be found in the management of a theater. The venture with the St. James's was to result in considerable loss; but at the moment prospects were good, and the theatrical public was interested, Dickens amongst them. He, as it happened, had two friends who were associated with the new manager. One of these was John Pritt Harley—a popular actor chiefly renowned for his representations of the more comic amongst Shakespearean characters—whom Dickens had known and liked for some years; the other was John Hullah, a young man of his own age who had already written some tuneful music and whose acquaintance he had probably made through his sister Fanny.

Hullah, it seems, had been at work on an opera with a foreign setting, to be called "The Gondolier," when, sometime in 1835, he sought Dickens's assistance. Part of the music had already been composed. Dickens agreed to collaborate, but took exception to Hullah's libretto, and proposed to substitute for it a story of his own. In this way "The Village Coquettes" came to be written, and possibly at George Hogarth's suggestion, the opera was submitted to Braham.

The new manager agreed to produce it with himself in one of the chief parts, and there is news of its forthcoming performance in a letter of Dickens's written in June or July, 1836. Mr. Hogarth, he told Hullah, had been with Braham, who spoke "highly of my works and 'fame' (!)," and expressed "an earnest desire to be the first to introduce me to the public as a dramatic writer. He said that he intended opening at Michaelmas; and added (unasked) that it was his intention to produce the opera within one month of his first night. He wants," an obviously excited Dickens concluded, "a low comedy part introduced—without singing—thinking it will tell with the audience."

The low comedy part was duly introduced, but when at the end of August it was found that "The Village Coquettes" could not be ready for presentation on September 29, other arrangements had to be made. It was then, I fancy, that Pritt Harley told Braham that Boz had a farce ready which, he thought, would meet with success. According to one account, the actor had a particular interest in this farce, inasmuch as it had been on his suggestion that it had been written. Amongst the "Sketches" you will find one called "The Great Winglebury Duel." It is the poorest and most artificial of them all, but it possesses just that touch of staginess which would have appealed to Harley. Here, he is supposed to have said, was most admirable material for a farce—with, incidentally, a first-rate part for himself, and Dickens, by this time most expert of amateur adapters, had converted the sketch into "The Strange Gentleman," certainly before the first chapter of "Pickwick" had been completed, and probably sometime in 1835.

Braham approved of the farce, and on September 29 it was duly produced, with Harley as the strange gentleman himself, and Madame Sala, the mother of George Augustus, afterwards to be one of Dickens's "young men," playing Julia Dobbs, a young lady very keen to find a husband. Harley made a hit, and the "comic burletta," as it was called, possibly because Hullah had written a song or two for it, ran for more than sixty nights, during which, it was said, Dickens was constantly in the theater and on one occasion took the part of a waiter.

Behold, then, Boz the author of a successful farce! There cannot have been much money for him—those were the days when most dramatic authors were expected to feel amply repaid by the occasional present of a few pounds or a small weekly wage—but it was a pleasant beginning. Also there was the forthcoming production of "The Village Coquettes," which in every way was to be regarded as a much more important occasion. Braham himself was taking a part, Hullah's music was thought to be exceedingly good, and all those who had anything to do with the production were "delighted."

Rehearsals began early in October, and on December 6 it was played for the first time with "The Strange Gentleman," although on the following night the farce was temporarily withdrawn. The critics were not too kind—I do not blame them—but the public enjoyed this early form of musical comedy with its eighteenth-century costumes, which continued for some little time to fill the bill of the St. James's, and was afterwards transferred to an Edinburgh theater.

Incidentally it was during the London run that John Forster, then dramatic critic of the Examiner, was personally introduced to the ex-reporter whom he had seen at the time of the Chronicle strike . . .

I have said that in later years Dickens did not care to talk of this early stage work. He wished it to be entirely forgotten. In 1843 somebody wanted to see "The Village Coquettes" revived. Dickens wrote to a friend demanding that the opera be allowed to sink into its native obscurity. "I did it," he wrote, "in a fit of damnable good nature . . . I just put down for everybody what everybody at the St. James's Theatre wanted to say and do best, and I have been most sincerely repentant ever since." Quite so: that is the usual and intelligible standpoint of the successful author about his early work if it happens not to be on a par with what has followed.

At the time, however, he undoubtedly took this dramatic work very seriously indeed. As early as February, 1836, he was writing to Chapman & Hall, who had already begun the publication of certain popular plays in cheap pamphlet form, to say that he wished to publish "The Strange Gentleman."

"If you have no objection to doing it," he told them, "I should be happy to let you have the refusal of it. I need not say that nobody else has seen nor heard of it." The play was not actually printed until the following year, but in December, 1836, Bentley printed the "drama" of "The Village Coquettes," dedicated to Harley, and in the preface the warmest thanks were given to Braham and all the performers who had assisted him for "their zealous efforts in his behalf—efforts which have crowned it with a degree of success far exceeding his most sanguine anticipations." He added a reply to his critics. The libretto of an opera, he thought, "must be, to a certain extent, a mere vehicle for the music," for which reason "it is scarcely fair or reasonable to judge it by those strict rules of criticism which would be justly applicable to a five-act tragedy or a finished comedy."

So early, then, he was showing his sensitiveness to criticism, but at the time when these words were written, that amazing gallop into world-wide fame had begun. Mr. Samuel Weller had made his appearance, and "Pickwick" was selling in its tens of thousands. Yet it is to be noted that a third "burletta" of his was to be produced at the St. James Theatre in the following year. It is also to be noted that by this time Boz had fully realized his own financial value. Braham was naturally keen to produce a new play by the most popular author of the day. Boz was begged to state his own terms. He did so in a letter to Harley, and it is amusing to note the new air of calm assurance.

"I have considered the terms," he wrote, "on which I could afford just now to sell to Mr. Braham the acting copyright in London of an entirely new play for the St. James's Theatre; and I could not sit down to write one in a single act of about an hour long, under a hundred pounds. For a new piece in two acts, a hundred and fifty pounds would be the sum I should require. I do not know whether, with reference to arrangements that were made with any other writers, this may or may not appear a large item. I state it merely with regard to the value of my own time and writings at this moment; and in doing so I assure you I place the remuneration below the mark rather than above it."

Well, well, how pleasant to be able to write such a letter! The terms, I imagine, were accepted, for "Is She His Wife?" duly appeared in March, 1837. On Harley's benefit night, moreover, a Pickwickian item was expressly written for him, but that must have been meant as a gesture of private friendship.

It is time, however, to turn to Mr. Pickwick himself.

Chapter V

PICKWICK

[1]

"HOW did you first come to think of the thing?" That is the sort of question which is flung at embarrassed novelists after they have achieved a more than ordinary success. "Did you know from the beginning how it was all going to end? Had you planned out every chapter and made up your mind about each of the characters, or did you just write on and see what happened?" Well, I do not suppose that any two novelists set to work in precisely the same way. To some a theme will suggest itself first; to others one or two of the characters, if sufficiently vivid, will suggest the right story that should be woven about them. To some there must be the most detailed synopsis before a word can be written; to others no more will be necessary than the haziest notion that this or that may possibly happen. And sometimes, of course, the characters mutiny, and altogether refuse to carry out their author's commands. . . .

As it happens, "Pickwick," which has many claims to be considered the most remarkable work of fiction in the English language, has a history that is almost as remarkable as itself. Like Topsy it may be said to have "just growed." At the beginning neither Dickens (for all that he may have hinted to the contrary) nor anybody else had any very clear idea of what it was to become. Not only did there come a gradual alteration in its outlook and technique, but the character of its hero materially changed. The precise definition or proper scope of a novel may never have been satisfactorily decided, but even so few critics would be inclined to call "Pickwick"—I may be excused if I use the abbreviated title—a novel at all. It has no beginning and no end: it is just one great mass of glorious stuff which somehow got itself written.

And the joke of the thing is that it was not at first intended to be anything more than another Sketch by Boz, lengthened for the purposes of serial publication, and more or less as an accompaniment to certain projected prints of a sporting nature, which required some sort of textual embroidery. So much is very generally admitted.

Unfortunately the artist concerned committed suicide after only a few of the drawings had been completed, there arose an absurd controversy over the business, and even to this day queer little books appear which endeavor to prove some solemn thesis belittling Dickens's share in the conception of his masterpiece. As if it mattered twopence how many sporting sketches had been in existence before he "thought of Mr. Pickwick"! But there was created a high old rumpus, and everybody, including Dickens, wrote to the papers, and a sinister significance was attached to the suicide, and, as often happens, the controversy over "Pickwick" led to at least one other controversy that was equally stupid.

The historians of "Pickwick" are many, and at moments they can be charmingly contradictory, but the history itself, if peculiar and dramatic, is not really complicated at all. It begins, it is true, with Robert Seymour, who for the last twenty years had been producing a steady stream of more or less comical, and generally sporting, sketches. As an illustrator he enjoyed a very fair reputation, although his efforts at more ambitious work with the brush had not been successful. You will find his work in publications like Figaro in London, Hood's Comic Almanacs, and The Looking Glass.

If, moreover, you care to consult a little book called "Maxims and Hints for an Angler," which was issued in 1833, you will find other work of his which is not without some small interest to readers of "Pickwick." This book was the (anonymous) work of one Richard Penn, and professed to be a reprint of the "Minutes of the Common Place Book of the Houghton Fishing Club." With a little good-will you may discover in the fat, cheery, bespectacled old boy who is to be found in several of the plates some faint resemblance to Mr. Pickwick as we know him. It is to be noticed, however, that every sketch does not show the same old boy. In some he is comparatively young, in others he has very thick and most un-Pickwickian lips. He wears all sorts of clothes, including, I admit, the Pickwickian gaiters.

In this series of plates there is also a long thin gentleman (not unlike Mr. Jingle) who is shown playing chess and, again, fishing with a slightly Wellerian and cockaded servant in attendance. Very well. Two years after the appearance of this little fishing book, a bookseller called Charles Tilt (who afterwards gave Dickens a commission for certain minor but well-paid work) published a series of lithographs by Seymour called "New Readings of Old Authors." Here, too, you will find a fat old boy and a long thin man. They were, as a matter of fact, two of the artist's favorite stock figures.

In the same year another book called the "Squib

'Annual," containing Seymour's work, and incidentally another faintly Pickwickian figure, was published by Chapman & Hall, who engaged him, early in 1836, to provide sketches for their new Magazine of Fiction, to which, by the way, Dickens was a contributor. And one day Seymour, no doubt thinking of the success which high-spirited publications like Life in London and The English Spy had enjoyed, conceived the notion of printing the chronicles of a Nimrod Club, which should relate the comical misadventures of some vainglorious and unskilful cockney "sportsmen."

What happened then? No controversy would ever have arisen had not Seymour's family endeavored, after his death, to extort money from Dickens on the ground that the artist's share in the great success of "Pickwick" had never been adequately (in the financial sense) acknowledged. According to them Seymour made four etchings for his Nimrod Club, and showed them to a print-seller called Spooner, who suggested that Theodore Hook should be invited to provide letterpress. On Hook's refusal, Henry Mayhew, then editing the Figaro, and Moncrieff, the theatrical hack, were approached. Finally, the artist took his suggestion to Chapman, who thought well of the proposal.

I see no reason to doubt this much of the Seymour version, although Chapman takes credit for having suggested that the plates should be accompanied by letterpress and be issued in monthly parts. In any case, the publisher invited a Mr. William Clarke, the author of a facetious book called "Three Courses and a Dessert," to collaborate in the scheme. Clarke did not reply, and for a while the proposal was dropped. Then Seymour wrote to say that he had been offered some work which, were he to accept it, would occupy his whole time, and pressed for an immediate decision.

If we are to believe one of the accounts, several writers were written to before Dickens was approached. Leigh Hunt is mentioned in this connection, although the choice sounds sufficiently odd, as well as Charles Whitehead, the editor of the Magazine of Fiction. Whitehead was a clever enough writer—his book on Richard Savage deserves to be better known than it is —but he refused the commission, and recommended Boz. To Dickens, therefore, Mr. Hall was sent, and a bargain was struck.

One clear reservation, however, was made. "I objected," wrote Dickens in the 1847 preface to "Pickwick," "on consideration that, although born and partly bred in the country, I was no great sportsman . . . that the idea was not novel, and had been already much used; that it would be infinitely better for the plates to arise naturally out of the text; and that I should like to take my own way, with a freer range of English scenes and people, and was afraid I should ultimately do so in any case, whatever course I might prescribe to myself at starting. My views being deferred to, I thought of Mr. Pickwick, and wrote the first number; from the proof sheets of which Mr. Seymour made his drawing of the club and that happy portrait of its founder by which he is always recognized, and which may be said to have made him a reality. I connected Mr. Pickwick with a club because of the original suggestion, and I put in Mr. Winkle expressly for the use of Mr. Seymour."

What, then, of the controversy? Well, it was suggested that the sketches had been shown to Dickens before he wrote a single word of "Pickwick." It was pointed out that the design for the cover showed a fat bespectacled man asleep in a boat with a fishing-rod by his side, and a long thin man shooting (and missing) a robin or a sparrow on a twig within a few feet of his gun. But Mr. Pickwick never went fishing. Therefore —what? Therefore Mr. Pickwick was Seymour's own invention, and his unfortunate suicide was due to disappointment at his idea being coolly appropriated by a pushing young writer. What a preposterous business!

Suppose, as is likely, that Dickens had been shown some of Seymour's sketches for a Nimrod Club. Suppose he had seen the cover with Mr. Pickwick asleep in a boat before he wrote a line of his book. What then? It is known that there was much re-etching of the Pickwick plates on Seymour's part; it is known that Dickens very courteously insisted on certain alterations being made. What could it matter who gave to Mr. Pickwick his particular girth or even his gaiters?

Yet the whole business was taken so seriously that after the Seymour family had issued a pamphlet, giving their version of the proceedings, Chapman, at Dickens's request, wrote out his own account of these early transactions, and incidentally claimed for himself Mr. Pickwick's portly figure. Seymour's first portrait, he said, had been of a long thin man, but on his describing a personal friend of his own who lived at Richmond—"a fat old beau who would wear, in spite of the ladies' protests, drab tights and black gaiters"— a different drawing was made. Whereupon Dickens took the trouble to alter a portion of his statement, as printed in the 1847 preface, and henceforth allowed Chapman's claim.

What did happen, of course, was that Seymour was badly piqued. Here he was, well-known and sought after, with the clearest idea of what he wanted done. There was a regular procedure in the business. You drew your plates, and some hack was engaged to write a story about them. Yet here was this youngster taking his own line from the beginning, getting rid of the Nimrod Club and allowing him no more than a poor morsel in the shape of Mr. Winkle. How was he to know that this new piece of hackwork was to be unlike any other hackwork that had ever been written?

His family declared that he was the most genial and ordinary of men, but I see him as an ill-balanced, excitable fellow, subject to fits of depression which came near to acute melancholia. Yet surely he may be allowed his fat man? It is not too much to give him. And we may give him Mr. Pickwick's peculiar figure all the more readily when we find that Chapman's account of the proceedings, admittedly obtained verbally from his partner, who had been dead for some time, is not too accurate in other details. As for the gaiters—but enough of this tragi-comical business.

[2]

"There was no agreement about Pickwick, except a verbal one." So wrote Chapman in 1849, but he had forgotten a short correspondence between Dickens and the firm that included a very definite agreement indeed. There is still in existence a letter dated February 12, 1836, which sets forth the exact terms agreed upon. Nine guineas were to be paid for each sheet of sixteen pages, and each page was to contain about five hundred words. A sheet and a half were to be issued each month, and in the event of the publication proving very successful, the firm would "be happy to increase the amount in a proportionate degree." "Copy" was to be delivered two months before the date of publication, payments were to made monthly, and Dickens was invited to write a prospectus for immediate issue.

To this letter Dickens replied in four days' time. He took exception to only one of these terms: he did not think it necessary for his "copy" to be ready so long before it was to be issued, and suggested that five weeks in advance of publication would be enough. As for the new prospectus, he proposed to have it ready by the following week, when he would have moved into the larger suite in Furnival's Inn. From this letter, by the way, you learn that so far no title had been found for the book; it was still "unchristened."

On April 1, No. I of "The Posthumous Papers of the Pickwick Club" duly appeared, with four plates by Seymour; and one wonders exactly how sucessful it was. How many copies did Chapman & Hall expect to sell? How many copies were actually sold in the month? According to Forster, this first number attracted far less attention than had been given to the "Sketches." James Grant speaks of it as "a signal failure."

Many years afterwards the binder employed by Chapman & Hall stated that there had been a first order for only four hundred copies to be bound, contrasting this very moderate number with the forty thousand included in the first order for No. XV. This, however, hardly helps us, for we do not know when or to what extent that first order was repeated. Charles Tilt, the bookseller, is supposed to have attempted to push the sales, and to have distributed, personally, fifteen hundred copies of the earlier numbers to the trade, but this may not be true. It is impossible to be at all definite, but we will suppose that there was only a moderate sale. Why, indeed, should there have been much more? Boz had not yet got into anything like his true Pickwickian stride, and to a number of not particularly interested people, it must have seemed that here was only the beginning of yet another of those semi-sporting books: probably the usual Seymourish affair.

At the same time I cannot think that the publishers *ever* regretted their venture as some people have suggested, for even before the second number had appeared, they were listening sympathetically to Dickens's proposal that he should be paid ten instead of nine guineas a sheet, and in May or June of this year—sometime before Mr. Samuel Weller had made his appearance—the young writer was acknowledging their new and "very handsome terms . . . relative to our mutual friend Mr. Pickwick." After No. VIII, that is to say, £25 was to be paid for a number containing thirty-two pages.

This increase in letterpress had followed on the tragic affair of April 20. Dickens had returned from his brief honeymoon, and soon found it necessary to speak frankly to Seymour. He sent the artist a very polite, but very firm letter. A drawing had been submitted that was "not quite my idea," and would Seymour greatly oblige by making a new sketch? He explained in some detail the alterations he required, and invited the artist to take a glass of grog with him and his publishers on the following Sunday evening.

On that Sunday Seymour went to the chambers in Furnival's Inn. For some reason the publishers were not present, but Mrs. Dickens was there, and Frederick Dickens, then a boy of sixteen. The interview, Dickens informs us, was "short," and his visitor "certainly offered no suggestion whatsoever." But I think that Seymour must have made up his mind to utter a final protest. . . .

I can see the two men. They have never met before; they are never to meet again. Seymour, ill at ease in the presence of this most juvenile writer, makes some endeavor to stand on his dignity. Such treatment as this, he points out, is not that usually accorded to men with established reputations. He is very willing to meet Mr. Dickens half-way; but, after all, the original idea was his, and if there are to be no sporting scenes, if his own powers of invention are never to be used, why continue? There must be other and possibly younger men better qualified to play second string. And Dickens himself, not unmindful, I hope, of the promised glass of grog, stands there, very handsome, very finely dressed, very happy, outwardly calm, although he is really in a state of the greatest excitement, for already he has talked matters over with "many literary friends" and the true Pickwickian panorama is beginning to unfold itself in his mind.

What does he say? He quite understands Mr. Seymour's position, he is delighted with Mr. Seymour's portrait of Mr. Pickwick, but it will be impossible for him to circumscribe himself in any way. For the future he must reserve to himself the right to issue such instructions to his illustrator as may be necessary. His publishers are entirely at one with him in this matter. It may seem a little strange that so young a man should be talking in this way, but Mr. Seymour must understand. . . .

Mr. Seymour understands, and at an early hour two mornings later, young Frederick Dickens with a newspaper in his hands is knocking loudly on the bedroom door and in horrified tones informing his brother that the artist has shot himself in his Islington garden.

It was very dreadful, but Dickens was in no way to blame. There was only one thing to be done. Seymour had left three finished drawings to be used in No. II, but a successor would have to be found at once. This, it seems, was no easy matter, and it is a little curious to find so many candidates for the post. Indeed, I am minded to see in their number proof that No. I had made more of an impression than some people suppose. The obvious person was George Cruikshank, but at the time he had about as much work on his hands as he could conveniently manage, and there was also the strong possibility that he would be even less willing than Seymour to play second string.

He did, however, send a young man to Furnival's Inn who, he thought, might be suitable. This was John Leech, afterwards to become a great friend of Dickens, but at the moment only nineteen years old and not too accomplished a craftsman. Leech, as it happened, was too late, but in any case he would not have been chosen. Others were applying for the position, amongst them, divertingly enough, young Thackeray, who personally took some of his drawing to Dickens. They were not found suitable.

There followed a harassed week or ten days, and then John Jackson, an engraver working for Chapman & Hall, recommended a certain Robert Buss, some of whose work he was engraving at the time for the Magazine of Fiction. Buss submitted a drawing, it was found acceptable, and he was installed in Seymour's position. Poor Buss! He was very far from being the right man. Two of his drawings appeared in No. III, but they would not do. He was summarily dismissed. Afterwards he confessed that his etchings had been "abominably bad," and in the ordinary editions of "Pickwick" you will not find them; but at the time he felt his dismissal keenly enough. In those days, however, the book illustrator was of rather more importance than he is today, and if "Pickwick" were to succeed, it was believed, the drawings must be of the first class.

Fortunately John Jackson had found another young

man to recommend, and with the arrival of Hablot Knight Browne—the "Phiz" who will be forever associated with "Pickwick" completed—all troubles of the kind were at an end. Quite naturally this youngster —he was only twenty at the time—fell into the exact degree of subordination that Dickens, exacting as he was from this time forth, desired from his illustrator, and it was many years before a growing carelessness on the artist's part brought their partnership to an end. Browne produced that sparkling sketch of Sam Weller cleaning the boots, and within a very few months all England was laughing. . . .

What happened? What does happen to make a work of fiction that in one month is selling quietly in its hundreds sell in the next in its tens of thousands? With "Pickwick" there was no colossal advertising campaign. Huge posters were not disfiguring the roadside. The critics were not shouting themselves hoarse over the advent of a new literary genius. On the contrary, they had been distinctly lukewarm. This new kind of humor might be all very well, but was it not rather vulgar? That, you will find, was the general trend of such criticisms as had already found their way into print. Then what was the detonator which caused so sudden and so overwhelming an avalanche of orders from every part of the country? By what miracle did it happen that over every dinner table, whether it was standing beautifully polished in a west-end mansion, or a plain thing of deal in a country cottage, two people, a master and a man, neither of whom had ever existed outside the covers of a book, were monopolizing the conversation?

You can answer such questions only in the vaguest way. With the meeting of Mr. Pickwick and Sam Weller, not only had two quaint folk made friends:

they were demanding to make friends with all the world. Not a man, woman, or schoolboy but wanted to shake Mr. Pickwick by the hand and listen to Sam's cockney wisdom. They were so real, moreover, that it seemed ever possible that you would find them round the corner, laughing together and delighted to meet you. And their adventures! The world they lived in! You knew it quite well, and yet it was a new world of enchantments.

Your starchified critics in their starchified journals might talk of ounces of Sterne and pounds of Smollett and handfuls of Hook, but where else could you find another Pickwick or another Weller? Nowhere at all. They had come, and every month you had an opportunity of getting to know them much better, and assuredly they were the two people of all others to meet whom everybody must, unconsciously, have been waiting for years.

And what of Dickens himself, the hard-working and newly married young man who only a month or two ago had been "doing" the parliamentary reports for the Chronicle? How was he taking this amazing success? What were his feelings when Chapman or Hall or both of them would come rushing round with very fat checks and the news that the printing-presses had to be worked day and night to cope with the orders for "Pickwick"? Did he lose his head when the name of Boz was on everybody's lips, when famous men were asking to meet him, when Braham was wanting more plays and publishers were tempting him with new agreements? Did he, perchance, think once again of the pretty girl who, more than anybody else, I feel, had been responsible for his success? Did he remember a fine house on a hill on the road to Gravesend? I wonder?

I think that in those days he must have found himself in a new sort of dream-stage, where everything that had seemed impossible was happening as a matter of course, and where nothing to which he set his hand could go wrong. Most men, it seems to me, would for a little while have been almost aghast, for success of the kind that Dickens was tasting means very much more than mere enjoyment of well-merited applause. It means a bunch of new and difficult responsibilities. It means that you no longer belong wholly to yourself. You may be courted and fêted, but you will also be pestered. You are there to be stared at, and thanked, and be talked of, but sometimes the talk will be ill-natured, and there may be a slander or two.

Yet I fancy that Dickens found his new responsibilities not too irksome. On a sudden the curtain had gone up to show a new figure alone on the stage, but that figure already knew much of the footlights. Naturally, effortlessly, he made the required bow and appeared in the heroic character of Charles Dickens, the eminent novelist as though he had been carefully rehearsing the part (as I suppose in a way he had) for years past. With no stage-fright at all he struck the appointed attitude, and like all good actors took an artistic pleasure in the performance that followed.

For all that, there did come a moment even in these early days when the new favorite was forced to take stock of himself. All this roar and bustle about him was splendidly exhilarating, but if he were not very careful his work would soon be in serious arrears. As it was, Chapman & Hall became anxious, and with one of their checks sent a letter of protest.

Dickens replied on November 1. He was well aware, he told them in his playful way, of the "lingering disease" under which Mr. Pickwick had "recently laboured, and of the great aggravation of the symptoms" which had "gradually taken place." But they were to rest assured that the disease had reached its height and would now "take a favourable turn." They must remember that he had many other occupations, and "spirits" were "not to be forced up to Pickwick point, every day. . . . Although, thank God," he concluded, "I have as few worldly cares as most people, you would scarcely believe how often I sit down to begin a number, and feeling unequal to the task do what is far better than writing, under such circumstances—get up, and wait till I am." Grimly, however, he set himself to understand the kind of schedule to which he would be obliged to work, and for years kept more or less closely to it.

What, too, of his family? What were they thinking of it all—the Dickenses and the Barrows and the Hogarths? On the day before his marriage Dickens had written in the most manly way to his uncle Thomas Barrow. His father, it seems, had not yet been forgiven, and he had no intention, he said, of visiting a house, even that of a near relation, where his father was not welcome. Was this old quarrel patched up during the marvelous autumn that followed? It may be so, but I fancy not, for Mr. Dickens was still having his "moments." Even at this time, you ask, when Charles was receiving considerable sums every month, when, in fact, he was "making a fortune"? Well, I am afraid that just now Mr. Dickens was being even less reliable than usual, and Dickens, in his new independence, was minded to speak out. . . .

And here, it may be, is the place to state very bluntly that few men have been unluckier in their families than Dickens. For all his genial temper and gracious manners, his father was little more than a wastrel, and a not very honest wastrel at that. His brothers did little or nothing for themselves, and more than once there was serious trouble. Dickens himself was never really free of these limpets, and time after time he was driven nearly wild by their extravagant follies. Nor in later years was he too fortunate in his own sons, who, with one marked exception, made little enough of their lives.

It is not pleasant to speak of these matters, but it is not only stupid to omit them, as Forster does: it is also unfair to Dickens. When the eyes of the world were upon him, you will find him often enough behaving in the most extraordinary way. He would do things which no man of sense, you would have thought, certainly no man of the world, such as Dickens was, could possibly bring himself to do. By nature he was an excitable person, and his occasional bursts of temper are understandable, but there would come moments of absolute frenzy, and to understand these it is necessary to realize the almost continuous family troubles and family shortcomings which he was unable to ignore.

They never left him alone; they expected him to do everything for them; they regarded him as "fair game." You are sometimes told that he cared too much for money; you are less often told what he did for his family. In point of fact he was extraordinarily generous. Time and again he allowed himself to give when it might have been better to refuse, and time and again there was to come only the bitterest disappointment. He did take charge of his family, and did for them far more than they deserved, but there were times when even he was forced to turn a deaf ear to requests that as often as not ought never to have been made. And so at this time of "Pickwick," you have the unlovely spectacle of two members of his family going behind Dickens's back to his publishers and begging for presents or loans.

Mr. Dickens, of course, went about it in his usual grandiloquent way. In February, 1837, he was writing to Chapman & Hall from a house he had taken in Edward Street, Portman Square. There was a little debt of four pounds to them at the time. It had "occurred" to him, he wrote, that "at a moment of some difficulty," the publishers might be willing to extend their "obliging assistance," and he begged them to accept a bill for twenty pounds, due in April, and forward him the balance at once. "Do not suppose," he wrote, "I ask this on any other footing than that of obligation conferred upon me; and I assure you, though small in amount, its effects to me are matters of grave consideration, because anything that would occasion my absence from the Gallery"—he was still carrying on his reporting work, although with what regularity we do not know—"would be productive of fatal effects." The publishers, he added, might consider it "an intrusion that I should apply to you in a moment of difficulty. I feel it to be so; but, recollecting how much your interests are bound up with those of my son . . ."

You can imagine how the letter concluded. And, of course, when the bill became due, Chapman & Hall were requested to continue their good offices. Moreover, at regular intervals during the following months, he was taking the fullest advantage of "Pickwick's" success.

At the end of July the want of fifteen pounds was placing him "in a situation of the most peculiar difficulty—as regards home affairs: if it was any matter less urgent than a question of rent, nothing would induce me to intrude my affairs on your notice. Mind," he continued in his amiable way, "the subject is one of settlement by 2 o'clock, and unless I can so arrange it, I am lost."

'And there followed a typical passage. Only this new loan would enable him to reduce his expenses "without the appearance of disgrace, and without that annoyance to Mrs. Dickens and my family which would be painful indeed." Why should there be any appearance of disgrace because you moved into a smaller house? Why indeed? But Mr. Dickens belonged to that queerly sensitive division of the middle class which looked, and still looks, upon "gentility" as the brightest virtue of all.

He wrote on this occasion "with overwhelmed feelings" and duly obtained his loan, apparently on the security of his navy pay office pension. But it is doubtful whether he ever repaid the money, for a little later he was writing again, picturesquely enough, "to offer some explanation of my conduct in obtaining, as it were, from you money under false pretenses." By this time he owed them fifty-five pounds, but unfortunately required a further fifty pounds to be saved "from perdition." Would it satisfy them if he insured his life in their favor for three years? He had no right, he knew, to ask this at their hands, "but when a man is placed in the situation in which I have placed myself, all but subjected himself to the laws of his country, he will snatch at a straw to save himself not from drowning, but a scarcely milder sentence." And as usual the fifty pounds was required "by one o'clock tomorrow," if the "most awful consequences" were to be prevented.

Serious words! We are not surprised to find him writing "under feelings of the most pregnant and heart-rending distress at my own want of common honesty," nor are we astonished to see him concluding with one of those charming little precepts which seem so often, and so unhelpfully, to have been on his lips. "To what a state of ignominy does one false step lead those who under strong pressure have not the power to resist temptation!" Unfortunately there had been more than one false step, and this was by no means to be the last. At the beginning of the following year there was further trouble.

"All sorts of annoyances," he was writing, had almost driven him to madness, and would dear Chapman & Hall renew their last bill once again? Later on there came further arrests for debt, and the publishers were very coolly invited to "do the needful." And as with Mr. Dickens so with his son Alfred, who seems to have slipped very easily into the parental way of conducting financial affairs. A large bill had to be paid at once, and would Mr. Hall be good enough to let him have five pounds, to relieve him "from a most awkward dilemma"?

It is perhaps just as well that we do not know too many details about these false steps, but they were so far from decreasing in seriousness as to force Dickens at last to take legal steps. In 1841 his solicitor Mitton inserted a notice in the papers, which for all its intentional vagueness shows very well what had happened. "Certain persons," ran this announcement, "having or purporting to have the surname of our said client have put into circulation, with a view of more readily obtaining credit thereon, certain acceptances made payable at his private residence or at the offices of his business agents." And for the future no debts, other than those of his own or his wife's contracting, would be paid.

I mention this disagreeable business in some detail to show the kind of thing that was going on behind the scenes while Mr. Pickwick was conquering England. It helps to explain not a little that was to happen in the future.

[3]

The art of showmanship is not always given a high place, but the perfect showman, who must take himself and his work very seriously indeed, requires genius. Dickens, it seems to me, was quite possibly the greatest showman who ever lived. No writer gaged the public taste more accurately than he did; no man took greater pains to "keep faith" with his readers.

All his writing life he remained, very particularly, what the theater manager of today likes you to think that he is—a "servant of the public." He was *theirs,* and so much they must be made to understand. For which reason there came one or two quite legitimate little tricks of the trade. He had been ordained to play an arduous and heroic part: very well, everything possible—even the clothes that he wore—must be used to help him play it.

It was part of his showmanship, for instance, that he should periodically appear to be taking the public very fully into his confidence. There would come addresses of a more or less personal nature, generally judicious and sometimes playful, although once at least incredibly foolish. The first of these addresses, issued with "Pickwick" in December, 1836, merely gave notice that in spite of great temptation that work would not be continued beyond its twentieth number, but the second was of a very different nature. . . .

The new year opened auspiciously enough for him. A son was born on January 6, and christened Charles Culliford Boz: Charles Culliford had, I fancy, married one of the Barrow sisters, and the Boz, according to one account, was Mr. Dickens's suggestion. The monthly circulation of "Pickwick" had passed the twenty-thousand mark, and was shortly to be more than doubled. The "Sketches" were still selling, and the beginning of "Oliver Twist" had been written, the first book to show him in his guise as social reformer.

In March his new farce was produced, and a dinner was held to celebrate "Pickwick's" anniversary, at which a check for £500 changed hands. In the same month he moved into the house in Doughty Street which is now the home of the world-wide Fellowship with which his name is associated. He had discovered a man after his own heart in John Forster, and Ainsworth was introducing him to half fashionable London. Except for his father's foibles, he seemed to have no cares in the world. But when June came, there was no No. XV of "Pickwick."

Immediately the absurdest rumors arose. Although all literary London knew by this time who Boz really was, it was solemnly asserted that "Pickwick" could not be the work of one man, but must have been the joint invention of an association which for some unknown reason had disbanded itself. Alternately it was maintained that the author was a youth of eighteen who had broken down under the strain and been sent to a madhouse: which meant, of course, that there would be no more of Mr. Pickwick. It was said that he had been sent abroad, presumably for his country's good. It was even said that he was dead.

What had happened? On May 7, Mary Hogarth, who had now joined the household, had died, after a very brief illness, in Dickens's arms. It was a shock from which he did not recover for many years. The child-goddess had been suddenly snatched away, and his success, "Pickwick," "Oliver," the stage—all went for nothing. He was utterly unnerved and distraught. Work was impossible. It would, indeed, be difficult to overestimate his grief. On the day before the funeral he confessed to Chapman that he could make up his mind to nothing at all.

"I feel that as tomorrow draws nigh," he wrote, "the bitterest part of this calamity is at hand. I hope that for that one day at all events I may be able to bear my part in it with fortitude and console those about me— it will be no harder trial to any one than myself."

To Ainsworth he wrote in much the same terms. "I have been so much unnerved and hurt by the loss of the dear girl whom I loved, after my wife, more deeply and fervently than any one on earth, that I have been compelled for once to give up all idea of my monthly work, and to try a fortnight's rest and quiet."

He went to Hampstead, where for the first time Forster received his entire confidence and slipped into the position for which he was so admirably qualified: it was that of honorary business adviser and literary agent. He was to retain it throughout Dickens's life. . . .

A pathetic business, this lovely girl's death. "I have never had her ring off my finger," Dickens was writing a few months later to his mother-in-law, "by day or night, except for an instant at a time to wash my hands, since she died. . . . I can solemnly say that, waking or sleeping, I have never lost the recollection of our hard trial and sorrow, and I feel that I never shall. It will be a great relief to my heart when I find you sufficiently calm upon this sad subject to claim the promise I made you when she lay dead in this house, never to shrink from speaking of her, as if her memory were to be avoided, but rather to take a melancholy pleasure in recalling the times when we were all so happy —so happy that increase of fame and prosperity has only widened the gap in my affections, by causing me to think how she would have shared and enhanced all our joys, and how proud I should have been (as God knows I always was) to possess the affections of the gentlest and purest creature that ever shed a light on earth."

And it is the fact that her memory never was avoided. You will find her shadow hovering over more than one of the novels. The unworldliness of Little Nell, who for all her tender years, seems to be so surprisingly adult, is but the reflection of Dickens's idealization of Mary Hogarth. He confessed that he found it hard to bring himself to the point of killing off Little Nell; with the sad beauty of his much-loved Mary in our minds, it is not difficult to understand why.

It was to contradict the absurd rumors which had arisen that the second address was issued at the end of June, but from that date there was to be no further interruption. At the beginning of November the last two numbers of "Pickwick" appeared together, and the world satisfied itself that a work had been completed which would belong to the ages. Even the starchier critics were coming to heel, although a few of them continued to find what fault they could with the construction of the book, conveniently forgetting the way in which it had been written and issued.

On this matter Dickens defended himself with some skill, by pointing out "that though the mere oddity of a new acquaintance was apt to impress one at first, the more serious qualities were discovered when we became friends with the man." The words are Forster's, and he was probably right in drawing attention to Dickens's indifference to any criticism of his work "on the merely literary side." It is amusing to see how he took a lengthy notice of "Pickwick" in the staid Quarterly.

"Indications are not wanting," its reviewer had written, "that the particular vein of humour which has hitherto yielded so much attractive metal, is worked out. . . . The fact is, Mr. Dickens writes too often and too fast. . . . If he persists much longer in this course, it requires no gift of prophecy to foretell his fate—he has risen like a rocket, and he will come down like the stick."

Dickens mentions the review in a letter to Talfourd. "Murray," he wrote, "supposing, I presume, that any notice in the Quarterly must drive so young a man as myself nearly distracted with delight, sent me the Quarterly yesterday. I think Hayward has rather visited upon me his recollection of my declining his intimate acquaintance, but as the notice contains a great deal that I know to be true, and much more which may be, but of which I am no impartial judge, I find little fault with it. I hope I may truly say," he added, "that no writer ever had less vanity than I have; and that my only anxiety to stand well with the world in that capacity originated in authorship being unhappily my trade, as it is happily my pleasure."

At the same time there was considerable criticism on another score, and the smart journalist who deplored the absence of "gentlemanlike accomplishment" was probably voicing the opinions of many good folk. In "Pickwick" you will find a great deal about drinking and a pleasant deal about kissing. Why not? Both the warm brandies and the kisses were very much in the picture. But—was all this kissing and this drinking quite genteel? Was it even quite proper?

Yes, they really did ask such questions in those days —perhaps they do so no less today—and the Grundy tribe continued for some time to find fault with Dickens for his "lowness." But Dickens himself never disguised his liking for good cheer, and made no fetish of correct behavior. He could take his glass with the best of them, and enjoy it; and he had no patience with those early prohibitionists who were just now making their voices heard. For him, too, the puritan outlook held no appeal, for he knew intuitively what it took the psychologists half a century to discover, the unpleasant foundations upon which it is generally built. A pamphlet called "Sunday Under Three Heads," published while "Pickwick" was being issued, exhibited his dislike of religious bigotry, and almost every short paper of his showed how little sympathy the ultra-respectable household, with its artificial routine and its narrow views, could expect from him: he could see only its ridiculous side. . . .

Vulgar or not, however, Mr. Pickwick had come, and he had conquered, and such was his triumph that he stepped almost straightway out of literature into the general life of the time. Only in the distant future were clever innkeepers to exhibit, with results most satisfactory to themselves, "the very room where Mr. Pickwick slept"; but already tradesmen were discovering his value and making good use of his name. His words and those of his friends were creeping into ordinary conversation, and even being quoted by learned judges on the bench.

Altogether he must have brought at this time nearly £3,000 to his author and more than four times that sum to the publishers. And when at the end of the year there came a second Pickwick dinner, few writers can ever have been in a more enviable position than was Dickens. That celebration took place at the Prince of Wales off Leicester Square, and seven covers were laid. Boz himself, of course, was in the chair, and Talfourd, to whom "Pickwick" had just been dedicated, occupied the next most important seat. Ainsworth and Forster were there, and both the partners of the firm in the Strand. There were also two new friends: William Jerdan, the editor of the Literary Gazette, a well-known critic who had written to Dickens on the first appearance of Sam Weller, exhorting him to elaborate so splendid a character, and Macready, the actor, whose acquaintance he had made within the last few months.

"A capital dinner," Ainsworth told a friend, "with capital wine and capital speeches," and no less cheerful, I imagine, because Dickens had just been presented with another check for £750 by his publishers. Talfourd proposed the toast of the evening, and just before his speech the head waiter had come in "and placed a glittering temple of confectionary on the table, beneath the canopy of which stood a little figure of the illustrious Mr. Pickwick. This was the work of the landlord."

An historical feast! I could wish that one of its chairman's old parliamentary colleagues had been present with pencil and note-book, to record those capital speeches. It was, however, only one of a series of such celebrations, at which, according to all accounts, those who were privileged to be present, invariably saw Dickens in his gayest and most sparkling mood.

[4]

So "Pickwick" was finished, and its author was fêted and famous, but as usual there was something to pay. The pirates arrived. They came in swarms—in prints, in books, in pamphlets, on the stage. There were "sequels" and "additions" and imitations so close to the original as to deceive hundreds of readers—until they had read a page or two. The wretched Pickwick was taken abroad (by G. W. M. Reynolds, whose book was the only imitation of any merit at all) and even to the United States. His servant was tortured into the most frightful caricatures of his real self, and made to speak as no true Weller possibly could. The Pickwickians themselves were transformed into dreadful folk whose adventures were fitted only for a fifth-rate provincial stage.

There were the "Posthumous papers of the Cadger Club," and similar reports of the "Wonderful Discovery Club, formerly of Camden Town." There were "The Posthumous Notes of the Pickwickian Club," edited by a gutter-hack who had the monstrous impertinence to call himself Bos. There was a "Pickwick Comic Almanac," a "Pickwick Jest Book," a "Sam Weller Favourite Song Book." Others besides Phiz attempted to illustrate the original book, and issued their own portfolios. There was even a "Penny Pickwick," which ran for months and was no doubt read aloud to thousands of illiterate people who believed that they were listening to the words of Dickens. Nor was this all. The "Sketches" were likewise mangled, and a "Sketch-Book by Bos" made its appearance in monthly parts. Apparently you had only to put forth something that seemed to be connected with Mr. Pickwick or his author, to sell it without trouble.

On the stage, too, it was even worse. At that time there was nothing to prevent you from making (and producing) what play you pleased from a novel. You took the material you wanted, and the author was expected to be grateful for the advertisement. It sounds curious, but even while "Pickwick" was still appearing in numbers, three or four distinct versions were produced on the stage. So early as October, 1836, "The

Peregrinations of Pickwick" was put on at the Adelphi. This, the work of William Leman Rede, was described as "an original Serio-Comic Burletta, in Three Acts, interspersed with music, founded on the celebrated Papers written by Boz." Rather surprisingly we find it stated that "a great portion of the comic dialogue is extracted from the papers, by the express permission of the Author, C. Dickens." This may have been so, but I suspect showman's license. In any case it made little difference whether Dickens gave permission or not: he was not in a position to prevent the production.

It is amusing to note, by the way, that Rede originally intended his play to be taken as more or less serious drama—an old miser called Clutchley was introduced for that purpose—but in a short while it was turned into a farce, and with Buckstone as Jingle, and Yates—the father of Edmund, afterwards to be another of Dickens's young men—as Mr. Pickwick, it enjoyed some success. Rede published his drama, and I should imagine that it would make curious reading today.

A second version was produced at the City of London Theatre on Easter Monday, 1837. "The Pickwick Club; or the Age We Live In" was the work of Edward Stirling, who also printed it in the same year. It was succeeded three months later by "Sam Weller; or the Pickwickians" at the Strand Theatre. This had been written by an impudent hack (of the kind that Mr. Crummles sometimes employed) called William Moncrieff, from whom, indeed, for some years no novelist had been safe. It was in this version that W. J. Hammond made a hit as Sam, but what Dickens thought when he saw (if he did see) Mrs. Bardell being sent to prison for bigamy, her real husband being no other than the unfortunate Jingle, we have no means of knowing.

Serious protests, however, were raised, and Moncrieff defended himself in a preface when he printed his play. We need not believe him when he says that "it would have been a much more easy and genial task for me to have written an entirely original work," nor, indeed, when he explains that he had been "piqued" into dramatizing "Pickwick" on account of the alleged impossibility of the task.

But he is interesting and not a little informative when he complains of the "twaddle" printed in the newspapers by those high intellectuals—the highbrow, unfortunately for him, had not yet been invented—"who so pathetically condole with Mr. Dickens on the penalties he pays for his popularity in being put on the stage." Messrs. Chapman & Hall were invited to state whether "Pickwick's" sales had not increased wonderfully since his version had appeared on the stage. Undoubtedly the sales had increased, but whether Mr. Moncrieff had had anything to do with it may be doubted.

As to Dickens, he took no notice of the man. "If the Pickwick," he wrote to Forster, "has been the means of putting a few shillings in the vermin-eaten pockets of so miserable a creature, and has saved him from a workhouse or a jail, let him empty out his little pot of filth and welcome."

Chapter VI

A More Serious Note, and Some Quarrels

[1]

IT needed a cool head to deal with this sudden acquisition of wealth and this sudden widespread popularity, and had Dickens succumbed, little surprise would have been felt. Yet for all his excitability, he settled down to his good fortune as though every incident in his life had been preparing him for it. He banked his money at Coutts's, incidentally becoming a great personal friend of Angela Coutts, afterwards the Baroness Burdett-Coutts, who in 1837 was left two million pounds; he insured his life; he made his will.

The little luxuries, of course, he allowed himself. He joined the ranks of the "carriage folk." Forster mentions his first purchase—"a small chaise, with a small pair of ponies" for his wife's use, which was soon changed for "a more suitable equipage." Further details are to be found in a letter to Mitton which mentions "the Craven Street turn-out." This is to be bought, and some fifteen pounds are to be spent on its decoration.

The waistcoats, it is true, did not become soberer in hue, nor was his brown hair allowed to become shorter, but in general he assumed all the respectabilities then, as now, considered proper for the successful professional man. His portrait was painted, more than once, Maclise and Stanfield, both to be Academicians, becoming very dear friends. And, indeed, as more and more distinguished men were introduced to him, there was hardly one who found it possible to resist his fascinations. He was, they found, as good company as his books, which is by no means always the case.

There was "no nonsense" about him. He was the jolliest, cheeriest companion, not in the least "stuck up," without unpleasant fads, fond of his glass, fonder of a good joke. Boz, as his old schoolmaster said, was "inimitable," and an invitation to the house in Doughty Street was a privilege to be highly prized.

His health was fair at the time, though the old attacks were persisting. "I was seized last night with a violent pain in my head," he wrote to one of his uncles early in 1837, "(fortunately just as I had concluded my month's work) and was immediately ordered as much medicine as would confine an ordinary sized horse to his stall for a week." (It is possible, by the way, that he was not always ordered so much physic, for his medical man was that Dr. Elliotson who had actively interested himself in hypnotism. The two men became friends, and from this time there were frequent hypnotic seances in the Dickens household, in which the novelist was not only the "subject" but sometimes played doctor himself.)

He was wise enough not to neglect physical exercise. The long walks had not been given up, but they were now supplemented by almost daily rides, Ainsworth and Forster being his usual companions. They would go out to Jack Straw's Castle at Hampstead, or to Richmond and Twickenham, or eastwards to Greenwich. Sometimes, too, a longer spell away from work was found advisable. There came the first of many jaunts abroad—his wife and young Hablot Browne accompanied him to Belgium—and a flight from London now and then for a breath of sea air. Broadstairs was tried, and proved so much to his liking that for some years he paid it regular visits. His letters to Forster at this time are full of his joy in the place, and it was here that a Mrs. Christian, who had met Dickens in London, came to know him fairly well.

She has recorded her impressions in some detail, and I know of no more intimate picture of the family as it was in these early days. She seems to have been brought in the first place to the Doughty Street house for dinner, on a night when Forster happened to be there. Mrs. Dickens she found "a pretty little woman, plump and fresh-coloured with the large, heavy-lidded blue eyes so much admired by men." There was "a genial smiling expression" on her face, "notwithstanding the sleepy look of the slow-moving eyes."

Then at dinner she met Dickens and at once noticed what so many others have commented upon, "the marvellous power of his eyes." She herself calls them "nondescript in colour, though inclining to warm grey in repose," but most of his friends speak of them as deep blue. And then, of course, follow details of his dress. "The collar and lapels of his surtout were very wide, and thrown back so as to give full effect to a vast expanse of white waistcoat. He wore drab-coloured trousers, ditto boots, with patent-leather toes, all most inconsistent with the poetic head and its flowing locks."

She was surprised, however, that he talked comparatively little during the evening—Forster was there, and he was never disinclined to listen to his own sonorous words—but commented upon "a certain thickness" in his speech "as if the tongue was too large for the mouth." There was, indeed, the suspicion of a lisp. . . .

In Broadstairs itself she met the whole family, including Dickens's mother: "very agreeable" and entering "into youthful amusements with much enjoyment," though showing the results of what she had been obliged to go through. Mr. Dickens, she thought, "appeared younger than his wife: a plump, good-looking man, rather 'an old buck' in dress" who "indulged occasionally in fine sentiments and long-worded sentences, and seemed to take an airy, sunny-sided view of things in general."

There follows a passage that illustrates very well the family's feelings about their unexpected good fortune. "It was wonderful how the whole family had emancipated themselves from their antecedents, and contrived to fit easily into their improved position. They appeared to be less at ease with Charles than with anyone else, and seemed in fear of offending him. There was a subdued manner, a kind of restraint in his presence, not merely the result of admiration of his genius, and respect for his opinion, but because his moods were very variable." Well, I do not wonder at that "kind of restraint" in his presence, in whatever mood he might choose to be.

Money continued to flow in. A little pseudonymously issued book called "Sketches of Young Gentlemen" brought him £125, which—as he wrote in a diary he was attempting to keep early in 1838—was "pretty well" for a very thin book without either Boz or his real name on its title-page, and it was not the only piece of "extra" work that he was doing. He seems to have been concerned in some way with Jerdan in the Literary Gazette, and wrote a booklet or two for Charles Tilt. There was a regular editorial salary coming from Bentley, and Chapman & Hall had given him a share in the Pickwick copyright. There came a time, however, when he woke up to the fact that although he might be making a great deal of money himself, the various publishers were making more—much more, in his opinion, than was meet; and it was this discovery that led to one business quarrel after another.

Is it necessary to describe these quarrels in any detail? Well, with any ordinary writer, I should say that his business dealings are of no general interest, but in the case of Dickens it happens not only that they are dramatic and, incidentally, very seldom understood, but also that the worries they produced had very definite effects upon Dickens himself. . . .

[2]

The publisher of books, a philanthropist who belongs to a much-misunderstood race of men, will tell you that an author is a very difficult creature who requires the most delicate handling. He will assert that many years of experience are necessary to understand the natural reactions of an author to his rather exceptional environment. The optimism of an author in particular, he will complain, is unbelievably great, while his vanity and conceit, however heavily veiled on occasion, are altogether beyond words. According to this view, an author is a suspicious, jealous, slightly effeminate and lamentably ill-balanced being with a deplorable and, indeed, indecent craving for gold. At a public dinner or in the course of a newspaper interview, he may appear swathed in modesty, but in the publisher's office all the polite veneer disappears, to leave a fretful, unbusinesslike Narcissus, incapable of seeing any reflection but his own.

It is further hinted, when the publisher is in a facetious mood, that if the author could only be eliminated altogether, the publishing business would assuredly improve to a very remarkable extent. At the same time it will be found that the author has very decided and not too favorable opinions about the man who publishes his book. To him the fellow is a soulless merchant, a parsimonious wretch living solely on other men's brains, a profiteering capitalist without courage or vision, afraid of all legitimate advertisement (of the author's own books), and in league with the booksellers to keep him in a state of penurious hackdom.

Now on the whole Dickens was exceedingly lucky with the four publishers who were concerned with his more important work, but it is a fact that he quarreled with every one of them. True, at the beginning, as at the end, of his career, he could say very nice things about Chapman & Hall, but even they came in for harsh words when affairs were not going as well as usual, and as a race, I am inclined to think, he came to view publishers with the usual suspicion. (I like the reply that he gave to Sala who had asked his opinion about one of the tribe. *Physically,* said Dickens, the gentleman in question was "very like a fraudulent butler.")

His quarrels, moreover, could be taken to a stage of bitterness that is explicable only when you remember what a man of extremes he was. The least misunderstanding would prey on his mind until it had been magnified into an intolerable insult to himself. There could be only one side to a question: his own. He was soon in a position to make his own terms, but he cannot be altogether acquitted of the charge of taking advantage of that position and treating his publishers in too casual a manner.

He is not, I think, to be blamed for driving a hard

bargain, for he was most shamefully pirated all his life; and these piracies, with which, of course, his own publishers had nothing to do, added not a little to the general irritability that came to characterize all his business dealings, but there were times when his publishers had reasonable grounds for complaint.

It has been suggested, however, that Forster is not wholly free of responsibility in the matter, and this may be so. I look upon Forster as a man even surer of himself than was Dickens: as a man very fond of laying down his own interpretation of the law, and intolerant of any opposition. That his advice was almost always the best (for Dickens) I cannot doubt, but it seems to me that he enjoyed his position as adviser too much. You hear of him in later years strutting—a burly man in a tight-fitting coat—through Chapman & Hall's establishment as though it belonged to him. Publishers, moreover, were not the only folk to call him a blustering bully. At the same time it may not unreasonably be argued that he was, as often as not, only following implicitly Dickens's instructions. But, whatever the responsibility that may have been his, it was never the publishers who were really to blame when a crisis came.

Take the case of Macrone. He was, you will remember, expecting a novel called "Gabriel Vardon" at the end of 1836. In August he had been surprised to learn from Ainsworth that Dickens, not content with the work he was doing for Chapman & Hall, was signing some agreement with Bentley. He seems to have done nothing until November. Then he wrote for news of the novel. I have not seen Dickens's reply, but I cannot doubt that it stated very plainly not only that no word of "Gabriel Vardon" had been written, but also that he did not consider himself morally bound to write it.

Immediately Macrone's hot temper led him to write a whole series of injudicious and impolite letters to everybody in any way concerned in the business. His behavior drew a rebuke from Ainsworth. He was not at all surprised, the novelist wrote, at what had happened, and months ago had warned Macrone what was afoot. But he thought it a mistake to attempt to widen the quarrel, which properly concerned Dickens alone. "I differ from you," he added, "in thinking you have kept your temper, though I own the circumstances are sufficient to endanger one's equanimity; and I find it hard to blame Mr. Bentley or any other spirited publisher (yourself, for instance) for patronizing rising talent."

But there could be no doubt that Dickens had agreed to write the novel, and two days later he was writing again "in the strictest confidence," advising Macrone to put the matter into legal hands. Ainsworth's position, I can see, must have been one of great delicacy. It was he who had introduced Boz to his first publisher, and both men were his friends. He believed that Dickens was in the wrong, but naturally wished to keep out of the dispute himself. The publisher took legal advice, and threatened Dickens, who, seeing that he might lose any case in the courts, proposed a compromise.

Writing three years later to Mitton, he explained what was done. "A dispute," he said, "arose between myself and Mr. Macrone whether an agreement for a novel, which we had together, was not understood to be cancelled between us. As it was not actually cancelled, he had the legal power of enforcing it, or claiming damages against me. . . . I gave up to Mr. Macrone the copyright of both series of Sketches on getting back the agreement."

This transaction must have taken place after the second series of "Sketches" had been hurriedly printed and published, for "Gabriel Vardon" was still being advertised as "forthcoming" in the first edition of that book.

Very well. Macrone had obtained the copyright—it seems that he had paid £100 for it in addition to forgoing the novel—and on seeing the enormous success of "Pickwick" quite legitimately proposed to reissue the sketches in monthly parts. Whatever profits he had already made—admittedly they were large—he saw no reason why he should not attempt to make more.

As soon as his intentions became known, however, Dickens chose to think that the publication would "most seriously" injure him. "I have," he told Forster, "a very natural and most decided objection to being supposed to presume on the success of Pickwick, and thus foist this old work upon the public in its new dress for the mere purpose of putting money in my own pocket." With memories of the Quarterly's warning, no doubt, in his mind, he considered—quite rightly—that to have his name attached concurrently to three separate publications would be prejudicial to his reputation. He therefore begged Forster to see what could be done in the matter.

Forster did what he could. According to instructions he reminded Macrone that no intention of publishing the "Sketches" in this new form had been "in the remotest manner" hinted to Dickens "by him or on his behalf when he obtained possession of the copyright." Very naturally Macrone told his visitor that he had every right to do as he pleased with his own property, and if he talked at some length of the transactions which had led to the acquisition of that property I should not be surprised.

Forster was obliged to accept the situation, but made

a suggestion. Would Macrone be willing to sell back the copyright to Dickens? Certainly he would—on terms. A few hundreds perhaps? Oh, dear, no: now that Pickwick "had made its author famous, a few thousands would be required. Forster refused to discuss any such figure, and counseled Dickens "to keep quiet for a time." But, as you will already have realized, this was the one thing that Dickens never could do.

He had decided that at all costs a monthly reissue of the "Sketches" must be stopped, and until this had been done, there could be no peace for him. Consequently there was nothing to be done but to curse Macrone for a money-grubbing knave and pay him the £2,000, which was the lowest figure he would accept. Against Forster's advice this sum was paid jointly by Dickens and Chapman & Hall, and—what followed? Within a few months the "Sketches" were being reissued in monthly parts.

I do not doubt that Chapman & Hall were in a better position than Macrone to make a success of the venture—all the Pickwick machinery was at their disposal—but the whole transaction is a little odd. True, it was Chapman & Hall who persuaded Dickens to agree to their proposal to reprint, but that Macrone should have been so bitterly assailed for not being as generous as they seems to me a little hard.

Yet here again you have a chance of seeing the real Dickens: impulsive, hot-tempered, easily swayed, but at heart the most generous of men. For a little while no words could be found too bad for this iniquitous fellow who had dared to buy the "Sketches" outright. When, too, on Macrone's sudden death this same year, there was an attempt on the part of his chief creditor, a printer called Hansard, to obtain money from Dickens on the alleged ground that he had been a "partner" in the "Sketches," there came an additional and wholly undeserved worry. But when it was found that Macrone had ruined himself by mad speculations, Dickens forgot his old feelings and went out of his way to help, by editing the "Pic-nic Papers" for the benefit of his widow and children.

Take the case of Bentley. There seem to have been constant misunderstandings extending over a period of nearly four years, during which time no less than six separate agreements were signed, each more favorable to Dickens than the last. Like Macrone, Bentley was called all sorts of names; but did he really deserve them? You will recollect that the original agreement of August, 1836, embraced a scheme for the editorship of a new magazine at £20 a month, and a serial story to be bought for £500.

The Wit's Miscellany was duly put in hand, but was rechristened Bentley's Miscellany before publication, in spite of some wag's objection that the change meant "going to the other extreme." The first number appeared at the New Year. In February the first instalment of "Oliver Twist" was printed, and in March there was a second agreement, whereby Dickens undertook to write for Bentley two other novels, the first to be delivered at "an early specified date." He was to be paid £500 each for these novels, though this figure was soon raised to £750. His editorial salary was also to be increased to £360 a year.

In the summer Bentley began to worry about the first of these novels—the much-delayed "Gabriel Vardon" (soon to be renamed "Barnaby Rudge"). Dickens became alarmed. He was taking his editorial duties very seriously, he had not yet finished "Pickwick," and he was in the middle of "Oliver Twist." How could he possibly think of any other work? Bentley, however, was insistent, and as usual Dickens went to Forster.

It seems that he had no copy of either of the agreements, though he had made some memoranda about them. "I fear," he wrote, "he has my second novel on the same terms . . . a bad look-out, but we must try to mend it. You will tell me that you are very much surprised at my doing business in this way. So am I, for in most matters of labour and application I am punctuality itself. The truth is . . . that if I had allowed myself to be worried by these things, I could never have done as much as I have. But I much fear, in my desire to avoid present vexations, I have laid up a bitter store for the future."

Forster saw Bentley, and attempted to show him how greatly it would be to everybody's advantage were the publisher to agree "to more equitable adjustment of their relations." I confess I do not understand how Bentley was expected to see where any advantage would accrue to himself in this way, and I am not surprised to learn that "some misunderstandings followed." It is impossible not to sympathize with Dickens, but it is also difficult to blame Bentley, particularly as at each crisis he allowed himself to recede a little farther from the position that was legally his.

In September, 1837, there came a compromise: not a good one. The third novel was to be abandoned altogether, but "Barnaby Rudge" was to be delivered by November, 1838, and Dickens agreed to edit Grimaldi's memoirs, then in manuscript, for Bentley. Forster was not too pleased at this new arrangement, which meant not only that "Barnaby Rudge" would have to be written before "Oliver Twist" was finished, but that the successor to "Pickwick," for which Chapman & Hall were naturally clamoring, might be seriously delayed. Nevertheless, in November, 1837, Dickens was agreeing to provide Chapman & Hall with another serial—"Nicholas Nickleby"—the first number of which was to be delivered by the following March.

What a business! Naturally, there was "something hanging over him like a hideous nightmare." Naturally, he was forced to see that he had attempted the impossible. He was obliged to appeal once again to Bentley. Would it not be better if instead of appearing in the first place as a three-volume novel "Barnaby Rudge" were to follow "Oliver Twist" in the Miscellany?

"The conduct of three different stories at the same time," he wrote, "and the production of a large portion of each, every month, would have been beyond Scott himself."

Bentley was not too pleased at this new interference with his plans, and there came "six months' wrangling," which included legal threats, before Dickens had his own way. Even so, however, the "nightmare" refused to disappear, and "Barnaby Rudge" refused to be written—at any rate on the agreed terms.

At the beginning of 1839 he was summarizing his position to Forster. "It is not fiction to say that at present I *cannot* write this tale. The immense profits which Oliver has realized to its publisher and is still realizing; the paltry, wretched, miserable sum it brought to me (not equal to what is every day paid for a novel that sells fifteen hundred copies at most); the recollection of this, and the consciousness that I have still the slavery and drudgery of another work on the same journeyman-terms; the consciousness that my books are enriching everybody associated with them but myself; and that I, with such a popularity as I have acquired, am struggling in old toils, and wasting my energies in the very height and freshness of my fame, and the best part of my life, to fill the pockets of others, while for those who are nearest and dearest to me I can realize little more than a genteel subsistence: all this puts me out of heart and spirits; and I cannot—cannot and will not—under such circumstances that keep me down with an iron hand, distress myself by beginning this tale until I have had time to breathe; and until the intervention of the summer, and some cheerful days in the country, shall have restored me to a more genial and composed state of feeling. . . . I do solemnly declare, that morally before God and man, I hold myself released from such hard bargains as these, after I have done so much for those who drove them."

Certainly one may sympathize with him, though the hand was not quite so metallic as he seemed to think, but—what of Bentley? He behaved very well. When the last number of "Oliver Twist" had appeared in the Miscellany, he released Dickens from the editorship, and on his advice appointed Ainsworth in his place. (There is an amusing letter from Dickens to Ainsworth written at seven in the morning, exhorting him to see Bentley at once and apply for the post.)

Finally, in the following year, "that noblest work of God in New Burlington Street"—I quote Dickens's ironical description of the publisher—agreed to forego all his rights in the still unwritten "Barnaby Rudge," in return for Dickens's agreeing to repurchase (with the help of the ever-willing Chapman & Hall) the copyright of "Oliver Twist." Forster and Jerdan met to arrange the terms, and a sum of £2,250, which included payment for certain unsold stocks, was agreed upon. From that time Bentley dropped out.

As for Chapman & Hall themselves, the time had

not yet come for any serious misunderstanding. They, indeed, could afford to be generous. . . .

[3]

I must speak briefly of the two books that belong to this time. Unlike "Pickwick" they were "serious," and that in itself was a serious matter for Dickens. It marked his sense of his responsibilities to the public. "Pickwick," wrote Forster, "in teaching him what his power was, had made him conscious of what would be expected from its use; and this never afterwards quitted him." There you have the plain truth. Dickens, indeed, came to take himself with extreme seriousness. At the age of twenty-six he was behaving like a veteran of fifty. His letters to the various members of his family suggest that they might have been written by a grandfather. It is as though at a bound he had come to middle age.

You have a glimpse of the kind of thing that was happening in an account of Dickens in the Doughty Street days written by George Henry Lewes, then a very young man who was dividing his interest, rather curiously, between philosophy and the stage. He is, incidentally, one of the few people who have anything to say of what was to be found in Dickens's house. There were, he records, a number of books on the shelves, but they were mostly three-volume novels, many of them presentation copies from their authors.

When, however, he returned from a two years' stay in Germany, and found Dickens in a larger house in Devonshire Terrace, the books had changed. In the place of the novels were standard editions of the classical authors. Dickens himself, too, had changed with his books; he now showed a graver mien.

"He still remained outside philosophy, science, and the higher literature," wrote Lewes, "and was too unaffected a man to pretend to feel any interest in them. But the vivacity and sagacity which gave a charm to intercourse with him had become weighted with a seriousness which from that time forward became more and more prominent in his conversations and writings."

And indeed, this new seriousness, in his writings at any rate, was almost inevitable. The public had laughed over "Pickwick," as it was meant to laugh, for the book had been written to entertain and amuse, but from its great writers the public demands something besides humor if they are to be "taken seriously," and so soon as Dickens had made his name, he very wisely prepared himself to write what was wanted.

Here there is a point to be noticed. Many good novelists attempt to do the same thing, but do not succeed. Their failure may be due to various causes, but it generally comes from incomplete sincerity. It was Dickens's good fortune to share to a greater degree than do most men of his craft the commoner ideas and ideals of humanity. For all his love of a joke and his pleasure in the good things of life, he was, fundamentally, a serious man. He felt deeply the things that his thousands of readers felt deeply. Cruelty and injustice and hypocrisy made his blood boil, and he wrote about these things because he wanted to write about them. But he knew that he was writing for a public whose blood also boiled at these iniquities, and that meant, though he may not have realized it at the time, certain limitations.

The temptation to show virtue ever triumphant and vice duly punished is great, and Dickens never really resisted it. There did come moments when he attempted to check his inclination for the more conventional forms of romance—I think of the Golden

Dustman in particular—but they were only moments. Why, indeed, should he have resisted? Did not the big public demand in its fiction a world that they would like to believe in? Did not Dickens himself demand, and in a way believe in, such a world? I cannot doubt it. Ever since Chatham days he had liked to wear spectacles of his own manufacture. But he was no ordinary writer, and the spectacles resembled the rimless pince-nez of our own day: they escaped very general notice.

So it was that when with "Oliver Twist" he turned his attention to the unhappier aspects of life, he was able not only to find a new public, but also to set in motion new machinery to deal with the evils of which he was writing. Many writers before him had attacked a civilized community which could permit such disgraces as the ill-treatment of children and the workhouse. Dickens attacked by ridicule, and succeeded where his predecessors had failed.

It is to be noticed, however, that for a little while the old criticisms continued to be hurled at him. When "Oliver Twist" was appearing in the pages of Bentley's Miscellany objections were seriously raised to the introduction of such figures as Fagin and Sikes. They really were most particular in those days. It is a fact that Ainsworth was blackballed about this time for a club solely because he had written "Jack Sheppard," not on account of its historical inexactitude, but because it made a romantic hero out of a convicted felon.

Dickens, it is true, was elected to the Athenæum, no doubt without opposition, but it was felt in many respectable quarters that although he had never actually made vice alluring, he had had no business to give such a curious attraction to murderers and thieves. On the other hand, the general public was delighted to find that there were no signs of his "coming down with the stick." The creatures into whose clutches poor Oliver strayed might be very dreadful and even grotesque, but they were quite as "real" as any of Mr. Pickwick's friends. The same eager interest, moreover, was being taken in their fortunes. So, for instance, the fate of the Artful Dodger was matter for the most serious debates with Forster, and Talfourd could deliver a brief on Charley Bates's behalf quite as impassioned as any he would declaim in the Courts. But, whereas with "Pickwick" there had been no cause for distress, it was impossible for anyone to read its successor without asking himself whether things were quite so bad as they were made out to be.

As a matter of fact they were very bad indeed, and though it is difficult to believe that Fagin or Sikes could ever be found off the stage, there was little enough exaggeration in the description of their environment. Most important of all, here was Dickens paying attention to "plot" and providing the public with what it always craves—a story: a highly dramatic story, told in a way that was new; and if there were improbabilities in it, why not? It is the improbable things that give the greatest delight and are easiest to remember. Obviously the author of "Pickwick" had come to stay. . . .

About "Oliver Twist" little more need be said. There were two interruptions during its serial appearance, and it was published in book form five or six months before the last number had been printed in the Miscellany. There is a vignette of the author at the time, written by Henry Burnett—Fanny Dickens's husband —which speaks of his "mind and muscles working (or, if you please, *playing*) in company, as new thoughts were being dropped upon the paper"; and you are told that he was muttering to himself as he worked. The novel was acting itself for him.

You hear, too, of more rides with Forster, though sometimes an outing must be postponed, because there is something more dramatic than usual to be written. "No, no, don't, don't let us ride till tomorrow," he is writing on one occasion, "not yet having disposed of the Jew, who is such an out-and-outer that I don't know what to make of him." But of course he knew well enough. If ever a man had been born to be decently hanged it was Fagin, and hanged he must be, if the Doughty Street house was not to be attacked by an infuriated mob bent on seeing justice done. Which is not quite so absurd as it sounds, for the merry old Jew had taken hold of men's minds in true Pickwickian fashion.

Incidentally, Dickens went out of his way to secure a background that should be accurate, and in doing so showed for the first time the power of his words. He wanted for his story a harsh and insolent magistrate, and as it happened there was a Mr. Laing in Hatton Garden who was exactly suited to his purpose. He was smuggled into the little court, obtained the material that he wanted, and, shortly after his sketch of the man had appeared in print, the tyrannical Mr. Laing was removed from the bench.

As with "Pickwick," moreover, there were more or less scandalous imitations and two various theatrical adaptations. An Oliver Twiss and a Blue Coat Boy made their appearance in print, and before the end of 1838 no less than six separate dramas with Oliver for their hero were produced on the stage. The St. James's was first in the field in March, and Jerdan was probably voicing Dickens's opinion when his Literary Gazette regretted that the acting was so good, "for a thing more unfit for any stage except that of a Penny Theatre we never saw."

There was a performance at the Surrey Theatre, and Dickens was taken to see it; but he saw very little indeed, for, as Forster tells us, half-way through the first scene he lay down on the floor of the box and refused to move until the curtain fell. At the Adelphi Mrs. Keeley took the part of Oliver, and seems to have had some success. Of more interest, however, is the fact that Dickens, so far from losing interest in the stage, twice made proposals to dramatize the novel himself.

In November he approached Macready on the matter, but the actor thought the suggestion impracticable. Whereupon Dickens wrote to the elder Yates. "I don't see any possibility," he said, "of any other house doing it before your next opening night. If they do, it must be done in a most extraordinary manner, as the story, unlike that of Pickwick, is an involved and complicated one. I am quite certain that no one can have heard what I am going to do with the different characters in the end, inasmuch as at present I don't quite know myself. So we are tolerably safe on that head. I am quite sure that your name as the Jew, and mine as the author, would knock any other attempts out of the field."

Yates duly produced a new version in the following year, but Dickens had nothing to do with it.

A word may be added about "Oliver's" illustrator. George Cruikshank had been engaged for the purpose, and long afterwards he conceived the notion that, like Seymour with "Pickwick," he had not been done justice. He published a pamphlet which related how Dickens had happened to come one day to his studio and picked up a portfolio of drawings—twenty or thirty in number—which showed Fagin and all his gang and were intended to illustrate the life of a London thief. Whereupon Dickens decided to bring Oliver up from the country and introduce him into a thieves' den. Probably he did see some such portfolio. The thieves' den may even have been Cruikshank's suggestion. But once Fagin had really been born, it was not the illustrator who developed his character, and at least one of the plates was redesigned at Dickens's urgent request. Cruikshank, however, did not commit suicide, and he was wise enough to say nothing until Dickens was dead.

[4]

"I hereby nominate and appoint William Hall and Edward Chapman . . . my periodical publishers, until I am advertised in the daily papers as having been compressed into my last edition—one volume, boards, with brass plates."

So wrote Dickens to the publishers of "Pickwick," when it seemed possible that Bentley might snatch him away from them; but, as we have seen, affairs were ultimately settled in their favor, and when the time came for "Pickwick's" successor, it was no longer a question of what were fair terms but only one of deciding upon a theme.

Of what nature was the new story to be? Serious? Comic? A mixture of the two? He had soon made up his mind. His aim, no less than before, would be to amuse, but in the new story there would be a serious strain, and he hoped to enlist the "kindliest sympathies" of his readers as well as their "heartiest merriment." At the same time he had an idea for a purely comic work, which he proposed should be issued at Christmas. Chapman & Hall were agreeable, and terms were fixed. We learn details from a letter that Dickens sent to his publishers at the time when he was at work on the first chapter of "Nicholas Nickleby."

"Don's Annual Register and Obituary of Blue Devils" was to be issued as an octavo volume at Christmas. Dickens was to receive £300 on its appearance and half the profits, in return for which Chapman & Hall were to have a half-share in the copyright. One wonders who on earth the Blue Devils were to be, but, so far as I know, this is the only mention of them in a letter. The project—like a previous proposal to collaborate with Ainsworth in a work to be called "The Lions of London"—must have been abandoned almost at once, but it is interesting to see thus early an idea for a special Christmas book.

What, then, was the new theme to be? Well, the greatest interest had been aroused in the misfortunes of Oliver Twist. Were there, perhaps, other malpractices in which children, not necessarily of the poorest classes, were concerned? Dickens must have asked himself some such question, and recalled to mind an old Chatham experience of his own. A boy had returned from a Yorkshire school not only with tales of ill-treatment and oppression but bearing physical marks of the grossest neglect.

He had marveled at the time that there could be schools so different from "Giles's Cats." And of course! He had seen cases of the kind reported in the newspapers: one of them—in which a man named Shaw of Bowes Academy, Greta Bridge, had been concerned—being particularly horrible. Boys had been starved and bullied and even allowed to go blind from lack of proper attention. He must have another look at that case.

He did have a second look at that case, and found

others as well. There could be no doubt about it; there were private schools where the most hideous cruelty was practiced, and the worst of them all were in Yorkshire. In that county, it seemed, they catered more especially for parents who were anxious to be relieved altogether of their children during schooldays, "no vacations" being a common feature in the advertisements. Obviously a scandalous business. Very well then, it should be investigated. He would go up to Yorkshire himself, and take a careful look round, and if some sort of story could not be woven about such iniquities—well, he must have strangely overrated his powers.

It was necessary, however, to proceed with caution. These Yorkshire schoolmasters must suspect neither his identity nor his purpose, and for this reason he sheltered himself behind a friend's name. Armed with letters of introduction which spoke of "a supposititious little boy who had been left with a widowed mother," he set out with young Browne for a companion on a tour of exploration. They arrived at Greta Bridge on the last day of January, 1838, met Shaw in person at Bowes, interviewed others not too different from him on the Durham border, and had ample opportunity of seeing the conditions under which these far-away schools were being run. And when Dickens returned to town, he was accompanied by the image of Wackford Squeers of Dotheboys Hall.

Here, perhaps, I may speak for a moment of a question which has worried good Dickensians to an almost unbelievable degree. How far, I mean, did he carry his habit of modeling his characters upon real men and women? That he often did work from such living "originals" is, of course, very well known. Already we have seen him appropriating Mr. Laing for a satisfactory ogre. But what of the others? What, in partic-

A More Serious Note, and Some Quarrels

ular, of Squeers and young Nickleby's other employers, the gorgeous Mr. Crummles and the Cheeryble brothers?

Well, there were times when Dickens could be almost photographic and consequently guilty, I suppose, of what today would be called a lapse of good taste, but in general he did what other novelists are accustomed to do. He followed the tea-merchant's example, and *blended*. Sometimes, to be sure, the blending would be slight—just a pinch of Pekoe dropped lightly on to a great mass of Ceylon—but more often some care was taken in the process.

In "Nickleby," as it happened, there were several recognizable portraits, and this led to much wordy warfare. Dickens's mother, it is true, could ask him whether a woman like Mrs. Nickleby had ever existed; but there were others who did not fail to see themselves, as they complained, more or less cruelly caricatured. When Mr. Squeers made his appearance, there was a hullabaloo. Mr. Shaw may not have been quite so bad as Mr. Squeers was painted, but he was certainly brought near to ruin. This, you may say, was just as it should be, for even though they did put up a stained-glass window to his memory when he was dead, he had not come too well out of the charge of cruelty brought against him years before. But was it quite fair to pillory real people in a work of fiction where the truth could so easily, and unnoticeably, be distorted?

Dickens replied to this charge in a preface to "Nickleby," where he stated that Squeers was "a representative of a class, and not of an individual"; and nobody is really in a position to say that he was not speaking the truth. He *did* meet Squeers, as he admitted to friends, and it *was* that "identical scoundrel" who was in his mind when he was describing the amenities of Dotheboys Hall; but who is to say how much blending there was?

There came trouble, too, when Mr. Crummles and his astonishing family burst on the scene. One Davenport, an actor-manager with provincial interests, professed to see himself guyed; and it did happen that a small daughter of his had made her first public appearance the previous year in a theater at Richmond which he had leased. Well, there are those who believe that Dickens had some reason to feel a grudge against this man. They declare, on evidence which was first brought forward more than sixty years later by the adopted son of Davenport's daughter, that at some early period in his career the novelist had belonged to Davenport's company, and been told bluntly to go back to his scribbling. Even so, however, was the revenge that he took too brutal?

Moncrieff, in the same way, complained of the "intemperate and vulgar caricature" of himself, but had he not for a long time been laying himself open to some such attack? Besides, in his case it was the man's actions, rather than the man himself, that were held up to ridicule. No, I confess that except in a few instances where a useful autobiographical note is to be found, I can take little interest in this business of probing for "originals," and prefer to think of my tea-merchant.

But what *is* really interesting is the fact, only recently brought to light by that amiable historian Mr. F. J. Harvey Darton, that so far from the Crummles scenes being absurd exaggerations they were singularly accurate. The Othello who blacked himself all over really did exist. So did the pumps and the wash-tubs. There were third-rate actor-managers like Crummles on every "circuit," and their programs were unbelievably crude. Dickens, as usual, was only transcribing what he had seen. . . .

It was in February, 1838, that "Nickleby" was begun, in spite, as he said, of much playgoing and "a thousand blandishments." Two months later the first number appeared, and the success of the book was never in doubt. Nearly fifty thousand copies of that first number were sold, and Dickens may well have believed that the £150 he was to receive each month was not an undeservedly large sum. The story was finished during the last months of 1839, and when it was ready to appear in book form there was an agreeable bonus of £1,500 for its author.

It was with "Nickleby," moreover, that criticism on the older lines definitely came to an end. There was nothing about the new story which could be called vulgar or low. True, a critic or two might reasonably lament the inclusion of high-falutin' passages too reminiscent of the stage and of a villain too close to the conventional theatrical type; but only Dickens could have invented Mrs. Nickleby and Crummles and Tim Linkinwater and Newman Noggs and the faithful Smike. They were a glorious crew, and they broke down all opposition. Even Sydney Smith succumbed. He had stuck out, he said, as long as he could, but now confessed that he was conquered.

Letters poured in from an excited public. Dickens was implored not to "kill" Smike. When that unfortunate youth was dead, distracted mothers who had lost sons poured out their souls in long letters which choked up the Doughty Street box. They were less lucky than one adventurous boy who had written to Dickens giving his views on the rewards and punishments to be given the characters: he, at any rate, received a reply.

The pirates, of course, remained busy, in spite of Talfourd's efforts in parliament. They had certainly not been frightened away by the amusing parody of an official proclamation that had ushered in the new story. Dickens might claim to be "the only true and lawful 'Boz'," whose delectable works were being imitated by "dishonest dullards" lurking in mean streets and living in cellars; he might threaten these villains with gibbets "so lofty and enduring that their remains" should be "a monument to all succeeding ages"; but nothing could prevent the wretched "Bos" from producing his "Nichelas Nickelberry," or a scoundrelly publisher called Lloyd from issuing a "Nickleby Married," with the name of "Boz" so arranged on the titlepage as to suggest that Dickens had written this wretched sequel.

As usual, too, the stage-adapters were making the most of their opportunity. There was an Infant Phenomenon billed at one of the theaters almost as soon as that remarkable person had made her appearance in print. By November, 1838, Edward Stirling had a two-act farce ready for Yates, who played Mantalini himself and gave the part of Smike to Mrs. Keeley. Forster confessed that he was "amazed" at Dickens finding much to say in its favor.

There followed the inevitable Moncrieff drama, which led to even more than the usual amount of abuse, and at a later date Stirling was responsible for a dramatic sequel to the book called "The Fortunes of Smike." Other versions were shown at the provincial theaters, and in one form or another "Nickleby" for years remained a stock piece for touring companies of the second class.

It was not until the book had been finished that Dickens freed himself altogether from Bentleyan complications, and most of it was written at high pressure. Nevertheless, with his editorship given up, he was able to enjoy a rest now and then, and spent two quiet summers in the country. In 1838 he took a small house at Twickenham. Here, with his own two small children—a daughter had been born earlier in the year—and his younger brothers, there were games and sports—devised of course primarily for them, but thoroughly enjoyed by their elders.

You hear, in particular, of a Balloon Club with Forster as its president (on the very proper condition that he provided the balloons) and the small Charley and Mamie—known respectively as the Snodgering Blee and the Popem Jee—as its most important supporters. You hear of rather more boisterous pastimes at Petersham, near Richmond, whither he went the following year. Here there were races of various kinds, in which Tom Beard and Maclise seem to have been the most accomplished performers, though in the matter of "keeping it up" their host was unbeatable.

To these pleasant retreats there would come a regular stream of friends, most of them fellow members of the Garrick or Athenæum clubs. Ainsworth was still on very intimate terms, Thackeray was a frequent visitor, and Douglas Jerrold, though not yet of the inner circle, was very welcome. "Phiz" of course would drive out; and another good craftsman, George Cattermole, who had married some distant relation of his host or hostess, was often to be found at the cheery dinners that Dickens always delighted to give to his friends.

Most of "Nickleby," however, was written in Doughty Street, and in London there seem to have been a steady round of gay parties. A Shakespeare Club had been founded, and there were Shakespeare Club dinners. Macready resigned the management of Covent Garden Theatre, and there was a dinner to him. There were birthday dinners, and a "Nickleby" dinner, and dinners with the fashionable world, at Gore House and elsewhere; though Dickens always preferred the less formal meals—"snugger," he would call them—with his own little circle. Pleasantly full days. . . .

And what, you wonder, of Mr. Dickens and his family? We have had a glimpse of them at Broadstairs, but the time had now come for Dickens, very definitely the head of the family, to shoulder further responsibilities on their behalf. It was due to him that a post was found for young Frederick in a government office and another in some engineering works in the Midlands for Alfred.

What of Mr. Dickens himself? Well, I fancy that he was still "working" in his careless, good-humored way; I know that he was still having his "moments." Obviously something must be done for him. It was decided that as the father of a famous man, he might now retire and become a country gentleman. For this reason a house must be found for him and his wife and younger children. Where? It is impossible not to smile when one hears where it was that Dickens had found a suitable house. It was a charming little house in beautiful country. . . . Near London perhaps? I can hear Mr. Dickens's inquiry, when it becomes clear to him that further expectations are about to be realized. No, the new house is at Alphington, a village near Exeter, which is certainly a long way from London. But if they are not pleased with it, Dickens will be "grievously disappointed."

Mrs. Dickens, I dare say, is pleased, but is Mr. Dickens so sure? Exeter is the deuce of a long way away, and, as he asks Chapman & Hall, what on earth is he expected to do with himself in a place like Alphington? After all, he is only fifty-three. But it is a wise move on his son's part. London can do very well without the "prodigal father," and in a Devon village there can hardly be much opportunity for "moments." And so—for a while—Mr. Dickens goes down into the west. . . .

[5]

In November, 1839, Dickens moved into the larger house he had found for himself in Devonshire Terrace, Regent's Park. It was, he told Macready, to whom, by the way, he had dedicated "Nickleby," "a house of great promise (and great premium), undeniable situation, and excessive splendour." And its occupation by Dickens may be said to have marked the beginning of that curiously reverent attitude henceforth paid to him by the public. He was no longer the mirth-provoking "Boz": he was Dickens, without the Charles; a great moral force in the land; in fact, an institution.

Chapter VII

MASTER HUMPHREY'S CLOCK

[1]

BEHOLD, then, in Dickens at twenty-seven the most popular novelist that his country had yet known. His position seemed to be as secure as the Bank of England. He had only to write, and people would read. He could make his own terms, and the publishers cheerfully would pay. As it was, several of them were making him princely offers. But although as yet there were few signs of that unhappy restlessness that in later years was to drive him to such desperate lengths, Dickens at no time was content for very long to be a mere story-teller.

Most men, I suppose, finding themselves in the position which at this time was his, would have been content to produce at most a new novel each year. They would have found the strain of monthly numbers too great, and waited for the completion of a story before allowing any portion of it to be printed. Dickens, it is true, was finding this strain very great, yet he could cheerfully propose to make it greater. It was not enough to write new stories: in the old Chatham way he must needs see himself in some monarchial post, which would allow him unlimited scope for his powers. He wanted to play editor again, but with a new sort of

magazine in which he would be his only contributor:
a contributor, moreover, who would not be content to
tell stories, but who would play critic and commentator
and satirist and perhaps playwright as well. He saw
himself as a kind of literary universal provider. . . .
It was no doubt a magnificent scheme, but one factor
of the greatest importance was forgotten. The public is
a conservative body with very clear ideas as to what it
requires, and from its novelists it demands only novels.
And even Dickens, beloved though he might be, could
not persuade it to fall in with his new program.

The experiment of "Master Humphrey's Clock,"
however, is of real biographical interest, for it shows
Dickens not only in the light of literary pioneer, but
also as the excellent showman who can recognize failure and—almost with a wave of his wand—turn it into
his greatest success.

You begin to hear of this new scheme in Petersham
days, when "Nickleby" was within measurable distance
of its end. A beginning had even then been made with
"Barnaby Rudge," but it had been put aside until
affairs with Bentley were settled. What, then, was to
follow "Nickleby"? In the first place, of course, it was
necessary to be quite certain about Chapman & Hall.
By this time Forster had made himself indispensable,
and it was Forster who was asked to approach them.
What, in effect, would they be prepared to pay for a
new work conceived on entirely new lines: a threepenny
weekly publication, in fact, roughly on the lines of the
old Spectators and Tatlers, though written in a more
popular vein? Dickens was in no doubt as to his own
monetary value, and he put things bluntly.

"If they do something handsome," he told Forster,
"even handsomer perhaps than they dreamt of doing,
they will find it their interest, and will find me trac-

table." Would they, therefore, "step gallantly forward" with an offer?

Chapman & Hall proposed terms which, if not quite so gallant as Forster would have wished, were acceptable, and asked for further information. Whereupon Dickens set forth in detail what he was proposing to do. He intended, he said, "to introduce a little club or knot of characters and to carry their personal histories and proceedings through the work; to introduce fresh characters constantly; to introduce Mr. Pickwick and Sam Weller . . . to write amusing essays on the various foibles of the day as they arise; to take advantage of all passing events; and to vary the form of the papers by throwing them into sketches, essays, tales, adventures, letters from imaginary correspondents, and so forth, so as to diversify the contents as much as possible."

Particular details were also mentioned. Remembering the project with Ainsworth to write about London through the ages, he now suggested a new sort of "Arabian Nights" with Gog and Magog for the narrators. He also proposed to include "Savage Chronicles" purporting to "describe the administration of justice in some country that never existed," but which were really to be satirical comments on the maladministration of justice at home. Most interesting of all was the suggestion that he should go (at the publishers' expense) to some place abroad, Ireland, for instance, or America, and send home papers written there after the style of Washington Irving's "Alhambra." By now, too, it seemed likely that he might require assistance, but he would agree to a certain specified portion of each number being his own work.

There were further discussions, and Chapman & Hall agreed to pay £50 each week, no matter what the sales might be, and half of the profits. Browne and Cattermole were to be the illustrators, and it only remained for Dickens to decide on a title. He had a notion, he was telling Forster in a little while, of an "old file" in a queer house, with a great affection for an "old quaint queer-cased" grandfather-clock, in whose recesses various manuscripts were to be discovered and their contents related to the old boy's friends. Within a few days he had made his choice, and in January, 1840, wrote the first number. At the beginning of April "Master Humphrey's Clock" was wound up for the first time in public, and seventy thousand copies were sold.

[2]

Meanwhile there had come a visit to Bath that was not without its importance to Dickens. In a solid house in a solid square in that singularly beautiful city lived the poet Landor. He was now in his sixty-fifth year and separated from his wife: a lonely and cantankerous and rather violent but warm-hearted man. Between him and Dickens there had existed since "Pickwick" days a mutual admiration and affection, and in this year he began the custom of inviting the novelist and his wife and a few other intimate friends to a birthday celebration.

At the time of this visit Dickens himself was in the wildest possible spirits—the old "slavery" was now finished and done with—and it is interesting and not uninstructive to find him playing a queer kind of elaborate joke with his friends, and giving to it all the careful attention to detail that he invariably bestowed on his work. The queen's marriage had taken place on February 10, and the whole country was talking of little else.

Two days later Landor was astounded to receive an apparently serious letter from Dickens with the startling news that he, Dickens, had fallen hopelessly in love with his sovereign and proposed in despair to elope with one of her maids of honor.

Poor Landor was so puzzled that he sent on the letter to Forster, asking for an explanation, but Forster was already in the joke. He himself had just been informed, also by letter, that his friend could no longer bear the sight of his wife, loathed his parents, and hated his house. The distraught man, it seemed, was thinking of suicide or of joining the Chartists, and would probably murder both Chapman and Hall.

With Forster and Maclise to abet him, moreover, the joke was carried to such lengths that a rumor of Dickens's insanity did actually arise later on in the year. Indeed, I have seen it solemnly stated that no further proof than the letter to Landor is required to show that he had temporarily taken leave of his senses. Well, it may be making too much of a trifle, but I would hazard a guess that while the joke—Forster calls it a "daring delusion"—lasted, Dickens put such enthusiasm into the theatrical part that it amused him to play as almost to make him believe in its reality. He had not yet begun a new novel, and so he made of himself a new character for a novel: a man in love with the young queen who could never be his. . . .

In Bath, I imagine, the joke was carried on, and Landor probably enjoyed it with the rest, but before the four days' visit had come to an end, it may well have been forgotten. Perhaps, however, it might be more correct to say that it had merged itself into a more serious fancy. I may be accused of absurdity, but behind the figure of the girl queen who was lost to him, I see the image of another girl—also a queen in her way—who was lost: the Mary who was so constantly in his dreams. And so perhaps the joke was not really so meaningless as it might seem to be, more especially as we learn from Forster that it was in Landor's house on this occasion "that the fancy which took the form of little Nell in the 'Curiosity Shop' first dawned on the genius of its creator."

You will have noticed that in the preparations for "Master Humphrey's Clock" nothing had been said about a new novel, and "the little child-story" which Dickens now proposed to incorporate in the new weekly publication was at first intended to be merely a "Personal Adventure of Master Humphrey." As such, indeed, it began, but already the public had shown that it was not too enthusiastic about the "Clock." After the first number, which gave no signs of a new serial story, there was an ominous drop in the sales, and not even the revival of Mr. Pickwick and Sam with an amusing small son could materially increase them.

It became necessary to make the most radical change, and Dickens, ever sensitive to public opinion, lost no time in making it. Returning from a holiday in the Midlands, during which, by the way, Forster and he found themselves without money and were forced to pawn their gold watches, he ruthlessly banished Gog and Magog and allowed the ill-fated Humphrey to look after himself. All ideas of Savage Chronicles or foreign papers were forgotten, and his whole attention was given to "The Old Curiosity Shop." Some skill was required to adapt the "little child-story" to the altered conditions, and as yet it had not taken full shape in his mind; but the machinery applied was not too noticeable, and in a little while all England was enjoying the pathetic adventures of Little Nell, and had made the acquaintance of Dick Swiveller and the

Marchioness, the delightful Kit, and the wholly abominable Quilp.

We have fairly full reports of its progress from Forster who incidentally was responsible for the "killing" of poor Nell—a matter of the deepest concern at the time to a large number of people. While the earlier chapters were being written, Dickens was summoned to sit as a juryman at the inquest on a baby supposed to have been murdered by its mother. He duly appeared, and seems to have been greatly affected by the harrowing business—which may or may not be the reason why for the rest of his life he very coolly and quite unjustifiably ignored every summons of the kind. (The authorities seem to have been strangely indulgent.)

In the summer he was at Broadstairs, and he was there again in September; but in August there was an incident at his London house that Forster does not record. I include an account of it, because it may serve to stand for the many little quarrels between Dickens and Forster of which their common friends so often speak but so seldom give details. The two men remained friends until Dickens's death, but there were those who could not understand the friendship, and there were certainly times—notably in 1847—when Dickens was near to severing all relations.

Yet, though he might find his chief friend altogether too domineering, he could not conceal from himself his very great worth. Forster might patronize or find fault, but he was doing what no other man could have done. And so, though there were frequent quarrels and harsh words, there never came an actual break. But these quarrels, I think, were not without their effect upon Dickens. I give Macready's account of the sorry affair of August 16 in full:

"Went to dine with Dickens, and was witness of a most painful scene after dinner. Forster, Maclise, and myself were the guests. Forster got to one of his head-long streams of talk (which he thinks argument), and waxed warm, and at last some sharp observation led to personal retorts between him and Dickens. He displayed his usual want of tact, and Dickens flew into so violent a passion as quite to forget himself, and give Forster to understand that he was in his house, which he should be very glad if he would leave.

"Forster behaved very foolishly. I stopped him; spoke to both of them, and observed that for an angry instant they were about to destroy a friendship valuable to both. I drew from Dickens the admission that he had spoken in passion and would not have said what he said could he have reflected; but he added that he could not answer for his temper under Forster's provocation, and that he should do just the same again. Forster behaved very *weakly;* would not accept the repeated acknowledgment communicated to him that Dickens regretted the passion, etc., but stayed skimble-skambling, and at last, finding he could obtain no more, made a sort of speech accepting what he had before declined. He was silent and not recovered—no wonder!—during the whole evening. Mrs. Dickens had gone out in tears. It was a very painful scene."

Yes, it must have been painful, but the reconciliation came speedily enough, and in a few days' time the affair was doubtless forgotten. When, too, in a little while, the Bentley squabbles had come to an end, Dickens, in sending his friend an antique silver-mounted wine-jug as a token of his affectionate gratitude, wrote a letter such as any man would have been proud to receive. . . .

There had been a brief visit to Alphington in this

same month, and in September Dickens was temporarily upset by new rumors about himself. These not only doubted his sanity, but announced his conversion to Rome. How such an idea could have arisen I do not know. He was never a keen churchman, although all his life he remained a religious man who took the greatest pains to see that his children were made familiar with true Christian ideals. But although on one occasion a difference of opinion with a clergyman sent him temporarily to a Unitarian chapel, where the minister, Edward Tagart, was a wholly exceptional man, he never left the established church, and at no time showed the least inclination towards Rome. Rumor, however, has a liking for flinging her cloak about men in Dickens's position, and at all times the wildest stories about him were widely believed.

It was about this time, too, that Carlyle met Dickens for the first time, and like most of the great men of the day at once acknowledged his exceptional charm. He had gone to a dinner party at the Stanleys, and met "lords and lions."

"Know, Pickwick too," he recounted in his characteristic way, "was of the same dinner party, though they did not seem to heed him overmuch. He is a fine little fellow—Boz, I think: clear blue intelligent eyes that he arches amazingly, large, protrusive, rather loose mouth, a face of the most extreme *mobility,* which he shuttles about—eyebrows, eyes, mouth and all—in a very singular manner while speaking. Surmount these with a coil of common coloured hair, and set it on a small compact figure very small and dressed à la D'Orsay, rather than well—this is Pickwick. For the rest, a quiet, shrewd-looking little fellow, who seems to guess pretty well what he is and what others are." Not a very faulty vignette, to be sure, and the prelude to yet another warm friendship.

There seems to be no doubt that "The Old Curiosity Shop," sold either as part of "Master Humphrey's Clock" or in a volume by itself—it had been finished, by the way, in the first month of 1841—was even more popular than any of its predecessors, and in America its success was immense. I cannot find mention of any imitations, although lengthy extracts from the novel appeared in a children's publication; and the theatrical adapters were less busy than usual. Somebody succeeded in making a "domestic drama" out of "Master Humphrey's Clock" two months after its first appearance, and Stirling produced his version of "The Old Curiosity Shop" in November, 1840, with Yates as Quilp and Mrs. Keeley as Little Nell, but some years were to elapse before the complete novel seems to have been dramatized.

Incidentally, I can discover no good reason why the queer little house in Portsmouth Street, Lincoln Inn's Fields, should pride itself on having once been the old curiosity shop in Dickens's mind. But it will probably continue so to pride itself until some severely practical authority orders its destruction.

[3]

The much-delayed "Barnaby Rudge" now began to be tackled in earnest. Two chapters had been written in 1839, but it was only after Chapman & Hall had signed the agreement for its publication in "Master Humphrey's Clock" that it progressed at the usual speed. It was finished in October, 1841, which must have meant very hard work, for there were many worries and distractions this year, including the two volumes of miscellaneous papers that Dickens had agreed to edit for Mrs. Macrone's benefit, a visit to Scotland, a serious illness, and the rather hurried preparations for an American tour. On the other hand, he had been thinking about "Barnaby" for four or five years, and must already have gathered all the historical material that he required. The book itself showed the author in a less familiar mood, but in no way interfered with his popularity. The stage versions included more than one musical arrangement, and the shameless "Bos" invited the public to read his "Barnaby Budge."

One or two other matters call for mention. A fourth child, and second son, Walter Landor, was born on February 8. In the following month there was a small tragedy in the household. You remember Barnaby's raven; it was not an imaginary bird. Dickens himself owned a real Grip. It does not seem to have been a universal favorite, being rather too fond of biting the children and Topping, the groom, but it talked a great deal and undoubtedly gave its owner much pleasure. In March, however, it died, apparently poisoned, either incautiously by itself or maliciously by an unfriendly butcher or other ill-disposed person, and the obsequies were sufficiently grandiose. It is typical of Dickens that with all his work he could write a long and detailed and very droll account of the poor bird's last hours to Maclise.

"This morning at daybreak," he wrote, "it appeared better; received (agreeably to the doctor's directions) another dose of castor-oil; and partook plentifully of some warm gruel, the flavour of which he appeared to relish. Towards eleven o'clock he was so much worse that it was found necessary to muffle the stable-knocker. At half-past, or thereabouts, he was heard talking to himself about the horse and Topping's family, and to add some incoherent expressions which are supposed to have been either a foreboding of his approaching dissolution, or some wishes relative to the dispersal of his little property; consisting chiefly of half-pence which he had buried in different parts of the garden. On the clock striking twelve he appeared slightly agitated, but he soon recovered, walked twice or thrice along the coach-house, stopped to bark, staggered, exclaimed *Halloa, old girl!* (his favourite expression), and died."

One is glad to know that another and larger and even more accomplished Grip was soon obtained, and managed to survive for three years. Incidentally the rather ludicrous story is told that some friends of the novelist spoke of him about this time as being raven-mad. "Raven" is not too dissimilar from "raving": hence one of the current rumors. . . .

It was about this time, too, that attention had to be given to the "Pic-Nic Papers," and here again it was Dickens's misfortune to be engaged in a quarrel—a very curious quarrel—with a publisher. There was no financial dispute, of course, for all the contributors were giving their services free, but there did arise a bitter controversy over the question of editorial responsibility, which led to prolonged delays.

Henry Colburn, it seems to me, behaved in a quite extraordinary manner: in just the way, indeed, that was most likely to drive Dickens to sullen fury. Why? Nobody knows. It seems to be generally assumed that Dickens did not himself make the original suggestion for the "Pic-Nic Papers," but responded to appeals put forth on Mrs. Macrone's behalf—quite conceivably in the first place by Colburn. But he offered to make an original contribution, and was either invited, or offered, to undertake the editorship of the two proposed volumes. In any case he was duly constituted their editor, and naturally demanded full editorial authority.

In the previous June, however, Colburn had taken objection, apparently on some religious ground, to a contribution of Landor's, and, as if this were not enough, at a later date he was ignoring another paper sent in by the equally distinguished Leigh Hunt. This interference may have been courageous, but it was hardly wise. It led to Dickens's temporary refusal to have anything further to do with the business and to the withholding of his own contribution.

"Mr. Colburn," he was explaining afterwards to Leigh Hunt, "exercised my duties, and accepted and rejected Papers at his most literary will and pleasure. I resisted this monstrous indecency in Mr. Colburn for a whole year"—nine months, to be exact—"and then wrote him that, as it was a work of charity, and I wanted the money for Mrs. Macrone, I would give him his way. . . . I damned his eyes (by implication and construction) at the same time; and declined to hold further correspondence with him, on any subject."

The actual damning, if we are to judge from his only letter to Colburn—dated April 1, 1841—that seems to have survived, was comparatively mild. The "sneaking vagabond"—so was the publisher described to Forster—was indeed given his way "in view of the urgent appeals of the lady for whose benefit our price is to be paid," but he was bidden to send back the Landor manuscript if he wished ever to see Dickens's own contribution. The rejected paper must have been returned without delay, for Dickens was busily engaged in the second week of the month transforming "The Lamplighter," a farce he had written for Macready three years before —the actor had very delicately refused it—into a short story.

Mrs. Macrone seems to have been told, presumably by Colburn, that it was only Dickens who had been responsible for the delay; and at the end of May, when the two volumes were still unpublished, she wrote him a letter of protest. His reply contained a dignified rebuke. He had done everything, he said, that he had had to do, and only the pressure of George Cruikshank's engagements was responsible for this further delay.

"If we live a few years," he concluded, "and you gain in the meantime a little experience of the world, I shall be glad to hear that you have found many friends as disinterested and true as I have sought to prove myself and less inclined to quarrel. . . ."

Had he been a little too careful of his dignity in the matter? The question occurs to one, but to my mind the blame in this case must be given to the publisher, who continued his curious behavior even after the quarrel. For when the "Pic-Nic Papers" appeared "Edited by Charles Dickens Esq.," a third volume had been added (containing matter already printed in America) about which Dickens had been told nothing at all. A queer enough business. . . .

The invitation to stand for parliament also belongs to this date. Some gentlemen in Reading asked him to be their candidate. As I have said, he refused, ostensibly on the sole ground of the expense; but to my mind this was merely a polite way of refusing an honor that, though it may have pleased his vanity, was so little to his liking. There was another honor, however, which he did not refuse, and this had an additional importance inasmuch as it may have helped him—I am convinced that it did help him—to his decision to visit America in the following year.

In April Lord Jeffrey, an old editor of the Edinburgh Review and now a Scottish judge, had arrived in London. He made no secret of his high admiration for Dickens's work—Little Nell, in particular, had aroused his enthusiasm—and he brought with him the news that Edinburgh would be delighted to pay the novelist the highest honors if he would visit the city. Dickens, it seems, had been proposing to spend a short vacation in Ireland, but changed his mind, arranged to go with his wife to the Highlands, and accepted Jeffrey's invitation.

In Edinburgh he had a foretaste of what was to happen in America. He was given a banquet which "beat all natur'," he attended a theatrical performance where he was received like royalty, and he was voted the freedom of the city. His triumph, indeed, was complete. Once again he was begged to stand for parliament. There were invitations to attend other banquets. He was dined and fêted every day.

He slipped away to the Highlands—incidentally engaging the services as guide of a rather ridiculous but most lovable ex-sculptor called Angus Fletcher, who was afterwards to accompany him abroad—returned south to Broadstairs to finish his book and wind up "Master Humphrey's Clock" for the last time, signed another agreement with Chapman & Hall, which would give him a year's freedom from novels, and turned his eyes toward America.

Chapter VIII

THE FIRST AMERICAN VISIT

[I]

OLD Mr. Weller, you may remember, suggested to Sam that a "pianner" might usefully be employed to convey Mr. Pickwick secretly out of the Fleet Prison. " 'There ain't no vurks in it,' whispered his father. 'It 'ull hold him easy, vith his hat and shoes on, and breathe through the legs, vich is holler. Have a passage ready taken for 'Merriker. The 'Merrikin gov'ment will never give him up, ven they finds as he's got money to spend, Sammy. Let the guv'ner stop there, till Mrs. Bardell's dead, or Mr. Dodson and Fogg's sung (wich last ewent I think is the most likely to happen first, Sammy), and then let him come back and write a book about the 'Merrikins as 'll pay all his expenses and more, if he blows 'em up enough.' "

In 1842 Dickens visited America, wrote a book about the Americans, and in various ways "blew them up." What, exactly, were his reasons for going?

Several suggestions have been made. His books had been sold in thousands throughout the States, and at prices which placed them within reach of even the poorest. With no international copyright law, however, there had been no American money for Dickens except, I believe, £25 from one firm of publishers, willing to pay for an early set of proofs in order to get ahead of their rivals. Was he then proposing to visit the States with the intention of conducting a campaign in favor of some new international agreement? He certainly lost no opportunity while there to speak out his mind on the question, and that even in the face of the fiercest opposition, but he unhesitatingly denied that there had been any such intention in his mind before crossing the Atlantic.

For a very definite reason, moreover, I do not think that he deceived himself on the point. His preparations for the tour were conducted with that attention to detail which marks the good showman, but no steps were taken to prepare for any such campaign; and it was only after he had spoken once or twice to American audiences that he came to understand the value of receiving support in the press from brother authors at home. No, it seems to me that he went out of his way to attack existing conditions in the book world, because for the first time he was understanding the actual extent of his own losses.

But there were other reasons why such a trip should appeal to him. At this time the United States was almost continuously in thinking men's minds. The politicians would find in American conditions subject-matter for the most varied debates. To the more radical sections America was standing for a standard of liberty denied to reactionary Britain. To the humanitarians on the other hand there was the ignoble spectacle of slavery. To the polite world there was the alleged (and most comic) lack of all the more gracious aspects of social life.

Ten years before, moreover, England had been entertained, and slightly shocked, by Mrs. Trollope's "Domestic Manners of the Americans"—surely the

The First American Visit

mildest book that ever caused a sensation on both sides of the Atlantic—and she was only one of several English writers, including Harriet Martineau, whose impressions of America were of a kind to raise very general curiosity. Of late, too, a few American authors, Washington Irving at their head, had been finding a large British public. And with his interest in so many social problems, his unorthodox radicalism, and his dislike of shams, Dickens more than most people must have found himself keen to see with his own eyes the American way of doing things.

They were constantly writing to him from the States, and if all accounts were true, he was even more popular there than in England. He needed an extended holiday; why not take one in the New World, where his reception ought at least to be as warm and affectionate as that which Edinburgh had given him? More important, why not combine pleasure with work, and find in America material for a new sort of book? There had been some such idea in his mind when he was elaborating his proposals for "Master Humphrey's Clock," and from that time, I dare say, it had never been permitted to be wholly banished.

A letter from Washington Irving, the one American writer whom he wholeheartedly admired, possibly decided him. Irving had written warmly about his work, and sought his friendship. Dickens, not disguising his pleasure at the American's praise, wrote to say how gladly he would welcome Irving to England. This, apparently, could not be; and so, if they were to meet, it was Dickens who must cross the Atlantic.

There was, of course, opposition. His wife, with four small children to look after, did her best to dissuade him. The voyage would be dangerous, there would be no real advantage in going, and what was to happen to the children? Forster, possibly thinking of future misunderstandings with publishers, although at this time it really did seem as though matters were comfortably static, expressed no enthusiasm. But although Kate might weep whenever America was mentioned, and Forster might grumble, and Lady Holland might suggest that "third or fourth class people" of the kind that he would presumably meet in America, were discoverable nearer home in Bristol, Dickens by September, 1841, had made up his mind.

Immediately, of course, he was in a state of the greatest excitement. A new sort of play was to be enacted on a new sort of stage with, more important, a new sort of audience, and every detail must receive his personal attention. "The American preliminaries," he told Forster, "are necessarily startling, and to a gentleman of my temperament, destroy sleep, appetite, and work, unless definitely arranged."

Except, however, for a serious illness—more serious even than usual, for he was forced to undergo an operation which kept him in bed for some time—and the sudden and unexpected death of his wife's younger brother, rendered all the more poignant when it seemed that he would have to agree to the poor fellow sharing Mary Hogarth's grave—"it seems like losing her a second time," he wrote—the preparations were carried out with his usual sharp eye for detail.

From the first it was wisely decided that all expenses should be paid by himself, in order that he might be left free to say or write what he pleased. Chapman & Hall were asked what they thought of a note-book to be published on his return at half a guinea, and when they expressed their warm approval of the scheme, they were begged to make inquiries about fares and berths. The question of taking or leaving the children was a difficult one, but was finally solved by Macready's offer to look after them. Fred Dickens, of whom they were fond, was to go with them to his house. Kate was to be accompanied by her maid Anne, whose extraordinary smartness was subsequently to arouse general attention, and the house in Devonshire Terrace was to be let for six months.

As usual, too, there was to be a public announcement of his plans: this time in the "Clock." Clothes had to be bought, letters of introduction to be obtained, and a hundred minor matters to be settled. Dickens took the precaution to become personally acquainted with the American minister, witnessed his son Walter's christening in the presence of his godfather Landor, who had come up from Bath for the purpose, saw his winecellar well and truly sealed up, took the faithful Forster with him as far as Liverpool, and on January 4, 1842, steamed out on the SS. Britannia, John Hewitt, captain, bound for Boston, Mass.

His "American Notes," almost maddeningly impersonal though the book is, contains a fairly detailed description of conditions aboard the Britannia, and this is supplemented by one or two private letters. The paddle-boat was a good enough ship for her day, but her cabins were not very large. Dickens was momentarily "dashed" at the sight of his own, but was soon laughing loudly at such a "monstrous absurdity," and making the best of things.

There were eighty-six passengers aboard, including Lord Mulgrave, an officer returning from leave to his regiment in Montreal; and one is glad to be told that all the women were "unusually pretty." They were promised "a very fine passage," but actually experienced about the worst that the ship's officers could remember. The voyage took eighteen days, and for one dreadful moment they were in most serious danger. Dickens himself was ill for five days, and his wife remained in "the utmost terror all the way."

Nevertheless, there were cards and games, and a steward lent Dickens an accordion—to which instrument he became so attached as to buy one for himself in America—and there were the usual absurdities and minor mishaps without which no voyage is to be borne. Dickens sent playful descriptions home:

"As for news, we have more of that than you would think for. One man lost fourteen pounds at vingt-un in the saloon yesterday, or another got drunk before dinner was over, or another was blinded with lobster sauce spilt over him by the steward, or another had a fall on deck and fainted. The ship's cook was drunk yesterday morning (having got at some salt-water-damaged whiskey), and the captain ordered the boatswain to play upon him with the hose of the fire-engine until he roared for mercy—which he didn't get; for he was sentenced to lookout, for four hours at a stretch for four nights running, without a great coat, and to have his grog stopped.

"Four dozen plates were broken at dinner. One steward fell down the cabin-stairs with a round of beef, and injured his foot severely. Another steward fell down after him, and cut his eye open. The baker's taken ill: so is the pastry-cook. A new man, sick to death, has been required to fill the place of the latter officer, and has been dragged out of bed and propped up in a little house upon deck, between two casks, and ordered (the captain standing over him) to make and roll out pie-crust; which he protests, with tears in his eyes, it is death to him in his bilious state to look at." And so on in the most cheerful vein.

But as they were running at night into Halifax harbor, the ship struck a mud-bank, and for a short while Dickens believed that the end had come. "For half an hour we were throwing up rockets, burning blue lights, and fixing signals of distress, all of which remained unanswered, though we were so close to the shore that we could see the waving branches of the trees." The pilot seems to have lost his head, but the captain remained cool—he was officially thanked at the end of the voyage and given a piece of plate—and at high tide all danger was past.

At Halifax Dickens had a slight foretaste of what was to come in the way of ovations: "Crowds cheering the inimitable in the streets," introduction to the governor Lord Falkland, parliamentary courtesies, and the like. But his stay was short, and on Saturday, January 24, at five o'clock in the afternoon, he reached Boston, there to meet with a reception the like of which had never before been accorded to any one man.

[2]

On the American side preparation had been made on no ordinary scale. Boz was coming, and to the Americans Boz was much more than a widely popular European writer; he was even more than another of those "very remarkable men" with whom at the time America knew herself to be singularly well provided; he was a phenomenon. He had given great pleasure equally to learned professors in the East and to illiterate pioneers in the Far West.

Men who were rarely seen with a book in their hands had laughed over Sam Weller, and brushed a tear away at the death of Little Nell. Mr. Pickwick might be wholly British, but, unlike a large number of his countrymen, ne had been able to steal every American heart. There was this, too, about Boz: he was, like his Pickwick, wholly British, but it was obvious that he stood for ideals which America had made, or chose to think she had made, her own. He was coming, and he should be shown that the New World knew how to treat its heroes. That, at any rate, was the official view, and if it happened that there were those who cared little for Boz but had no intention of missing any raree-show for which there was nothing to pay—well, even the most honored visitor must be prepared to take the nation as he found it.

The lead fell to Boston, and that city of culture and tradition was determined to make the most of its opportunity. It had many men in its midst who either had achieved fame already or were to become world-famous in the future. Longfellow was a professor at Harvard. Prescott had begun his career as an historian. Young Richard Dana had delighted readers on both sides of the Atlantic with his "Two Years Before the Mast." James Russell Lowell and Charles Sumner (just home from Europe) were at the bar. In the intervals of writing lyrics and singing songs, Oliver Wendell Holmes was practicing medicine, and Cornelius Felton, afterwards one of Dickens's greatest friends, was a most unusual professor of Greek.

Committees of such men were hurriedly formed to decide precisely what should be done. Obviously there must be an official banquet with speeches; and the presence of Mrs. Dickens suggested the propriety of holding a grand ball. The managers of Boston's two theaters prepared gala performances with a strongly Dickensian flavor; and the editors of the six newspapers, not, as it happened, on the best of terms with each other, found it convenient, at any rate on this occasion, to usurp the functions of their reporters, and board the Britannia themselves for that strange preliminary ordeal upon which Americans insist to this day, a first interview with "the nation's guest."

Dickens was amused at this, the first honor paid him. "I was standing," he wrote to Forster, "in full fig on the paddle-box beside the captain, staring about me, when suddenly, long before we were moored to the wharf, a dozen men came leaping on board at the peril of their lives, with great bundles of newspapers under their arms; worsted comforters (very much the worse for wear) round their necks; and so forth. 'Aha!' says I, 'this is like our London Bridge'; believing of course that these visitors were news-boys. But what do you think of their being EDITORS? And what do you think of their tearing violently up to see me and beginning to shake hands, like madmen? Oh! if you could have seen how I wrung their wrists! And if you could but know how I hated one man in very dirty gaiters, and with very protruding upper teeth, who said to all comers after him, 'So you've been introduced to our friend Dickens—eh?'"

He had cause, however, to be grateful to one of their number. Dr. Palmer, then acting-editor of the Boston Transcript, learned that no rooms had been engaged at the Tremont House, and rushed off to engage the best suite at that fine hotel. Then, when the ship had been moored, Francis Alexander, the painter, who had already arranged for a portrait, arrived, and took the Dickens party and Lord Mulgrave off in his carriage "through cheering crowds."

Almost immediately the triumph began. By this time Dickens must have become well-used to adulation, but he had yet to learn much. On the Sunday, it is true, he was left more or less to himself, for no newspapers were published on the Sabbath, and he was able to see something of the city with Mulgrave and Colley Grattan, the British Consul. From an early hour, however, on the Monday morning he was rarely again left alone, and his program had to be drawn up as meticulously as any of those to which modern royalties are obliged to submit.

It was, indeed, more or less as a king that he was received. Not only was his hotel besieged by strangers eager to shake his hand, but already there was a small avalanche of letters. Most of these were requests for his autograph, but many contained more or less official invitations that required immediate reply. Good-humoredly on that first morning he sat down to his correspondence, the while at least one artist was busily sketching in his room; but he was soon to find it necessary not only to engage a secretary to attend to his correspondence, but also to refuse three-quarters of the invitations he received.

There were two public engagements for that Monday: a visit to the senate, and the first of the gala performances. This last was timed to begin at 6:30, and when Dickens with his wife and Mulgrave, who must have been highly amused at all the rumpus, came out of the hotel, the police had some difficulty in clearing a space for them to cross the road to the theater. In the theater itself the scene was dramatic enough. Every seat was occupied, for it had been widely advertised that Boz was to be present, and on his appearance in one of the private boxes, the whole audience rose up and gave him a round of nine cheers. He acknowledged the compliment "with a smile and a bow," and settled down to witness a performance of Charles O'Malley.

What he thought of it we do not know, but he must

have been amused, and perhaps touched, by the two items that followed. The manager J. M. Field not only had dramatized "Nickleby" for the occasion, but had devised a Dickensian pageant to which he had given the curious title of "The Masque Phrenologic, Boz." The manuscript of this masque was sent to Dickens at midnight, and he acknowledged the "most ingenious compliment which afforded him very high satisfaction and entertainment" the next morning.

From that moment Boston went slightly mad about its guest. The newspapers reported his every movement. When he walked out to Alexander's studio to sit for his portrait, crowds lined the streets and even the steps leading up to the studio; and, if we are to believe one account, written by a nephew of Dr. Holmes, some of the women behaved very oddly in the studio itself.

"What devilish fools," he wrote, "folks are making themselves about Boz. . . . Alexander got the privilege of taking Dickens's portrait. The ladies pressed in to stare at him, so that at last he couldn't bear it, swore a big oath that he wouldn't sit there to be gazed at and bolted for the door. . . . Really it is too bad that he should get such ideas of the ill-breeding of our people."

It would seem, too, that after the interrupted sitting these ladies did not cease their pursuit, but closed about him, seized his hand, touched his coat, and no doubt cast covetous eyes on that very long hair. Yet I fancy that Dickens had not yet tired of being the center of attraction, and when he had engaged the secretarial services of a pupil of Alexander called Putnam, he settled down to play lion with his usual intention of giving the public, so far as he could, what it wanted.

The most trifling affairs took on the importance of real news. There was, for instance, the ridiculous business of the pocket-comb. It may not be true, though I see no reason to doubt it. Dickens attended a semi-private dinner at some big and socially important house. He caught sight of himself in a mirror, did not like the "set" of his hair, took out a comb, and coolly "combed his hair at the table," an act which still seems to be causing Bostonians no little astonishment.

To speak of his hair, it is interesting to note the contradictory reports about it at the time. The Alexander portrait certainly suggests a much darker tint than it is generally supposed to have shown, and when Richard Dana described his first meeting with Dickens he made particular mention of his "matted, curling, wet-looking black hair."

Dana, by the way, was sadly disappointed with the novelist's personal appearance. He had expected "the handsomest man in London," but found "a dissipated-looking mouth with a vulgar draw to it, a muddy, olive complexion, stubby fingers and a hand by no means patrician." Patrician, however, was what Dickens never had been and never would be, but even Dana had to admit his fascination. "He has," he wrote in his diary, "what I suppose to be the true Cockney cut."

More criticisms of the kind followed when on January 26 the grand ball was held at Papanti's Hall. The ladies could not quite forgive his vivid waistcoats—it was a time for sober black waistcoats in polite America —nor, indeed, were they too sure that he was quite genteel. At a dinner given by Prescott's father, the aristocratic Miss Wormely was seriously distressed at something he said.

"In the course of the entertainment," she wrote, "a discussion arose among the gentlemen as to which was the more beautiful woman, the Duchess of Sutherland or Mrs. Caroline Norton. 'Well, I don't know,' said

> Devonshire Terrace
> Fourteenth December 1842
>
> My Dear Pettigrew.
>
> I cannot tell you how much I regret the being obliged to say that I have received letters this morning which oblige me to leave town by Railroad immediately on some family business (not the most pleasant in its nature) which will detain me until tomorrow.
> In haste
> Believe me
> always faithfully yours
> Charles Dickens

An unpublished letter of Dickens
mentioning his family troubles
In the collection of Charles J. Sawyer

Dickens, expanding himself in his green velvet waistcoat, 'Mrs. Norton perhaps is the more beautiful, but the Duchess, to my mind, is the more kissable person.' Had a bomb-shell dropped upon Judge Prescott's dinner-table it could hardly have startled the company more than this remark."

But Boz had never hidden his liking for the good things of the world, amongst which most people, I imagine, would include kisses, and well used to good society though he was, a certain bluff heartiness was rarely absent from his conversation.

Meanwhile the Bostonians were not alone in their preparations. New York might pretend to deprecate the "beslavering" of Boz, who must surely be disgusted with "such liquorice doses" as he was being given, and Boston itself might be rechristened Boz-town by contemptuous rivals, but almost every city was imploring the novelist to pay it a visit.

"I have had deputations," he wrote to Forster, "from the far West, who have come from two thousand miles distant! from the lakes, the rivers, the backwoods, the log houses, the cities, factories, valleys and towns. Authorities from nearly all the states have written to me. I have heard from Universities, Congress, Senate and bodies public and private of every sort and kind."

As usual, too, there were the grumblers, but it was only after the first of the great public banquets in his honor had been held, that definitely inimical expressions were heard. This Boston dinner took place on February 1, and it must have been an extraordinary feast. "Was there ever such a night in our staid city?" asked one of those present; and he was not alone in professing astonishment. Fifteen dollars a cover was charged, but for that sum you were given a choice of more than forty dishes. The president of the state senate was in the chair, and the speeches were both numerous and long, though singularly good of their kind.

Dickens's own speech makes interesting reading. After telling them that they had made his house an Aladdin's palace and very happily diverting the honors shown to himself to those downtrodden classes from which many of his favorite characters had been taken, he came boldly to the question of international copyright. The time, he hoped, was not far distant when American writers would "receive of right some substantial profit and return in England from their labors, and when we, in England, shall receive some substantial profit and return in America from ours." England, he asserted, had done her part and it remained for America to do hers.

The challenge had been thrown down, but for a little while Dickens did not realize the widespread indignation that his words had aroused. When he did, however, he showed his most pugnacious side. With him it was not a question of expediency or good taste; it was a matter of common honesty. And as with copyright, so with slavery: he spoke his mind bluntly, and made enemies by the thousand. But that was Dickens. The limelight may produce a pose now and then, and the author of "Pickwick" was not always above saying or writing what was expected of him; but if he felt really strongly about a particular matter, the whole audience might hiss him as much as it pleased without producing the slightest effect on himself. And, of course, it was because his tens of thousands of readers could see the sincerity of the man behind all the droll exaggeration in his books that they had taken him to their hearts. . . .

From Boston the nation's guest and "his lady"—in this way was Mrs. Dickens generally described, though on one occasion at least you find mention of "the Bozzess"—went to Worcester, where an enterprising editor gave about the finest display of journalese for which Dickens's visit to America was responsible. It is too good to be missed.

"We found," runs this passage, which was widely quoted at the time "a middle-sized person in a brown frock coat, a red figured vest, somewhat of the flash order, and a fancy scarf cravat, that concealed the collar and was fastened to the bosom in rather voluptuous folds by a double pin and chain. His proportions were well-rounded, and filled the dress suit he wore. His hair, which was long and dark, grew low upon the brow, had a wavy kink where it started from the head, and was naturally, or artificially, corkscrew, as it fell on either side of his face. His forehead retreated gradually from the eyes, without any marked protuberance save at the outer angle, the upper portion of which formed a prominent ridge, a little within the assigned position of the organ of ideality.

"The skin on that portion of the brow which was not concealed by the hair, instead of being light and smooth, flushed as readily as any part of the face, and partook of its general character and flexibility. The whole region about the eyes was prominent with noticeable development of nerves and vessels, indicating, say the phrenologists, great vigour in the intellectual organs with which they are connected. The eyeballs completely filled their sockets. The aperture of the lids was not large, nor the eye uncommonly clear or bright, but quick, moist and expressive.

"The nose was slightly aquiline, the mouth of moderate dimensions, making no great display of the teeth, the facial muscles occasionally drawing the upper lip most strongly on the left side, as the mouth opened in speaking. His features, taken together, were well-proportioned, of a glowing and cordial aspect, with more animation than grace, and more intelligence than beauty. . . . He wears a gold watchguard over his vest, and a shaggy greatcoat of bear or buffalo skin that would excite the admiration of a Kentucky huntsman. In short, you frequently meet with similar-looking men at the theatres and other public places, and you would infer that he found his enjoyments in the scenes of actual life, rather than in the retirement of a study. . . ."

In Hartford there was another banquet, and here again he spoke of the copyright question. They were not, he said, to believe him sordid, for he would rather that his children "trudged in the mud and knew by the general feeling of society that their father was beloved and of some use," than "ride in their carriages and know by their bankers' books that he was rich." But there was no reason why a man should not be paid for his work, and "if there had existed any law in this respect, Scott might not have sunk beneath the mighty pressure on his brain."

"I wish," he told Forster, "you could have seen the faces that I saw, down both sides of the table at Hartford, when I began to talk about Scott. I wish you could have heard how I gave it out. My blood so boiled as I thought of the monstrous injustice that I felt as if I were twelve feet high when I thrust it down their throats."

Mrs. Dickens, we are told, listened to this speech from the hall, and, going one better than Boston, Hartford had given its guest a choice of no less than seventy dishes at dinner. Here the newspapers hoped that Dickens would be treated "like a gentleman and not a show," but there seems to have been much the same curious scenes as at Boston, and at New Haven, where the students had a display of their own, the same wild scrambles were witnessed.

"Such was the desire to see him," wrote Dickens's American secretary, "that he was urgently requested to receive the throng assembled, and for hours the people filled the reception-room and held the halls and passages of the hotel. As the crowd increased the landlord found it necessary to put two stout porters on the main staircase, who locked their hands across the stairs, and kept the throng somewhat at bay."

So it went on. The visitor came with "his lady" to New York, and the Tribune announced that he had been "allowed with very little annoyance to proceed to his rooms at the Carlton House." There came a grand ball and a "superb" dinner. At the ball Dickens was in a suit of black "with a gay vest"—the waistcoats continued to excite the liveliest comment—and Mrs. Dickens was "in a white figured Irish tabinet trimmed with mazarin blue flowers."

The usual semiprivate functions followed. When he dined with David Colden, who was largely responsible for his reception in New York, the Daily Advertiser, announcing that the party to meet him would be "made up of the élite of the ancient régime," thought it "probable that Mr. Dickens was never, in England, admitted into such really good society as since he landed in this country."

Finally there came the great "Dickens Dinner," at which Washington Irving presided, and broke down, as he had always maintained that he would, through sheer nervousness. Here again the speeches make interesting reading, and in particular one delivered by Cornelius Matthews, an editor, who deplored the great influx of European books that was giving American authors so little chance to be heard, and who declared that Dickens ought certainly not to be blamed for proposing what was really "the only honest turnpike between the readers of two great countries."

Matthews was more courageous than most of his countrymen. He knew very well that nearly every right-thinking man, certainly every author of any distinction, privately agreed with his views, but he also knew that they were the kind of views which nobody was expected to mention in public. . . . It would be un-American and therefore improper to do so. The wholesale acquisition of the best foreign literature at no cost at all was surely one of the brightest signs of real American smartness. Very well then: let there be no such ridiculous talk, and if Boz chose to take advantage of his position to interfere in matters of purely American interest, why, he must not be surprised to hear a little plain speaking about himself. . . .

They tell a story, by the way, of Dickens in New York, which bears on this matter. It may or may not be true, and it has been fathered on to other British authors, including Thackeray, who visited America at the height of their fame. Dickens, it seems, was dining one night with a member of a firm, already in the front rank of American publishers, and after dinner he took a small child of the family on his knee. "You are a very fine boy," said he; "you are a very fine boy indeed. You are the son of the greatest pirate on earth!"

[3]

In a very short while the strain was beginning to tell. Daily receptions, evening parties, visits to prisons—always of peculiar interest to Dickens—and an ever-increasing correspondence, not all, one suspects, of the friendliest nature, for the newspaper attacks were becoming more virulent—no words, he told Forster, could exaggerate the immense worry and fatigue they all entailed. His wife, never, I fancy, too pleased at the part she was being called on to play, became ill. Dickens himself was suffering from a sore throat. He was forced, while still in New York, to refuse any further public entertainments, a resolution broken only in favor of St. Louis, the westernmost point of his tour. Already, too, he had booked his return passage in a sailing-ship, the George Washington, due out from New York on June 7, being determined, he said, never to trust himself again to a steamer.

From this time he was constantly traveling about, by road or river or rail, not always successfully avoiding long receptions with their hours of tiresome handshaking, rapidly tiring of a limelight that was so much more garish than any at home, longing for his children and the little excitements of London, ever more conscious of disappointment in what he was seeing, never muzzling his tongue, and relinquishing his efforts on behalf of a new copyright law only when he realized how hopeless it was to effect any immediate change.

You may read of the more serious side of the tour in his "American Notes," though there is no mention of international copyright in its pages, and of some of its more comical aspects in "Martin Chuzzlewit." Here the briefest outline is all that is needed. You catch glimpses of him in Philadelphia where, owing to an injudiciously worded paragraph in one of the newspapers "half the city besieged poor 'Boz' "; and you see him in Washington, at the President's levee, given a seat within the Bar of the House of Representatives, chatting with Irving, now appointed minister to Spain.

In Richmond, Virginia, he could not escape a more or less public "supper," and was not allowed, even if he had wished to do so, to avoid expressing his opinion on "the accursed and detested system" of slavery. At Baltimore he was realizing the extent of his disappointment.

To Macready, who had once rather surprisingly expressed a desire to end his days in America, he wrote with considerable bitterness. The press was "more mean, and paltry, and silly and disgraceful" than that of any country he knew. Everywhere there was political distrust and suspicion. He had been implored not to ruin himself outright by his speeches. He was disgusted at the everlasting chewing of tobacco and spitting. The Americans themselves might be "affectionate, generous, open-hearted, hospitable, enthusiastic, good-humoured, polite to women, frank and candid to all strangers, anxious to oblige," and not so prejudiced as some writers had made out, but America was not the republic he had come to see. If he had been born an American, he thought, he would have "lived and died poor, unnoticed, and a 'black sheep' to boot."

To Mitton, too, he gave a vivid description of the general routine. "In every town where we stay, though it be only for a day, we hold a regular levee or drawing-room, where I shake hands on an average with five or six hundred people, who pass on from me to Kate, and are shaken again by her. . . . Think of two hours of this every day, and the people coming in by hundreds, all fresh, and piping-hot, and full of questions, when we are literally exhausted and cannot stand. I really do believe that if I had not a lady with me, I should have been obliged to leave the country and go back to England. But for her they would never leave me alone by day or night, and, as it is, a slave comes to me now and then in the middle of the night with a letter, and waits at the bedroom door for an answer."

So the slow journey westwards continued, and the social amenities grew less, and the inhabitants became correspondingly more difficult to please. There came long hours spent on queer river boats. An alleged Eldorado called Cairo was passed at the point where the Ohio River runs into the Mississippi. Much British gold had gone to its making—perhaps some of Dickens's own—but the traveler found only a "detestable morass," which he afterwards described accurately enough as the dismal Eden in "Chuzzlewit." There followed a two-hundred-mile run up the "beastliest river in the world" to St. Louis. Here they showed him a bit of their prairie, and gave him a soirée—dancing not being considered quite proper in some quarters—and in general made the usual fuss of him.

But by this time Dickens was not only disillusioned and homesick; he was sullen and angry and bored. He was sick to death of the incessant chatter of dollars and politics and the slave question. Every day, too, he must have been understanding more clearly what all this widespread piracy meant to himself. He was no more mercenary than most of us are, but he had his father's children to look after as well as his own, and so far, I imagine, he had not been able to save very much. Yet here, in almost every state, publishers were making fortunes out of his books, while there was not a cent from their sales for himself. Worse, they could not see the gross unfairness of it all! To them it was just one example of the national smartness. Of course he was sullen and angry.

What, moreover, had he obtained from his visit? Little enough. A few new though very good friends, yes; and possibly material for more than one book, but what else? Had it been worth it? These Americans were delighted to stare at him and would even fight in their eagerness to shake his hand, but were they really friendly? They boasted all day long of their greatness and liberty, but if you dared to find fault, they attacked you for a fool and a liar. No, although he might well look back with pride all his life to those first few glorious days in the eastern states, the tour itself had not been altogether to his liking. . . . You are not surprised to hear that the accordion was brought out fairly often to play "Home, Sweet Home."

The last month of the tour, however, was to be spent in more delectable surroundings and in much more congenial company. On board the Britannia Dickens had promised Lord Mulgrave to go to Montreal and take part in some theatricals which that officer's regiment, the Coldstream Guards, was getting up for charity, and on leaving St. Louis he went north by Lake Erie, which he found unpleasantly rough, to Buffalo and the glories of Niagara. At the falls, at any rate, there was no disappointment, and when at length he reached Montreal, it was to forget for a while American worries and to throw himself into his favorite pastime with all the old enthusiasm.

Once again he played managerial tyrant. "Everybody was told they would have to submit to the most iron discipline," and for this occasion only "everybody" included his wife, who, much to her husband's surprise, gave a very creditable performance in one of the three farces that had been chosen to make up the program.

"I would give something," he was writing to Professor Felton during the preparations, "if you could only stumble into that very dark and dusky theatre in the day time . . . and see me with my coat off, the stage-manager and universal director, urging impracticable ladies and impossible gentlemen on to the very confines of insanity, shouting and diving about, in my own person, to an extent that would justify any philanthropic stranger in clapping me into a strait-waistcoat without further enquiry. . . . This kind of voluntary hard labour used to be my great delight. The *furor* has come strong upon me again, and I begin to be once more of the opinion that nature intended me for the lessee of a national theatre, and that pen, ink and paper have spoiled a manager." Perhaps there was just a little more than a joke in the words. From time to time during the next sixteen years he was turning to the amateur stage for relief from worries and disappointments, and when at last he was giving his professional readings, he was still "on the boards." There are those who have attempted to show that too much can be made of Dickens's fondness for "dressing up" and directing theatricals. To me it would seem that the theater gave him something that he was always asking of life, which was to be found nowhere else. He could not keep away from it. There was a fascination even in the smells peculiar to itself.

And it must have been in Montreal that he realized not only that the old enthusiasm was persisting but also that he had lost none of his old facility. The performance given once for the regiment's friends and once for the public with professional actresses "went with a roar." Dickens himself was hugely successful in the three parts that he played, and when he reached New York to step on board the George Washington, I believe that it was those hours spent in the Queen's Theatre, Montreal, which reconciled him more than could anything else to a tour that, for all its amazing scenes, had by no means been an unqualified triumph.

Chapter IX

DISAPPOINTMENTS

[1]

SO the wanderer returned—with a small shaggy dog, the gift of an American actor, for a trophy. The sailing-ship made the passage in twenty-three days, and, characteristically, Dickens established on board a semitheatrical club called the United Vagabonds, which dined by itself and indulged in much mock-serious ritual. The chief vagabond amused himself and others by playing doctor (with a Bob Sawyer and a Ben Allen, both dressed for the part, in solemn attendance), and in general made merry.

But there must have come moments when he was wondering what effect the American tour would be likely to have on himself. He was wholeheartedly glad to be nearing home, but had his recent experiences induced a taste for travel? Had they, perhaps, shown him the delights of a vagabondage? Already, I think, he was wondering what other countries he wanted to see. . . . He reached Liverpool on July 1, and "it is a curious fact," Thackeray wrote to Braham that day—he was on his way then to Ireland—"that both Boz and Titmarsh reached Liverpool the same day, but the Journals have not taken notice of the latter. Gross jealousy!" The journals might announce his arrival, but

Dickens with his wife and the very smart Anne slipped away quietly to London the same day.

It was a worried city at the time, bewildered by daily reports of Chartist agitations and strikes, and anxious about military disasters in Afghanistan. Political feeling was rising to almost American heights. Demented youths seemed determined to murder the queen. Incidentally a new copyright bill had just received the royal assent.

But Dickens can have had little time to worry himself about such things. Almost immediately he was overwhelmed in work. For a week or two he remained in his London house, being welcomed by friends and petting his children. They, poor dears, had not been too happy with Macready, whose strict views upon discipline, it seems, were not confined to the theater; but their father knew well how to make amends, and so you have glimpses of him at this time playing shuttlecock with them in the garden, singing gay songs at their bedside, and inventing for them more ridiculous nicknames. The five-year-old Charley was no longer the Snodgering Blee but Flaster Floby. Mamie's placid disposition had suggested Mild Glos'ter as a more suitable pet-name than the cryptical Popem Jee, Katie had become the Lucifer Box, and Walter, the baby, was dubbed Young Skull. This was the time, too, when Georgina Hogarth, Mrs. Dickens's younger sister, joined the household, never to leave it while Dickens was alive.

There was talk of a public banquet, but there had been enough of such things in America, and the returned traveler preferred the private dinner that a dozen or so of his particular friends gave him at his favorite Greenwich. It was after this joyous affair, by the way, that George Cruikshank, so soon to adopt extreme temperance views, insisted on going home in Dickens's phæton *on his head,* "to the mingled delight and indignation of the metropolitan police." Little time, however, was wasted on celebrations of this kind, and before he had been home a fortnight, Dickens had already done much to put his "American Notes" into order.

He was working, he told a friend, "like a dray-horse; to the great astonishment of my red face which is turning white with wonder." It had been decided that the "Notes" should be published in two volumes some time in October, and although for the most part they were to be "written up" from his letters home, there was a great deal of hard work to be fitted into a bare three months.

In August he was at Broadstairs, but there were frequent visits to London. "I date this from London," he was writing to Felton at the beginning of September, "where I have come as a good profligate, graceless bachelor, for a day or two, leaving my wife and babies, at the seaside. . . . Heavens, if you were but here at this minute! A piece of salmon and a steak are cooking in the kitchen; it's a very wet day, and I have had a fire lighted; the wine sparkles on a side table; the room looks more snug from being the only *un*-dismantled one in the house; plates are warming for Forster and Maclise, whose knock I am momentarily expecting; that groom I told you of, who never comes into the house, except when we are all out of town, is walking about in his shirt-sleeves without the smallest consciousness of impropriety; a great mound of proofs are waiting to be read aloud, after dinner." A very typical scene!

Dickens liked to read his work to his friends before it was given to the world, and it was not only vanity that had led to the custom. Valuable advice would be forthcoming, and in the case of "American Notes" it was particularly important that everything he had written should be carefully revised. Already a forged letter purporting to give some of his impressions had appeared in an American newspaper, and he was being widely attacked. He was determined to speak bluntly on matters which he considered to be of general interest—it was for this reason that slavery was mentioned though international copyright was not—and knew that he could hardly hope to avoid giving fresh offense in some quarters; but it was essential that nothing should be printed to which personal friends of his in America could take exception.

Thus there was a long discussion at the last moment about an introductory chapter which Dickens had written. He himself was strongly in favor of its inclusion, but Forster was as strongly against it. In the end it was omitted—to the delight of bibliographers with a weakness for oddities of pagination—though only on condition that Forster would see to its publication at "a more fitting moment." As a matter of fact he did not print it until he published the first volume of his "Life," though why he objected to words which might possibly have modified American criticism at the time it is difficult to determine.

The two volumes appeared on October 18, and in England met with the greatest success. Macaulay, it is true, found fault with the book, which could certainly have been made livelier than it was, but most of the critics considered that it had been very well done. As regarded its general accuracy there could be no two opinions. Mrs. Trollope was only one of many to send him the warmest congratulations. And he had his reward. Four editions were required before the end of the year and put a thousand pounds into his pocket. In America, of course, there was an uproar, and words were not minced. Dickens was accused of ingratitude, the grossest discourtesy, and deliberate falsehood. It did not matter that he was ready with chapter and verse for every one of his statements: they were in no mood to be told anything like the truth. He had insulted a nation. On the other hand, men like Emerson and Longfellow (who at this time was in England, and for a short while Dickens's guest) could praise its honesty and good-humor. There was to be a fiercer outcry when "Chuzzlewit" appeared in the following year, but one is not surprised to hear that it died down soon enough. In a little while America was very ready to forgive. . . .

At the end of the year there came a little bachelor jaunt into Cornwall, with Forster, Stanfield, and Maclise for companions. They traveled down to Devon by rail and then hired an open carriage, in which the four of them seem to have behaved like small schoolboys. Dickens admitted that he had never laughed so much before in his life. "I was choking and gasping," he wrote, "and bursting the buckle at the back of my stock, all the way."

The revelers returned home in time for Christmas and the preparations for a birthday party in young Charley's honor. This was to include a grand magic-lantern display and a conjuring entertainment provided by Dickens himself. "If you could see me," Felton was told, "conjuring the company's watches into impossible tea-caddies, and causing pieces of money to fly, and burning pocket-handkerchiefs without hurting 'em, and practising in my own room without anybody to admire, you would never forget it as long as you live." Stanfield, his confederate in the tricks, does not seem to have been particularly accomplished, but what did that matter? Here was Dickens in yet another theatrical rôle, and nobody knew better than he the best way to please an audience of small children.

By this time, however, the first number of a new novel had made its appearance, and therein the germs of new and grave troubles were lurking.

[2]

Many odd things happened to Dickens, and amongst them, I think, must be placed the reception given to "Martin Chuzzlewit." In its completed form the novel sold exceptionally well, but on its appearance in monthly numbers it was, regarded by Dickensian standards, a failure. At no time did the sale of these shilling numbers exceed twenty-three thousand copies. This might have sounded agreeable enough to most of his contemporaries, but not to Dickens and decidedly not to his publishers, who had framed their last agreement more or less on the assumption that the sales of the new novel would at least equal those of its predecessors.

What, then, was the cause of this failure, which was to prove, as Forster points out, a turning-point in Dickens's career? Here was a story which by common consent showed the novelist at his best. He himself at the time considered it to be "immeasurably" the finest piece of work he had done. It contained a gallery of portraits that could rival any of the others. The horrible Pecksniff pranced through its pages. So did the unhygienic, but immortal Mrs. Gamp and her intangible crony. Tom Pinch and Mark Tapley and young Mr. Bailey formed an incomparable trio. And, at least, the story was as dramatic as "Nickleby" or "The Old Curiosity Shop." Yet it obstinately refused to create another sensation, even after Dickens, changing his plans for the story, had sent his hero to America and thereby written its finest scenes. Why?

Forster believed that a public now accustomed to take its Dickens in weekly doses disliked the change back to monthly numbers. He also suggested that the novelist's absence in America was not "favourable to an immediate resumption by his readers of their old and intimate relations." Mr. Chesterton finds the opening chapters "sad," but would this explain? Somebody has advanced the theory that Pecksniff himself was responsible—there being too many Pecksniffs about—but this will not do. There was no dropping off of sales after an enormously successful first number, as had been the case with "Master Humphrey's Clock": on the contrary there was a slight increase after Martin and Mark had embarked for America. No, it was just one of those unaccountable affairs which have a habit of making their appearance at the most inconvenient moments.

To Dickens, at any rate, the failure of the new book brought him into very serious financial difficulties, and it must be held responsible, in part at least, for that restlessness which henceforth was to be so marked a feature of his life.

It was not that he had been unduly extravagant in his personal expenditure, but it did so happen that the financial arrangements made previous to the American tour depended for their own successful working much more upon the success of the new novel than either Dickens or Forster had realized. The repurchase of the older copyrights had not yet been completed, so far, that is to say, as Dickens himself was concerned, and the American tour had not been cheap. And of course Mr. Dickens *would* choose this time of all others to discover that Alphington was a little too cloistered for his liking and prepare to resume his "moments." His younger sons, too, were making fresh demands on their brother. When, moreover, the hitherto saintlike Chapman & Hall hinted that it might be necessary to keep very strictly to every clause in their agreement, the position became sufficiently alarming.

This agreement, signed in September, 1841, had taken into consideration the fact that for twelve months at least there would be no successor to "Barnaby Rudge." The publishers had agreed to advance monthly sums of £150 from the conclusion of the "Clock" until the first number of the new book should be ready, such sums to be deducted from Dickens's three-quarter share of the profits. While the numbers were appearing he was to receive £200 a month, but —and this was the clause destined to cause all the trouble—in the unlikely event of the sales of the new novel, as judged by those of the first five months, not reaching a particular figure, £50 might be deducted from these monthly payments. Forster had agreed to this clause, regarding its inclusion as a mere matter of form, and it was certainly fair. But when at the end of June, on the eve of the seventh number, Mr. Hall "dropped an inconsiderable hint" to Dickens that it might be necessary to put this clause into force, he can hardly have been prepared for what followed.

At the time there was nothing to show the world that Dickens was not his usual cheerful and good-humored self. He was constantly at social gatherings, at the theater, at semiofficial functions of one kind or another. He presided at a Printers' Pension Fund dinner and worked hard to obtain money for the children of an actor who had lost his life in a shipping disaster. He wrote a prologue for Macready, and gave detailed attention to a dinner at Greenwich in honor of his old editor John Black, whose connection with the Chronicle had been suddenly, and undeservedly, broken. He could joke with Douglas Jerrold over some ridiculous theatrical scheme, and tell Felton that he was working with all his old vigor, in the best of spirits and health, and well capable of dealing with a correspondence which, he said, meant for himself at least twelve necessary letters every day.

For all that, he was in one of his most excitable moods. Apart from the "constantly recurring claims from family quarters, not the more easily avoidable because unreasonable and unjust"—the words are Forster's—and the very natural irritation at the small sales of a book that his friends as well as himself placed so high, the campaign against him in America was at its height.

The absurdest lies about him were being printed. Abusive letters were pouring in. (It was really as a fitting challenge to all this abuse that he sent his hero to Eden and so caused, in Carlyle's words, "all Yankee-doodle-dom" to blaze up "like one universal soda-water bottle"; they actually burnt "Chuzzlewit" on the New York stage!) Moreover, although there had been a short holiday in Yorkshire, and much of "Chuzzlewit" had been written in a quiet Finchley cottage, he was working at very high pressure. It needed only Mr. Hall's injudicious remark—and that it had been injudicious both partners were the first to acknowledge—to act as a detonator.

Immediately Dickens flew into one of his worst rages. No words were too bad for Chapman & Hall.

The scaly-headed vultures might be within their strictly legal rights, but they owed everything to him, and their behavior was iniquitous. He would have nothing further to do with them—after the money that was still owing had been repaid. Other publishers must be secured at once. The printers, Bradbury & Evans, might be approached; he believed they would not be unwilling to enlarge their activities. As to the money that was owing, it should be found, and soon, even if he had to starve himself and his family. It was a monstrous business, and he would never rest until these things had been put right. . . .

"I am so irritated," he wrote to Forster, "so rubbed in the tenderest part of my eyelids with bay-salt, by what I told you yesterday, that a wrong kind of fire is burning in my head, and I don't think I *can* write."

Forster, as always, advised caution, and prevailed on him to do nothing until after the usual summer visit to Broadstairs. He did, however, approach the printers, who were interested but undetermined at first how far they would be willing to go. Tentatively, they suggested as a beginning a new magazine and cheap editions of all the novels, and these were the proposals which Dickens was considering while he took his furious walks by the sea, and tried to curb his fierce temper.

Now for the first time you hear of his inability to sleep. "I performed an insane match against time," he told Forster, "of eighteen miles by the milestones in four hours and a half, under a burning sun the whole way. . . . I could get no sleep at night, and really began to be afraid I was going to have a fever." He could still write placidly to Felton, and he managed somehow not to fall behind with his work, but he was still in a state of the greatest indignation and uncertainty. How was that money to be obtained which would allow him to be rid for all time of his scoundrelly publishers?

Sometimes the gods are kind. Dr. Johnson, wanting money to bury his mother and pay her debts, wrote "Rasselas" in a week, and Dodsley, his publisher, gave him £100 for it. Sometimes the gods make a show of being kind. Dickens, wanting money to pay his bills and be rid of the brutish Chapman & Hall, went to Manchester in the first week of October to open its Athenæum—Disraeli and Cobden "assisting"—and there conceived the idea for the first of his Christmas Books. Within a month he had written "A Christmas Carol."

Then, to be sure, he did not disguise his pleasurable excitement. Here, perchance, was the solution of all his problems. They might not buy his "Chuzzlewit"; but they would certainly buy his "Carol." They would laugh and weep over it as he was laughing and weeping over it himself. Never before, he knew, had he written just such a story as this: assuredly it must meet with an unprecedented success. He would publish it himself—in the circumstances it would not much matter which firm of publishers acted as his agents—and there ought to be at least £1,000 profit. . . .

With the little book finished, he impulsively sketched out a future for himself that Forster found sufficiently startling. He was afraid, he wrote, of a new magazine, and afraid of putting himself "before the town as writing tooth and nail for bread, headlong, after the close of a book taking so much out of me as "Chuzzlewit." He believed, too, that Bradbury & Evans' suggestion of cheap editions of his books could only damage him and his property, though some settlement must be made with them without too much delay. For him-

Miss Burdett Coutts
from
Charles Dickens

Seventeenth December 1843.

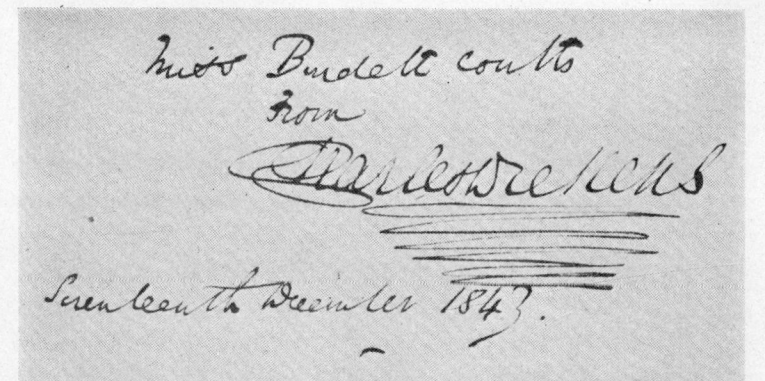

A CHRISTMAS CAROL.

IN PROSE.

BEING

𝔄 𝔊𝔥𝔬𝔰𝔱 𝔖𝔱𝔬𝔯𝔶 𝔬𝔣 ℭ𝔥𝔯𝔦𝔰𝔱𝔪𝔞𝔰.

From the earliest copy of "A Christmas Carol"
In the collection of Charles J. Sawyer

self, he had evolved a very definite scheme. As soon as he had written the last word of "Chuzzlewit" he would leave England, take his family to some cheap spot, travel about Europe and write further "Notes." He would let his house, cut down all possible expenses, live a wholly new sort of life. He anticipated no enjoyment from the scheme, but had come to look upon it as "a matter of policy and duty."

There were, however, to be further disappointments. The "Carol" sold well. It had, to use Dickens's words, "a most prodigious success—the greatest, I think, I have ever achieved." The little book, indeed, endeared him to thousands of new readers, and put him on a new sort of pedestal. The affectionate regard in which he had been held changed to something even warmer. Thackeray was expressing the general opinion when he wrote:

"Who can listen to objections regarding such a book as this? It seems to me a national benefit, and, to every man or woman who reads it, a personal kindness. The last two people I heard speak of it were women; neither knew the other, or the author, and both said, by way of criticism, 'God bless him!' "

But a great deal of money had been spent on the book. It was beautifully printed and produced. There were four colored etchings, besides woodcuts, by John Leech. (I do not know why this artist had been chosen —he was not yet on intimate terms with Dickens, though Jerrold may have urged his claims—and it is interesting to find that Cruikshank made at least one drawing for it, although it was never used.) Also it was sold at a cheap price. The sales were large, but they were not large enough, and the profits fell far short of the author's expectations.

"Such a night as I have passed!" he was complaining in February. "I really believed I should never get up again until I had passed through all the horrors of a fever. I found the Carol accounts awaiting me, and they were the cause of it."

One can sympathize with him. Not £500 had been earned. "I never was so knocked over in my life," he told Mitton, and confessed that he did not know where to turn for money. "What a wonderful thing it is," he was lamenting a day or two later to Forster, "that such a great success should occasion one such intolerable anxiety and disappointment! My year's bills, unpaid, are so terrific, that all the energy and determination I can possibly exert will be required to clear me before I go abroad." And even at the end of the following year, the £1,000 for which he had hoped had not yet been earned.

(The "Carol," by the way, had been entrusted to Chapman & Hall, and Forster wisely waited awhile before breaking off negotiations with the firm, but in the following year an agreement was signed with the printers—for fourteen years to be known affectionately as "B. and E."—who agreed to advance Dickens £2,800 in return for a fourth-share in any book that he might write during the next eight years. And so for a while Chapman & Hall faded out of the picture. . . .)

Finally, he was persuaded to take notice of some of the pirates and go to law. For some time Talfourd and Forster had been urging him to do so, and their advice, I suppose, had been sound. But even with the new copyright law in being, the author was not in too favorable a position; and although in one sense Dickens may be said to have won all along the line, he obtained only temporary satisfaction, and, financially speaking, was certainly a loser.

It was in January, 1844, that he applied in the vice-chancellor's court for an injunction to restrain one Lee and others from selling a children's weekly publication called Parley's Illuminated Library which sold for a penny. This, the forerunner, I presume, of the "Peter Parley's Annuals" that were afterwards so popular, was very coolly "reoriginating"—in other words, reprinting with two or three lines of introduction—more or less the complete "Carol."

Dickens himself was in court. The vice-chancellor, Knight Bruce, considered the case to be one of such "peculiar flagrancy" that he did not call on Talfourd —the novelist's counsel—to speak.

"The pirates," wrote Dickens immediately afterwards, "are beaten flat. They are bruised, bloody, battered, smashed, squelched, and utterly undone. Knight Bruce would not hear Talfourd, but instantly gave judgment. He had interrupted Anderton constantly by asking him to produce a passage which was not an expanded or contracted idea from my book."

Affairs, however, were not to continue so smoothly as he had expected. More affidavits were put in by the pirates. Talfourd was against any compromise at all, though Dickens seems willing to have been satisfied with a public apology and his costs. In the end the offenders did produce some sort of apology, and were "let go" without any inquiry into the profits they had made—profits which ought to have gone, and which Talfourd had always insisted must go, into Dickens's pocket. Costs were given against them, but unfortunately they took refuge in bankruptcy, and Dickens was obliged to pay all his costs.

Apparently, he was not too pleased at the vice-chancellor's methods of conducting the case after the first day's sitting. "I have dropped—dropped!—the action and the Chancery suit," he wrote to Talfourd at the beginning of May, "against the Bankrupt Pirates. We have had communication with the assignees, and found their case quite desperate. The four booksellers have come in and compounded, so that I lose nothing by them. By Lee and Haddock (the vagabonds) I *do* lose, of course, all my expenses, costs and charges in those suits. But it is something to know the worst of it and to be rid of Knight Bruce, whom I should call (if he were not a friend of yours) rather a pragmatical donkey—judicially speaking."

Indeed, he seems to have been treated very badly in the matter. In a little while the pirates had plucked up their courage again and were thieving as shamelessly as ever. On this occasion, however, Dickens wisely refused to proceed. "It *is* better," he said bluntly, "to suffer a great wrong than to have recourse to the much greater wrong of the law. I shall not easily forget the expense, and anxiety, and horrible injustice, of the Carol case, wherein, in asserting the plainest right on earth, I was really treated as if I were the robber instead of the robbed." Certainly after reading Mr. Lee's explanation in his Illuminated Library, you would think so. . . .

[3]

So we approach the days of wanderings abroad, and sudden changes of plan, and an unending search for distraction.

A fifth child had been born—christened Francis Jeffrey, but generally called Chickenstalker. There were visits to Liverpool and Birmingham, to take the chair at the opening of new technical institutions. A literary-minded carpenter called Overs, who had been introduced to Dickens by Dr. Elliotson, wrote a book when no longer able through illness to carry on his trade, and the novelist good-naturedly enriched it with a godfatherly preface. A few articles on serious matters were contributed to the Morning Chronicle, and a poem was given to Lady Blessington for her "Keepsake."

There were dramatic representations—four in 1844—of "Chuzzlewit," and more than one of the "Carol." Advice was sought as to the best place for a family about to go into voluntary exile, and the Devonshire Terrace house was let. There came the inevitable dinner of farewell, and at the end of June, with the shaggy dog, three maid servants "commanded by Anne of Broadstairs," Angus Fletcher as a sort of unofficial majordomo, and one, Roche, as the necessary courier, the family set out for the Mediterranean.

Chapter X

DISTRACTIONS

[1]

"I ADDRESS you with something of the lofty spirit of an exile—a banished commoner—a sort of Anglo Pole. I don't exactly know what I have done for my country in coming away from it; but I feel it is something—something great—something virtuous and heroic. Lofty emotions rise within me, when I see the sun set on the Mediterranean. I am the limpet on the rock. My father's name is Turner, and my boots are green."

In this way is Dickens writing to Maclise shortly after his arrival in Albaro on the outskirts of Genoa, and the words interpret his mood at the time. He had taken the plunge. How big a plunge it might prove to be he did not know, but a plunge it certainly was. Here he was once again in a strange country—delightfully different from America—ready to enjoy the blue skies and bluer seas, a free man. Or very nearly a free man. "Chuzzlewit" was off his hands, and there were excellent reports now of its sales. Bradbury and Evans had already shown that they were ready to behave like good men and true. There was no immediate hurry for a new long novel, though he would soon have to be thinking of a successor to the "Carol." Certainly it was a time for high spirits.

The house he had taken might resemble a "pink jail," and there might be too many inquisitive insects about, but without doubt Italy was a glorious place, and he had been wise to come. Enthusiastically he settled down to the new life. He learned to speak Italian, he explored Genoa, he became commendably fond of green figs, he walked and swam, and finally he sent for the little carved figures that for some time past had played mascot during working hours on his desk: sure sign that some new idea was afoot.

They were jolly days, marred only by a sharp attack of illness, with the old agonizing pains, brought on by a fall in the dark over a pole stretched across the street, and by a swimming mishap, in which his brother Frederick was carried out too far by the current and nearly lost his life. And for some reason—perhaps as an amusing distraction, perhaps to give tangible mark to the plunge—he allowed hair to appear for the first time on his face.

Progress was carefully recorded. "The moustaches are glorious, glorious," he was soon able to report. "I have cut them shorter, and trimmed them a little at the ends to improve their shape. They are charming, charming. Without them life would be a blank." Nothing in the world, of course, can be more exciting than a first mustache, even if you happen to be thirty-three at the time. . . .

Even so, however, ideas for work remained shy. Rooms were taken in a large house in Genoa itself, but this led him only to find the bright blues and greens not so attractive as they had been. It even occurred to him that the finest view in all Europe might be the one of the West Middlesex waterworks obtainable only from the study in Devonshire Terrace. Moreover, the heat was excessive, and little Mamie was seriously ill, and queer things were apparently happening to the shaggy dog's coat. When at last the new Christmas Book showed signs of molding itself into shape, and the "clash and clang" of Genoese bells had given him his title, he found that he missed having friends about him with whom to discuss his work.

"The Chimes" was finished at the beginning of November, and he believed that he had written "a tremendous book," but, as he told Mitton, none of his usual reliefs had been at hand, and he was "as nervous as a man who is dying of drink, and as haggard as a murderer." He did indulge in "what the women call 'a real good cry'"—I confess I am astonished at the number of Dickens's man friends who followed his example: those must have been the days when tears were fashionable—but what he really wanted was an audience. Very well, why not seek one? Nothing easier. He had only to go to London, and Forster would choose the right one. So, indeed, it was arranged.

To my mind, however, there was more in his visit to London—he was there for only a few days—than a desire to read "The Chimes" aloud to friends. In leaving England he had really taken a plunge, but it may be doubted whether he understood its true nature. Outwardly he remained the most jovial of men, but the feminine side that is to be found in nearly every great writer had now become very much stronger. Something had happened to leave him henceforth incapable of sustaining the same rôle—I purposely make use of a theatrical term—for more than a short while at a time. He had always been fond of change and excitement: they were now becoming necessities.

In roving through Italy as he did, before crossing Switzerland and France, he might believe that he was only taking a well-earned holiday, and in leaving his wife "shut up in her palace like a baron's lady in the time of the crusades," he might ascribe the separation only to the state of his purse; but already, I am convinced, there had been born in his mind some vague idea that he was not properly free. He adored his children, his home-life was happy, but was life giving him all that he asked of it?

From this time forward, indeed, you will find him at the mercy of some queer tyrant within him, forever forcing him to seek new excitements and new distractions. There is small evidence of this change in his letters—they continued to reflect his more masculine side, and remained the delightfully whimsical things they always had been—but it was there; and it was not only Forster who gradually became aware of its existence.

"The Chimes" was read aloud in Forster's house in December, and Maclise has immortalized the scene in a drawing which, in the reproductions, at any rate, provides the reader with a star-shaped halo. Carlyle was present in the seat of honor, and every member of the little audience seems to have been deeply affected, but the published book did not create quite the sensation for which Dickens had hoped. Nevertheless it sold very well, and in a short while there was £1,500 for him, a sum which, he told Mitton, would have been considerably greater if Bradbury & Evans (not yet provided, it would seem, with the necessary machinery) had not been obliged to seek assistance from the wretched Chapman & Hall.

By then, however, Dickens himself had returned to Italy, seeing Macready in Paris on his way. More explorations followed, this time with his wife, and sometimes Georgina Hogarth as well. He saw Rome in Holy Week, climbed Vesuvius in the snow, and visited Naples and Pompeii; and it was from his long letters home that "Pictures from Italy" was ultimately to emerge.

Then in June came another decision. A new novel showed no signs of presenting itself, but there were fresh and audacious schemes at the back of his head. A year ago Bradbury & Evans had spoken tentatively of a new magazine. He had fought shy of it at the time, but now it seemed suddenly attractive, even essential to his peace of mind. There must be a new magazine. That, of course, would mean London, but what better? He was pining, he found, for London. He wanted its theaters and its crowds and its queer grimy streets. Very well then, he would go; the exile had lasted long enough. And I can see him smiling as he recalled his last meeting with Forster and Jerrold at the big house in Lincoln's Inn Fields.

They had talked then of the possibility of forming some amateur dramatic club. More theatricals! A repetition of his Montreal success! Yes, there should certainly be another performance, and even the professionals might be astonished. He knew he could act. Once he had wanted to go on the stage, and the call was still strong. . . . Whereupon the great lumbering carriage that had brought them south was put into order, and boxes were packed, and the admirable Roche performed wonders, and the family were taken across Switzerland, with four horses pulling, and so by easy stages to Devonshire Terrace. . . .

[2]

In London the new magazine was duly christened, but, unnaturally, refused to be born. "The Cricket"—

"a cheerful creature that chirrups on the Hearth"—was to have been a weekly journal calculated to put everybody privileged to see it in the best of good tempers. It was intended to "take a personal and confidential position" with its readers, such as no other journal could hope to achieve; but it was just here that Forster, to whom the final decision had been left, felt more than doubtful. He could not forget what had happened with "Master Humphrey's Clock." And so the new magazine was temporarily allowed to be forgotten, although its title helped Dickens to find an idea for his new Christmas Book: that fairy-tale called "The Cricket on the Hearth," which sold much better than either of its predecessors and was the first of Dickens's stories to bear Bradbury & Evans's name alone on its title-page.

On the other hand, the theatricals were hugely successful. A little company of amateur players was brought into being, which was not really disbanded until its leader, thirteen years later, elected to become a professional entertainer. As I have already hinted, moreover, it is almost impossible to exaggerate the importance to Dickens of the various performances that were given during this period. It did not matter very much whether he was playing in his own drawing-room to a few friends or in public for some charitable purpose. He had only to assume his managerial duties, and straightway his worries, financial, domestic, or those connected with his writing, would disappear.

He was no ordinary actor-manager: he would shoulder the most varied responsibilities. It was not enough that he should be producer, stage-manager and "star": he must needs be business-manager, stage-carpenter, bandmaster, advance agent and publicity-man as well. It was he, and only he, who could infuse something like his own enthusiasm into the company; it was he, and only he, who knew how to deal with those little misunderstandings, outbursts of temper, petty jealousies and the like, from which no company of amateurs can be wholly immune. Away from the stage he could be moody, depressed, even sullen; surrounded by theatrical impedimenta he was never other than the most joyous of creatures. It was as though in some peculiar way the footlights were spelling home for him.

With his acting, too, there were no half-measures. He may not have been a great actor—on that point there is some difference of opinion—he may not even have been as good an actor as he believed himself to be; but once he had cast himself for a part, the man Dickens disappeared and did not always immediately emerge when the make-up was removed and the hired glories in which he had dressed himself were folded up for the night.

Before he had been in London three weeks a program had been arranged. Jonson's "Every Man in his Humour" is not the kind of play that amateurs usually attempt, but that fact only lent additional interest to the venture. It was to be followed by a farce, the one ultimately chosen being "Two O'clock in the Morning"—"as performed by the inimitable B. at Montreal." A congenial company of players was soon brought together. Forster was enthusiastic, and Douglas Jerrold produced half the staff of Punch. So there were burly Mark Lemon, its editor, soon to be known in the Dickens household as Uncle Mark, John Leech, Henry Mayhew, and, for a brief period, Gilbert à Becket. There was Frank Stone, the father of the better-known Marcus—he was a Manchester man, who seems to have met Dickens first at the Shakespeare

Club, of which he was the honorary secretary—and there was Mr. Evans of the printing firm.

Stanfield, in spite of the fact that as a middy with Jerrold he had produced and acted in plays long ago, preferred to confine his attention to the scenery. (Perhaps he was remembering his poor efforts as a conjuror's assistant.) Maclise was pressed to join, but "took fright" after a few rehearsals. Cattermole made at least one appearance, and both Frederick and Augustus Dickens were given a trial. As to the ladies, it seems to have been decided at an early date that professionals should be engaged when required, and the first of these was the well-known Miss Fortesque, afterwards Lady Gardner, who for some years had been distinguishing herself in various Dickensian parts.

Finally, a suitably small theater was found in Dean Street. It belonged to Miss Frances Kelly, once a friend of Lamb, an actress of the old school, whose fads and fancies caused Dickens considerable amusement. She was flustered at the idea of such well-known folk making use of her theater, and could not bear to think of them finding a speck of dirt within its precincts, but this did not prevent her from raging in the grand manner at the great expense she was being put to on that account. A difficult lady, the Kelly, but Dickens knew how to deal with her. Every few days he would write her the politest of notes. . . .

The first performance took place on Saturday, September 20, and Forster was probably not exaggerating when he said that its success "outran the wildest expectation; and turned our little enterprise into one of the small sensations of the day." Macready might sniff —"they seem to me," he recorded in his diary, "to be under a perfect delusion as to their degrees of skill and power in this art, of which they do not know what may be called the very rudiments"—but there were not many good amateurs at that time, and people talked, and there were paragraphs in the newspapers, and the company was invited to repeat the performance in public for charity. How many invitations were forthcoming I do not know—Count D'Orsay made great efforts to get them to appear on behalf of the Westminster Ophthalmic Hospital—but only one seems to have been accepted. For this the Dean Street theater was not large enough.

"I am sorry to say," Dickens wrote to Miss Kelly, "that for the Sanitorium representation we shall be obliged to go to the St. James's Theatre. Prince Albert is coming; and they have already exceeded your means of accommodation."

This was at the end of October, and on November 15 the performance, with but one small change in the cast, was repeated in the theater where Boz's first play had been staged. There was also a performance of Beaumont and Fletcher's "Elder Brother" given by the company at this theater at the beginning of the new year, for Miss Kelly's benefit, and it is surprising to find Dickens himself taking part, for at the time something else was requiring his attention—something so oddly unexpected as to cause the most widespread surprise.

A new morning newspaper was announced as about to appear. The Daily News was to combine all the best features of modern journalism. Many distinguished writers would contribute to its pages. It would be progressive, but free from mere party bias. It would be "devoted to the advocacy of all rational and honest means by which wrong might be redressed, just rights maintained, and the happiness and welfare of society promoted." And its editor was to be—of all people in the world—Charles Dickens.

[3]

Surely an amazing business! True, he had once been the star reporter on the Morning Chronicle. He was not ignorant of the complicated methods whereby a great daily was produced. He had played editor himself, more than once, with a magazine. He had written at various times serious articles on matters of public interest, and his "American Notes" had shown what a good journalist he could be. But that he ever imagined he would be able to sit comfortably in a Fleet Street editorial chair is extraordinary.

It was not as if he were merely lending his name. He was very much more than "in charge of the literary department" as some of the preliminary advertisements had announced: he was the editor of the Daily News at a salary of £2,000 a year. So far as the paper itself was concerned the moment was certainly propitious. The general unrest, the Corn Laws repeal agitation, the new fiscal policy that was about to be launched: yes, there was room for a newspaper run on politely radical lines. But—with Dickens as editor?

Justin McCarthy, remembering the "inspiring force" of the man and the "commanding figure" that he had become, did not hesitate to declare that he was "just the man to start such a venture as the Daily News"; but is he not speaking of a legendary Dickens? Forster knew well enough what a mad scheme it was—for Dickens. The conception might be great, and, so brave and outspoken a journal as the Daily News seemed likely to become would deserve the warmest support; but that its editorial chair should be occupied by a man physically as well as mentally overstrained—unfortunately there could be little doubt now that Dickens's health was becoming steadily poorer—was madness.

Almost from the beginning, when the ex-gardener, Joseph Paxton, and others had found the necessary capital, he was imploring Dickens, who had already confessed to being "sick, bothered and depressed," to withdraw and allow others to carry out his excellent scheme; but for once the novelist would not listen. Why not? Did he want the money so badly? Could he not resist enjoying the responsibilities that would naturally be his? Was he unable to bear the idea of allowing his own creation to be fathered on to others? No, it seems to me that he refused to withdraw because the Daily News was showing the way to a distraction that would be entirely and magnificently new. A fresh excitement was at hand, and it was one which, unlike the theatricals, would mean work of national importance. And so, when the attempt was made to dissuade him, he could think only of the new dream that had presented itself.

"I think I descry in these times," he wrote, "greater stimulants to such an effort; greater chance of some fair recognition of it; greater means of persevering in it or retiring from it unscratched by any weapon one should care for; than at any other period." He had before him, he said, "that possibility of failing health or failing popularity . . . which beckons me to such a venture when it comes within my reach." There was nothing more to be said.

Characteristically the newly appointed editor threw all his energies into the necessary preparations. Offices were taken in Fleet Street, and for a while Dickens was to be found there at all hours of the day and probably half the night. The engagement of a staff was no easy matter, but it was soon accomplished. Sorely against his inclination, I suspect, Forster agreed to accept a post, as did several of the Punch staff, including Jerrold, as leader-writer, and an exceptionally gifted man of business, W. H. Wills, who was afterwards to be Dickens's right-hand man on his two weekly papers. And at first all went well.

"I am regularly in harness now," he wrote to Paxton, "and we are getting on vigorously and steadily." One man whose services it was hoped could be procured, was about to be interviewed, and Dickens was determined to "nail him tight." A very good man had been obtained as Paris representative, and already he had distinguished himself, "being as familiar with the most secret moves upon the road, on the part of the other papers, as if he had done nothing else but receive their unlimited confidence from his cradle."

But there came endless worries and disappointments, and it is useless to disguise the fact that the Daily News owed little except its inception to Dickens. After the first splendid spurt he found himself unhappy and bored, forced to attend to a hundred trifling matters, and balked by obstacles whose very existence he could not have suspected. As Forster had anticipated, he had taken too much on himself. It is one thing to edit a literary weekly or monthly magazine; it is quite another to set in motion a vast organization like the Daily News. Even before the first number had appeared, he knew that he had made a bad mistake. All enthusiasm was gone, and the only question was how to be rid of the whole tiresome business.

There is no need to speak in detail of those three unlucky weeks during which Dickens was "editing" the Daily News. The first number appeared on January 21, 1846, and it was given a warm welcome, though the caricaturists were busy, and from that day to this it has pursued much the same policy. Dickens printed in it his own "Travelling Sketches—Written on the Road," which, later in the year, were to be republished in book form as "Pictures from Italy," but he did little else for the paper. The editorial functions were performed either by Forster or by the reliable Wills. Within a very few days Dickens was coming to the office only for an hour or so in the evenings. You hear from one of the staff the not very surprising information that work often did not begin until the editor had left the building.

At the end of the month he was thinking how much pleasanter it would be to write a new novel. More, he found himself becoming convinced that he would write that novel. On February 9 he resigned his editorship, and persuaded the unfortunate Forster to take his place. His "Travelling Sketches" continued to appear, and in addition he wrote a paper on the newly formed "Ragged Schools" and three letters on capital punishment, but within four months he had severed all connection with the paper.

Two little points are not without interest. By this time, I presume, the Alphington house had been permanently given up. At any rate Mr. Dickens reappears on the scene at this juncture, and very properly expresses his desire to be in harness again. His newspaper experience can surely be put to some use now that his son occupies an editorial chair. He is not yet sixty, and there must be some little niche for him. And so he is given the management of the reporting staff.

He takes his duties with commendable seriousness. He writes long-winded letters (which his son signs) to would-be reporters, and when these have been engaged, he sits in his managerial chair and plays superintendent. There is nobody else in the office who can watch others at work with such cheerful good humor. He is still fond of his glass of grog, and his diction has lost none of its polish. He is portly and "never given to much locomotion." Yet, as one of his colleagues tells us, he will always walk down Fleet Street on his way to the office, at eight o'clock in the evening, and this is unfortunate because at such times, according to his own account, he is invariably the victim of some artful dodger and loses his silk pocket-handkerchief.

"He would deplore the loss," relates Sir Joseph Crowe, the colleague in question, "in feeling terms when he tried to wipe the perspiration from his brow; for it was a peculiarity of his nature that he was always hot, whatever the weather might be. He maintained that he knew when his pocket was picked, but that he could not help himself, because the thief was too nimble, and he too stout." It must have made quite a nice little story. . . .

The other point concerns Dickens himself. He was the first to admit his mistake, and he washed his hands of the Daily News as soon as he possibly could, but he did not leave London to write his novel without a further search for distraction. It is almost unbelievable, but, according to Forster, he approached "a leading member of the Government to ascertain what chances there might be for his appointment, upon due qualification, to the paid magistracy of London." Dickens a police magistrate! I have not the least doubt that he would have made a most excellent one—for three months. Fortunately the reply was unfavorable.

Decidedly *something* had happened.

[4]

For the next pilgrimage Switzerland was chosen. A villa called Rosemont was found at Lausanne, and here in the summer of 1846 Dickens settled with his family.

It was quite a large household these days. Georgina Hogarth was with them, and a sixth child had been born at the end of the previous year. As before, too, the "brave" Roche was in attendance. And for a little while it seemed as though the vague mental worries had been banished.

There was beautiful scenery, there were congenial friends. It was here that he met the Richard Watsons of Rockingham Castle, William Haldimand, a former member of parliament who was the little king of the place, and the very likable M. de Cerjat. It was here, moreover, that he began the new novel "Dombey and Son," and wrote the new Christmas Book, "The Battle of Life." Yet, although he could declare that he liked the place "better and better," although there were long walks to be had and splendid explorations to be made, all was not well. For some years each new book had brought with it periods of feverish worry, but at Lausanne there was even more than the usual distress; there was something in the nature of an obsession. He found himself craving for crowded streets. He found that in his quiet retreat his brain was being deprived of something that was necessary for it, if it were to function as required.

Now, it is easy to make too much of such matters, but on the other hand they should not be too lightly dismissed. The unlikeliest folk may be at the mercy of such obsessions, though in general they prefer to say nothing about them. There are robust and apparently untroubled men who are secretly afraid of streets and large crowds, and others, outwardly contented and happy, who feel that their home is a prison. There is always a reason for such curious states of mind, though it is rarely understood by the victim.

The psychologists have their own names for such

phenomena, and they would find no difficulty in explaining the "case" of Charles Dickens. As yet, however, there was little cause for alarm. He might feel giddy and sick, be unable to sleep, find himself curiously despondent and aware of a vague anxiety about he did not know what—still there was the old will to work. Time and again he despaired of "The Battle of Life," but it was finished in time. Yet it is significant that he was able to do this only after a week by himself in Geneva, where, incidentally, he witnessed a bloodless revolution, and from which town he wrote to Macready that he had run away from a bad headache "as Tristram Shandy ran away from death."

Even now, I suspect, Forster was beginning to understand what had happened. "I dreamt all last week," Dickens wrote to him at the time, "that the Battle of Life was a series of chambers impossible to be got to rights or got out of, through which I wandered all night. . . . The mental distress, quite horrible."

Dickens, indeed, was already wanting to "get out," and it is interesting to find that to this time belongs his first idea of yet another possible means of distraction. "I was thinking the other day," he wrote, "that in these days of lecturing and readings, a great deal of money might possibly be made (if it were not infra dig) by one's having Readings of one's own books. It would be an *odd* thing. I think it would take immensely." But it was not only the money that was in his mind.

He was heartened by the splendid success of "Dombey," the first number of which had appeared in October, and when "The Battle of Life" was published it also enjoyed a huge success. For the next few months, moreover, there were such movings about and so many new excitements that he can have had little time to worry about himself. . . .

So you see him in Paris for the winter. "The queerest house in Europe" is taken, and to make fun of its architectural peculiarities is for some time his daily delight. He pays frequent visits to the morgue. He meets the most distinguished French writers, Victor Hugo amongst them. He rushes to London to see the rehearsals of a dramatization by Albert Smith of the new Christmas Book. The Keeleys are to stage it at the Lyceum, but he has heard poor accounts of its progress. And he is so "bothered to death" by the confounded thing that he is obliged to read the little book to the company. After which he coolly takes charge of the rehearsals.

On the same visit he arranges with B. and E. for cheap editions of his books, and dashes back to Paris. There he "kills" poor little Paul—a tragedy which "amazes all Paris" and causes Thackeray to lament his own limitations—but is obliged to return with Kate when news comes that young Charley, now at King's College School—Miss Coutts has made herself responsible for his education—is seriously ill. Presently the whole family is brought back by the estimable Roche, and as the Devonshire Terrace house is still let to Sir James Duke, another is taken in Chester Place, Regent's Park, where a seventh child, Sydney Smith Haldimand, alias the Ocean Spectre, alias Hoshen Peck, is born. All the while "Dombey" goes on, and if some people find it a little difficult to believe in Mr. Dombey, everybody loves Mr. Toots and Susan Nipper and Captain Cuttle. The circulation of the novel steadily increases—it has no serious rival: not even in that greater work, "Vanity Fair," which is also appearing in numbers at this time; and when it is finished Dickens finds that his financial embarrassments are at an end. Henceforth, indeed, he will be in a position to save money.

Incidentally he is particularly pleased by a review of his book in the Sun. He breaks his rule, and writes to thank the unknown reviewer. This man turns out to be Charles Kent, probably the most devoted of all his admirers, and so another warm friendship begins. Also the amateur dramatic company is summoned together again, this time to become "splendid strollers."

The occasion for this second venture was the straitened circumstances of Leigh Hunt. For some time there had been talk of a civil-list pension for him, but once long ago he had been imprisoned for libel, and there were difficulties in the way. A man of his eminence, however, could not be permitted to remain in want. Dickens bestirred himself. If the authorities refused to grant a pension, funds must be raised by private endeavor, and how better than by further theatricals in public?

He drew up his plans. There should be two performances in London, if a large enough theater could be procured, and one each at Liverpool and Manchester. There was to be a revival of the Jonson play, but "The Merry Wives of Windsor" was to be attempted as well. This was in the early summer of 1847, and certain preparations had already been made when the much delayed pension was suddenly granted.

It was therefore decided to forego the London performances and leave the Shakespeare comedy to the future. But as the pension was small and another case of distress had come to his knowledge—that of the dramatist John Poole, whose "Paul Pry" had given pleasure to thousands—Dickens decided that the two performances of "Every Man in his Humour" which he had already arranged to give in the north should not be canceled. Accordingly in June he once again assumed his managerial responsibilities. At the time he was in Broadstairs, which was to remain his headquarters until the autumn, and you catch pleasant glimpses of him at this congenial work. . . . The mornings must be devoted to "Dombey," when he is not to be disturbed. He *is* disturbed, because Broadstairs has developed "a season" and has grown noisy, but for the moment that cannot be helped. The rest of the day, however, may be given to theatrical business.

There are, of course, a thousand things to be done, if that £500 clear profit on which he has set his heart is to be obtained. Innumerable letters must be dispatched every post. Manchester and Liverpool must be placarded, and the right people interested in the venture. Also there is some little trouble with the cast, particularly as more than one farce is to be given after the play. Not all the old company is available. Miss Fortescue, for instance, cannot leave London. Who is to take her place? Mark Lemon is ordered to put matters right.

Mark Lemon, in fact, is ordered to do a great deal. Perhaps he had better run down to Broadstairs for a night. Punch can be left to look after itself. Uncle Mark stays in London, but he is by no means idle. More letters are written, and G. H. Lewes, Augustus Egg, the painter, and Cruikshank, no longer likely to stand on his head now that he has given up strong liquor and even smoking, are secured.

There come "all sorts of bedevilments." The casting is proceeding very well, and Uncle Mark has obtained Miss Montague—the future Mrs. Henry Compton—in Miss Fortescue's place, but Cruikshank is not at all sure that his histrionic talents are being properly appreciated, and in consequence is "a little discontented." Had he not better be given a larger part? He is given a good part in one of the farces because "his name is important," and all is well. So the days pass, and the time comes for rehearsals, and Miss Kelly, in graciously permitting her theater to be hired for the purpose, is able to add materially to her collection of Dickens's autograph letters.

Mere social engagements, of course, have to be refused. "I shall be continually going out and coming in at unholy hours," the worried manager is writing in excuse to a friend, a few days before he goes up to London with Kate and Georgina; "sounds of 'groans' will be heard while the inimitable Boz is 'getting' his words—which happens all day. . . . One hundred letters per diem will arrive from Manchester and Liverpool; and five actresses, in very limp bonnets, with extraordinary veils attached to them, will always be calling, protected by five mothers."

He does accept one invitation to Gore House where in Hans Andersen he meets a kindred soul, but that is an excusable exception. Otherwise there is no relaxation. Bulwer Lytton and Talfourd write prologues for him; Nathan produces his finest costumes; Miss Kelly is full of suggestions, which receive the greatest attention—until she is safely out of the way. The last rehearsal takes place, costumes and wigs are packed up, tickets are taken, and the company goes "on tour." . . .

It was not a long tour—two nights and no more—but it was a successful tour, and it gave the novelist a liking for "the road" that he never lost. Manchester and Liverpool were highly delighted, and although expenses were so high that there was only £400 to be divided between Leigh Hunt and Poole, the company's reputation was made.

This became perfectly clear some nine or ten months later, when an excellent excuse for another, more ambitious tour presented itself. Shakespeare's house in Stratford-on-Avon had recently come into the market, and committees were formed to arrange for its purchase and future preservation. The London committee, of which Dickens was a member, was also working hard to raise a fund to endow a perpetual curatorship. It desired to have the Irish dramatist Sheridan Knowles appointed to the position.

Knowles in his old age had rather surprisingly forsaken the stage for the Baptist pulpit, and the change of platform had not added to his material prosperity. On the contrary, he was now on the verge of bankruptcy. Dickens was terribly distressed at the time, for his sister, Fanny Burnett, was dying of consumption out at Hornsey; but he set to work to map out a tour which would provide the committee's fund with a good nucleus. It is not known exactly how many performances were projected at first. Leamington and Stratford were originally included in the scheme, but suitable dates could not be found for them. Newcastle asked for a performance—its theater manager addressed his letter to Dickens at the offices of Punch: an understandable mistake—but the invitation could not be accepted.

In the end nine performances were given, two in May at the Haymarket Theatre, four in June, at Manchester, Liverpool, and Birmingham (twice), and three times in July, at Edinburgh and Glasgow (twice). "The Merry Wives," with Dickens as Shallow and an unpadded Lemon as Falstaff, was now included in the company's repertoire. For some reason—probably illness—Douglas Jerrold could take no part, but a new amateur actress was found in Mrs. Cowden Clarke whose "Shakespeare Concordance" had been published three years before. She has left on record a vivid picture of Dickens at rehearsals, which shows what endless pains he took to get the most out of his company.

The queen and the prince consort attended one of the London performances, and the whole tour produced a net profit of more than £2,500. By this time Stratford itself had undertaken the management of the birthplace, and the idea of the curatorship being given to a distinguished man of letters was abandoned, but the proceeds were handed to Knowles, and Dickens may well have been pleased at the result of his efforts.

[5]

So we approach another landmark in his career.

After the theatrical excitements he retired to Broadstairs, there to work on his delayed Christmas Book. This was "The Haunted Man"—the last of the series—which was finished in London and immediately dramatized by Mark Lemon. That Christmas there came the first ideas for a new serial story, which in its completed form is generally considered to be the finest of all the Dickens novels. Here, too, there was a departure from custom that is not without its significance.

"David Copperfield" is largely autobiographical. It was not originally intended to be, but Forster had been shown some fragments of autobiography, quite as romantic as anything Dickens had written, and suggested their incorporation into the new book. Dickens accepted the suggestion, and in doing so must have found something in the nature of yet another distraction. There had been sketches from life in every one of his previous books, but little enough of his own emotional experiences. Now, however, when his mental distress was increasing, when his physical health was deteriorating, when, indeed, he was coming to think more and more about himself, he unconsciously hit upon the value of self-confession, which need be no less a relief because it may not be revealed without disguise.

Chapter XI

HIGH TENSION

[1]

THERE is a daguerreotype of Dickens taken in 1852 which for me has a curious fascination. Apart from the fact that a casual glance at it might lead you to suppose that the late Sir Charles Wyndham had made himself up as the novelist for a Drinkwater chronicle play, it helps to bridge the gulf between the earlier portraits of a handsome, if slightly effeminate, youth, and the later photographs of a bearded and deeply lined old man. In spite of the temporary disappearance of mustache, however, this daguerreotype belongs more properly to the second group. You see a middle-aged man, and would not be surprised to be told that his age is fifty-five, yet Dickens was only thirty-seven at the time.

But the terrific strain had told. Already he *was* middle-aged. Romping on the stage, amusing his children with conjuring tricks, dining snugly with particular friends, he could assume the irresponsibility of a schoolboy, but in reality he had long ago said good-by to youth. I am convinced that he now felt himself to be almost an old man. In those day, you will have realized, it was fashionable and dignified to be old. Married women of thirty would put on lace caps and play matron without apparent effort, and men of the same age could hardly hope to be taken seriously until they had assumed a more or less patriarchal appearance.

Dickens still hankered after unusual waistcoats, but there was now a more conventional air about him. It was as though he had come to understand what was expected of "an institution." He had still to do some of his best work, he had yet to come into close contact with Wilkie Collins, the man who was to exert the most curious influence upon him, but the golden days were definitely behind him. He was tired, and, in spite of his unprecedented success, vaguely disappointed. It was not that he did not find the old pleasure in his work, it was not that he was bored with adulation; it was, rather, that the routine now imposed upon him had become irksome. Not to have worked would have been impossible—like Dr. Manette he needed his tools. But there was something else that he was needing, and as yet, it may be, he would not admit to himself what this was.

Many imaginative writers, with less excuse than Dickens might have pleaded, experience something of the kind at one stage or another in their careers. Sometimes they come to grief. Dickens fought on for eight years before he could make up his mind to take any drastic step, and during all that restless time, there was nothing in his work which allowed his public to suspect that anything was wrong. Indeed, there was little enough to show even his own friends, except perhaps Forster himself, that anything was wrong. They knew that a new novel in the making invariably meant "a bad time" for him, and they could not fail to see that he was aging fast; but as yet they saw only the jovial, perhaps rather effusive, but genuine enthusiast whom they had always known. . . .

We come, then, to the "Copperfield year"—not in

itself a time of exceptional interest, but one which seems to mark off quite definitely the end of a period. The usual things happened. An eighth child—the present Sir Henry Fielding Dickens, K.C.—was born at the beginning of 1849, and on this occasion no living friend provided the necessary Christian names. You might have expected a John Forster Dickens, but it was not to be. A few days later Dickens himself was in Yarmouth, finding local color for the new novel. This, by the way, was to have been called "Mag's Diversions," but the Thomas Mag whose adventures were to be related became metamorphosed by gradual stages into the David Copperfield whom we know.

That the initials of his hero, thus finally named, were his own reversed, seems to have "startled" the novelist, who was always on the lookout for such coincidences, but it was not perhaps very surprising. He worked at the book fairly steadily for the next eighteen months. In February he was in Brighton, where his landlord and his landlord's daughter both elected to go suddenly mad. In the summer he was at Bonchurch in the Isle of Wight.

Here he tried the effect of mesmerism on his guest, Leech, who was seriously ill after a bathing mishap, watched his children play with a red-haired boy called Algernon Swinburne, and found the air so little to his liking that he was forced to move on to Broadstairs. Bonchurch, in fact, was blamed for having an atmosphere which no self-respecting British seaside resort ought to have endured for a single day. Naples, he declared, was hot and dirty, New York feverish, Washington bilious, Genoa exciting, Paris rainy, but Bonchurch was "smashing." One is glad to know that it has managed to survive. . . .

In November he was in London again, and witnessed

the public execution of the Mannings, a monstrous spectacle which caused him to write to the Times in expostulation. He was opposed on principle, he said, to capital punishment, but recognized that public sentiment regarded it as necessary in extreme cases. If, however, the death sentence was to be continued, it ought to be carried out only behind prison walls. His two letters undoubtedly played their part in helping to put an end to a revolting business.

But this time it had unfortunately become clear that the sales of "Copperfield" were not going to equal those of "Dombey." This is the more surprising inasmuch as the general verdict seemed to agree with Dickens's own—it was always his best-beloved child—and at the time he was at the height of his fame. Thackeray and Lytton were but two who found in it all the most engaging qualities that a novel could hope to possess. In later years, moreover, the sales were colossal, second only to those of "Pickwick," but during serial publication, from May, 1849, to November, 1850, there was at no time any marked increase in circulation.

It had been definitely decided that there were to be no more Christmas Books, and you are not altogether surprised to find Dickens once again thinking of a new magazine. He was in no financial embarrassment, though the calls on his purse were not becoming less, but he was naturally disappointed. The Copperfield accounts were "shy," and although B. and E. were fully confident about the future, Dickens decided that "the Periodical must be set going in the spring." Accordingly he set about devising a weekly journal that should not only give "all classes of readers" the kind of literary refreshment they wanted but also keep his name continually before them.

The result was Household Words, which must be

considered to be one of the most successful ventures in Victorian journalism. Its precise scope was not, of course, settled in a moment, and I cannot help thinking that much of the credit for deciding upon the form it finally assumed must be given to Forster. There were the usual long discussions and the usual voluminous correspondence. Dickens himself in groping about for a new idea made vague suggestions about a benevolent Shadow, which was to be omniscient and ubiquitous and under whose mantle all contributors might take temporary shelter; but Forster in his hard-headed way fought shy of any such ghost.

In the end it was decided that there should be a popular miscellany of general literature, issued weekly at twopence; in the usual way entertainment was to be tempered by instruction, and important social questions were not to be burked merely because they seemed to be unpleasant. Dickens's name was to appear as editor-in-chief, but all contributions were to be anonymous. This decision, by the way, led to one or two bibliographical "mistakes" and also to occasional irritation on the part of ambitious young writers who found their work being ascribed to the "Chief." As a matter of fact more than one "outside" contribution was subsequently reprinted in America as Dickens's work—the most important being Mrs. Gaskell's "Lizzie Leigh"—and Dickens himself did not hesitate to make full use of his editorial prerogative by "touching up" and sometimes materially adding to his "young men's" proofs. But on the whole the scheme worked very well. It remained only to choose a title, find offices and a staff, and make financial arrangements with the publishers. A score of titles were suggested—including the Forge and Charles Dickens—before the final choice was made. Forster was responsible for the appointment of W. H.

Wills as subeditor and manager. Offices were taken in Wellington Street North; and R. H. Horne, whose long poem "Orion" had been published a few years before at the unusual but perhaps not wholly unsuitable price of a farthing, and Henry Morley, afterwards professor of English Literature at King's College, were given places on the staff.

The first number appeared on March 30, 1850, and two days before, "the proprietors"—Dickens himself with a half share, B. and E. with a quarter, and Forster and Wills with an eighth each—had signed a document whereby they agreed to share proportionately the profits and losses. In addition Dickens was to receive an editorial salary of £500 a year, and Wills a weekly salary of £8.

From the beginning affairs went well. Wills was precisely the right man for the job, and Dickens himself was never content merely to lend his name and occasionally write a short paper. They both worked very hard, and came to understand one another so well that there was hardly ever a difference of opinion between them. The right kind of contributor made his appearance, and Dickens's judgment was rarely at fault.

It has been said of him that he was not much of a literary critic, but he was one of the first to appreciate the merits of George Eliot's work—he suspected her sex, by the way, before anything was known about her —he admired Meredith's "Shaving of Shagpat," and he encouraged Adelaide Procter. Nobody, indeed, who reads his long and detailed letters to Wills can doubt his marked ability to "spot" good work when he saw it. Gradually there was brought together a little band of writers whose united efforts and general loyalty to their chief gave to "Household Words" a position peculiarly its own. A few of them, like Sala, were

Devonshire Terrace. The lease was due to expire this year, and this was just as well. With his very numerous family, he wanted a larger house. It seems to have escaped his biographers' notice, but this March he thought of buying Balmoral House overlooking Regent's Park and near to the canal. He approached the agents, and made a definite offer of £2,700 for the freehold, on condition that a good-sized study was built out for him. His offer was not accepted, very luckily for himself, for a few years later there was an explosion on a barge as it passed behind the house, a great portion of which was destroyed. Instead he entered into negotiations with his friend Frank Stone for his house in Tavistock Square and into this he moved later on in the year.

Unfortunately the various preparations for the play coincided with a little series of private misfortunes. His wife was seriously ill. She had hurt her ankle during rehearsals for the Knebworth performances, and had been unable to take part in them, but there was other and graver trouble, perhaps not unconnected with the birth of Dora Annie. Exactly what the matter may have been it is difficult to say, but there is an unpublished letter of Dickens belonging to this time which in view of what happened in 1858, when in so many words he stated that his wife had had more than one mental breakdown, is of more than usual interest.

The doctors considered that she ought to try the air of Malvern, and Dickens found a suitable house there, but not before he and his wife had received an invitation from one of the local doctors to stay with him. "I am so anxious," he replied to this Dr. Wilson, "that Mrs. Dickens should begin with a favorable impression of Malvern, and I am so certain of the impossibility of engendering that impression if she be on any visit, or in any house but our own (from what I have lately observed when we have been staying in the country houses even of intimate friends) that I am obliged, however reluctantly, to decline your hospitable proposal in relation to ourselves." What had he observed? We do not know, but it is certainly a curious letter. . . .

It was now that Mr. Dickens took to his bed for the last time. What had he been doing with himself these last few years? You hear of him occasionally, sometimes in the unlikeliest places, no longer "disappearing" or having very bad "moments," but not, I fancy, too willing to do anything in particular. You gather that he was no longer the "prodigal father," but how long he remained on the Daily News, being nightly robbed in Fleet Street, or where he lived with his wife and younger children I do not know. Now, however, he lay on his death-bed in London, and Dickens was summoned from Malvern to see him. He arrived too late to be recognized. The old gentleman died on the last day of March, and only his more likable side was remembered.

But there was yet another loss to come. Only a fortnight later Dickens was again in London to take the chair at a dinner in aid of the General Theatrical Fund. For a little while in the afternoon he played with his baby girl. Then, half an hour before he was about to propose the toast of the evening—and at this time there were few men in England who could make a more gracious speech after dinner—Forster was called out of the hall to be told that Dora Annie was dead. Wisely he said nothing until after the speech had been delivered. . . .

But there could be no going back, and, indeed, the guild and all that it meant had come into being at the right moment. There was no new literary work to be done, and Household Words while not exactly running itself was in safe hands with Wills. The guild gave him just the distraction he needed, and he did not spare himself. Luckily he found a powerful ally in the Duke of Devonshire, who took the greatest interest in the scheme and put his great house in Piccadilly at Dickens's disposal.

Here there was no stage, but having discovered with what comparative ease a portable theater could be constructed, he obtained the help of Joseph Paxton, just now a very prominent figure as designer of the Crystal Palace in Hyde Park, when the Great Exhibition was due to open in May, to design a new theater of the kind. This was all the more necessary as it had been decided to arrange a lengthy provincial tour, though, very wisely, without making use of the regular theaters.

The Paxton theater did all that was required of it. Well-known painters were invited to paint the scenery, and were not shy in responding. Finally there was brought into the cast a new member, henceforth to be one of Dickens's most intimate friends. This was Wilkie Collins, not yet well known as a novelist but already showing signs of unusual ability. Dickens had met him once or twice as a friend of Egg's, and been greatly attracted. Collins agreed to play, and speedily stepped into a place in his stage-manager's affections which even Forster himself did not always hold.

It was a brilliant London season that year, when visitors were arriving from all parts of the world to see the exhibition, and there was no more brilliant function than the first performance on May 16 of "Not So Bad As We Seem" at Devonshire House. The queen and prince consort were there, and although Dickens himself does not seem to have been too happily cast, it was a splendid start for the guild. The sum of £1,000 was obtained that evening, and sufficient advertisement to secure the greatest success wherever the company should choose to appear in the future. A second performance was given at the end of the month, and this time "Mr. Nightingale's Diary," a farce written by Mark Lemon but so greatly altered and improved during the next few years by Dickens as to be more than half his own work, followed the Lytton play.

Two further public performances were given in June and July at the Hanover Square Rooms, and the provincial tour began. It lasted, on and off, until the autumn of 1852, and definitely gave Dickens that craving to *hear* the applause of the public which he never really lost. So you are to imagine him at this time in charge of his little company of friends and semiprofessional actresses, more or less "on circuit": in the west, at Reading or Bristol or Clifton, in the Midlands, at Birmingham or Derby or Nottingham, in the north, at Manchester or Liverpool or Newcastle.

He is often at his new home, Tavistock House, where you hear of him giving multitudinous orders, including one for false "book-backs" to be painted on the doors of his study, in Broadstairs (for the last time), and in Boulogne with his wife and Georgina. But he is always looking forward to the next performance and more chats with this most attractive young Collins, who is so easy to get on with and such an all-round good fellow. Never before, indeed, has the Call been so strong.

There is little else to be recorded in this place. A new novel has been begun; occasionally there is a chair to be taken. Then another child, Edward Bulwer Lytton, is born, soon to be known as Plornishmaroontigoonter, or, more simply, as the "noble Plorn." His coming does not seem to have given too much pleasure to his father. "My wife is quite well," he is telling Cerjat at the beginning of May, "after favoring me (I think I could have dispensed with the compliment) with No. 10." And later on in the year, during a visit to Dover, he is expressing whimsical surprise that any of his friends, not already supplied by him, can be wanting a godchild.

"May I never have the opportunity of giving you one!" he cries. "But if I had, if my cup (I mean my quiver) be not yet full, then shall you hear again from the undersigned camel that his back is broken by the addition of the last overbalancing straw. What strange kings there were in the Fairy times, who, with three thousand wives and four thousand seven hundred and fifty concubines found it necessary to put prayers in all the Temples for a prince as beautiful as the day! I have some idea," he adds, and there is perhaps something more than a joke in his words, "with only one wife and nothing particular in any other direction, of interceding with the Bishop of London to have a little service in Saint Paul's beseeching that I may be considered to have done enough towards my country's population." The quiver, however, was now full. . . .

A great deal of money, by the way, was obtained for the guild from the various performances, but it was never really a success. Houses were duly built on the ground that Lytton had given, but they remained empty for twenty years because nobody who was "suitable" seemed willing to live in them. It was part of the scheme, moreover, that the authors and artists whom it was designed to assist should do something toward helping themselves, but they seemed curiously shy of doing anything of the sort. The guild itself continued to function in a mild way for a considerable time, but all public interest soon evaporated, and in the nineties a special act of parliament was passed which enabled such funds as remained to be divided between two more recently founded institutions of a similar kind.

[3]

The new novel was "Bleak House." This had been begun in October, 1851, almost as soon as Dickens had settled into his new London house. It was continued in various places throughout the following year, and finished in Boulogne in August, 1853. Like "Copperfield" it was issued in monthly numbers—from March, 1852, to September, 1853—and Hablot Browne, not quite such a satisfactory artist these days, though still in regular partnership was again the illustrator.

Much has been written about this story, which is the first of the novels to be provided with what modern reviewers call a regular plot. In the novels that followed it you will always find some such plot, and there is no question that for this marked change in technique Wilkie Collins was largely responsible. With the building up of "Bleak House," however, he can have had little to do, for it was more than half written before the two men were on terms of any intimacy. It has been suggested that the editorial work on Household Words was having its effect, and this may be so. What is certain is that there was no longer the old easy flow of invention. True, with Household Words and the various guild performances, it is surprising that he was able to manage a new novel at all. He did manage it, and the tension proportionately increased.

"At this date," writes Forster, "it seemed to me that the overstrain of attempting too much, brought upon him by the necessities of his weekly periodical, became first apparent in Dickens." And indeed, when he was not with his players the old restlessness broke out afresh. Already in 1852 he had had wild ideas, he said, of running away and traveling aimlessly abroad. He had tried Dover for a month or two, and Boulogne, and in the new year he was forced to admit that he was not his old self.

"The spring does not seem to fly back again directly," he told Forster, "as it always did when I put my own work aside, and had nothing else to do." He felt, he said, as if his head would "split like a fired shell" if he did not find some new diversion. As it happened a new idea almost immediately presented itself. They gave him a banquet at Birmingham, at which he promised to give two public readings from his works the following Christmas in aid of the Midland Institute.

A year, however, was to pass before he experienced the rather dangerous delights of appearing alone on a public platform, and in the meantime his health suffered. He tried Brighton, and had one of his old attacks, with intense pain in the kidney. He tried Boulogne, and found himself pining for excitement. Collins was exhorted to join him, and it cannot be doubted that already this young man of twenty-nine with the rather commonplace outlook and almost patronizing airs was usurping Forster's position.

It is certainly curious, the eagerness with which Dickens henceforth turned to his new friend for companionship, though I have my own ideas about it. It seems to me that Collins was providing the overwrought man with a rougher, slightly more cynical philosophy. Collins liked to do himself well; he enjoyed the little adventures in which a man of not too scrupulous taste will sometimes indulge. I do not say that he led Dickens astray; but after Forster's starchified and ultra-respectable ways it must have been a relief to have somebody about you at once capable of holding his own in intellectual argument and not unwilling to be pleasantly vulgar on occasions. There are passages in Dickens's letters to Collins (invariably deleted in the printed versions) which you do not find in his other correspondence. And so, in these days of strain, when the little bachelor jaunts were becoming so frequent, it was almost invariably Collins who was his companion.

Dickens was now making another experiment. For the first and only time in his life he dictated a book to his sister-in-law. This was "A Child's History of England," intended primarily for his own children, but printed in Household Words. It was not a very satisfactory business, and is chiefly interesting as showing his desire to do more and more work these days. It was almost as though he could not bear the thought of not being overworked. . . . A word must also be added about the two recognizable portraits in "Bleak House." There was no objection to his use of Landor for Lawrence Boythorne, but he was attacked for the rather cruel caricature of Leigh Hunt in Harold Skimpole. Yet, although he made such amends as he could, it is to be noticed that Leigh Hunt himself continued to write for Household Words, and I do not believe that at the time of writing Dickens was aware that he had done anything but make the customary use of a few characteristics of a friend.

The strain did not become less when "Bleak House" was finished. There was a prolonged bachelor tour with Collins and Egg through Switzerland and Italy in the autumn. Young Charley Dickens had now decided in favor of a merchant's career, and been sent to complete his education in Leipzig. He joined the travelers on their return home. At Christmas the first two readings from the "Carol" and the "Cricket" were given, as promised, at Birmingham—Collins went with him—and they were such a success that a third was arranged for working-men.

Enormously pleased at his reception, followed as it was by many requests to give other readings, Dickens went home to arrange some theatricals for his own and Lemon's children at Tavistock House. "Tom Thumb," Fielding's old farce, was given, with the children themselves taking part with their parents; and Thackeray, who was present, rolled in his chair with merriment. Straightway plans were made for another novel to be printed as a serial in Household Words. This was "Hard Times," a shorter story than usual, which doubled the circulation of his paper, but left its author almost in a state of collapse.

It had been difficult enough to write "Bleak House" in monthly instalments, but to give each weekly part the required dramatic interest must have taxed his powers of invention to the utmost. Yet he not only finished the book in a few months, but he worked harder than ever at Household Words, arranged another benefit performance for the poor old Kelly, now past her acting days, at the St. James's Theatre, and allowed himself to play almoner for Miss Coutts—which, even with Wills's assistance, was these days no easy task. He had gone again to Boulogne in the summer, whence he could write without too much exaggeration that he was "three parts mad and the fourth delirious." And when he had written the last line of his "socialistic romance," which drew such warm praise from Ruskin, he could make up his mind to nothing at all.

"I feel," he wrote, "as if nothing in the world, in the way of intense and violent rushing hither and thither, could quite restore my balance."

He had said something of the sort more than once before, but soon found relief. Now, however, although he was to struggle on for a while, it was becoming clear to him that it was not only his work that was "stunning" him. His letters might not in general be changing in character, but there was a new Dickens on the threshold, an almost hysterical Dickens who would no longer be satisfied with the old routine, even sprinkled, as it might be, with more theatrical diversions, a Dickens who was demanding and determined to enjoy a new kind of freedom.

Chapter XII

Breaking-Point

[1]

THE story of the next three years is one of an almost frantic search for peace—for peace of mind at all costs. It was not a question of being unable to work: Dickens continued to work tremendously hard. It was not a question of losing his hold on the public: he had lost nothing of his great popularity. It was, rather, the growing conviction that things could not go on as they were. Gradually he had come to believe that he was being shut up in some sort of prison, from which he would have to escape—somehow.

It was splendid to be an illustrious man of letters, invited to take this or that part in public life, besought to read his own works to admiring crowds, prosperous and able to satisfy any whim that suggested itself. It was delightful to watch his children growing up, and to know that he was in a position to give them a fine start in life. But in his comfortable house in Tavistock Square all was far from being well. Poor Kate was getting on his nerves, and there you had the kernel of all his worries.

She had borne him ten children, and all that childbearing had had its effect. Her good looks were gone, and she was a tired and prematurely worn-out woman,

who seemed to him—and, indeed, not only to him—
to be taking little interest in her children and none at
all in his work. There was nothing *against* her, but—
how different from her sister! It was Georgina Hogarth
to whom the children naturally turned; it was Georgina
who was really running the house; it was only Georgina who was capable of understanding him.

It is not difficult to understand what had happened.
Catherine Dickens was a placid, good-natured, affectionate woman. Nobody who reads her letters to her
youngest son, the much-beloved Plorn, can doubt the
warmth of her feelings. But she was inclined to be
lazy, she was generally bearing a child or being ill—
occasionally, perhaps, she had been more than merely
"queer"—and, to say truth, her husband was a difficult
person to please. She had played her part as well as
she could, but it was not the part that Dickens required.

There was also the question of her sister. Little by
little she must have allowed the more active and certainly more intellectually alert Georgina to take hold
of the reins. In the early years, I have no doubt, she had
been delighted to have Georgina in the house, but there
must have come times of friction and jealousy, times
when she woke up to the fact that she was no longer
mistress in her own house. And then, I suspect, there
must have come some such air of tension as Dickens had
frequently witnessed long ago beneath his father's roof.
Nobody, I suppose, was to be blamed very much, but
when there is divided authority in a household, there
is almost bound to be trouble, and the trouble is no
less because the quarrels that are waged may have their
roots in trifles.

You do not hear of these quarrels; you do hear, indeed, of Georgina's attempts to relieve the ever-growing tension. But she could do nothing. If Dickens had ever loved his wife as he had loved Maria Beadnell or Mary Hogarth, that love was dead. More, the respect which a love that is dead will so often bring in its trail, was not there. What, then, was to be done? He could not or would not send Georgina away, and there was no accusation to be brought against his wife. He was not the kind of man who in the face of domestic disquiet can shrug his shoulders and shut himself up in a shell. He was forced to plunge wildly into new and feverish activities, rushing hither and thither, searching for some sort of freedom away from his home. And it was at just this unhappy time that Maria Beadnell, though that was no longer her name, made her reappearance.

For Dickens the year 1855 opened with preparations for a fairy play in the little theater that had been erected at Tavistock House. Once again both grown-ups and children were to take part. For days every room was "full of spangles, gas, Jew theatrical tailors, and pantomime carpenters." An adaptation of Planché's extravaganza "Fortunio, and His Seven Gifted Servants" was to be performed, and the play-bill was drawn up by Dickens in his sprightliest vein.

There was "the return of Mr. Charles Dickens, Junior, from his German engagements!" and "the first appearance on any stage of Mr. Plornishmaroontigoonter (who has been kept out of bed at a vast expence)." Mark Lemon was among the actors disguised as Mr. Mudperiod, Wilkie Collins's name was Italianized for the occasion, and Dickens chose to call himself Mr. Measley Servile.

The pantomime seems to have been a success, but the hard work it entailed did nothing to lessen the stage-manager's growing impatience. Almost immediately times. . . . People used to say to me how pretty all that was, and how fanciful it was, and how elevated it was above the little foolish loves of very young men and women. But they little thought what reason I had to know it was true and nothing more nor less." And again he asked for a letter "all to myself."

Since he was obliged to leave Paris before her reply could reach him, he arranged for it to be forwarded on to him at the earliest possible moment. Back in Tavistock Square he continued for a while to hug this new and delicious secret. "No one but myself," he was writing on February 22, "has the slightest knowledge of my correspondence . . . I could be nowhere addressed with stricter privacy or in more absolute confidence than in my own house."

By this time Mrs. Winter must have been very well pleased with herself. She had plucked up enough courage to write to the great man, and so far from being rebuffed, had received the warmest replies. A new kind of romantic friendship, it seemed, was about to begin, and she was ready enough to play her part. She told him that for all their old quarrels, she had really loved him, and she must have experienced a thrill of excitement when in the course of his third letter he could write:

"Though it is too late to read in the old hand what I never read before, I have read it with great emotion, and with the old tenderness softened to a more sorrowful remembrance, than I could easily tell you." If only she had told him before! That, of course, was the one thought which refused to be banished. With Maria as his wife and in his house now, he would not be wondering how to find peace.

It was a thought which permitted him to write to Mrs. Winter without too much discretion, almost, indeed, as though he were expecting—as, in a queer way, I think, he was—the old romance to continue from the point where it had been so abruptly broken off in the thirties.

"Lady Oliffe," he told her, "asked me in Paris the other day (we are, in our way, confidential, you must know) whether it was really true that I used to love Maria Beadnell so very, very, very much. I told her that there was no woman in the world, and there were very few men, who could ever imagine how much." And of course they must be friends and meet. Why not? She had set matters right "at once so courageously, so delicately, and gently, that you open the way to a confidence between us which still once more, in perfect innocence and good faith, may be between ourselves alone. All that you propose I accept with my whole heart." But—he was a dangerous man to be seen with, and it would be well to keep what was to be "the most cordial, the most comprehending of friendships" a secret. Yes, that perhaps would be best. And in secret they arranged to meet.

Poor Maria. Was she really blind to the fact that the little dark beauty had grown into an unusually plump matron? Did she really suppose that she could give Dickens the sympathy and understanding that he wanted? Was she seeing herself in the part of some Aspasia stimulating her hero on to new triumphs? I believe that she was. I think that she was expecting a real romance such as was so often to be found in the lives of men of genius. It is quite true that she became a friend of the Dickens family. She met Kate Dickens and was often at Tavistock House. But there was no romance.

When and where she met her old lover I do not know, but nobody else was with them at the time. Dickens

But although he might choose to think so, these were not precisely the usual preliminaries to a new book. It was the realization that affairs were working toward a crisis, which was forcing him to search for a new outlet for his emotional strain. This took the form of a fierce, though temporary, incursion into politics. He not only found fault with the government for its handling of the miserable Russian war, but with the whole of the nation for its supineness. To Austen Layard of Nineveh fame he poured out his contempt for the politicians in the bitterest words, and in June he made his first and last political speech, characteristically on the stage of Drury Lane Theatre.

It was, however, in "the smallest theater in the world" that he found most relief. Another performance took place at Tavistock House in June. Wilkie Collins had written a melodrama for him entitled "The Lighthouse"—an old-fashioned thing, but containing such a highly emotionalized part as would appeal to him—and Dickens threw himself into the preparations with even more than his usual eagerness. Stanfield was persuaded to paint the scenery, Forster was not to be told anything until the new little amateur company "burst on an astonished world," and for this occasion Mr. Measley Servile adopted the more honorable name of Mr. Crummles. Once again "Mr. Nightingale's Diary" concluded the entertainment, which was repeated a month later for charity at Campden House, Kensington.

In July, Dickens took his family to Folkestone, and managed to make a beginning with his book. But peace of mind was not coming, and the work was not "right." Probably for the first time in his life he was forced to tear up what he had written and begin again; certainly for the first time a book of memoranda was compiled. Even by September little enough had been done. He was in "a hideous state of mind," he told Collins, and could "settle to nothing." More jokingly he informed Forster that in two or three years' time his friends would probably find him living with the monks on the top of the Great St. Bernard.

Yet he had never allowed himself to be beaten, and he was not going to be beaten now. The first number of the new story, originally, by the way, intended to be called "Nobody's Fault," but altered on the eve of publication to "Little Dorrit," appeared in October, and he had at any rate the satisfaction of hearing of its very large sales. By this time, however, he had gone abroad again, first to Boulogne, and then with his brother Alfred and Georgina to Paris, to find a "doll's house" not too free from smells, for the winter. Meanwhile there had been one or two public engagements, including more readings for charity and the chairmanship of a dinner given to Thackeray on the eve of his departure on an American lecturing tour. Negotiations, too, were now in progress for the purchase of Gad's Hill Place, which had itself come into the market as well as the little freehold on the opposite side of the road, and in the following March he had fulfilled his father's half-joking prophecy.

He had persuaded Collins to come to Paris, and I cannot help thinking that Forster was now becoming more than a little jealous of the young man of whom, it seemed, Dickens could not at this time see too much. If, indeed, Forster had been anybody but the burly Podsnap that he was, I should be tempted to suggest that this jealousy may help to explain his "astonishing" marriage, which now took place, to the utter bewilderment of every one of his friends.

Collins, however, could give Dickens something that

Forster had never possessed. He shared with Dickens the keenest delight in exciting melodrama, the keenest pleasure in seeing new things, and the same sort of boisterous humor. And he was not straitlaced. In Paris he must have been an ideal companion. A room was found for him near to the doll's house, and every day he took his meals with the family.

Dickens himself was busily meeting French writers and a little group of his Household Words young men, including Sala and Jerrold's son, both then living in Paris, and as busily arranging for a complete edition of his writings in French. It was at this time that he met that extraordinary woman George Sand, whose appearance suggested to him that she was best fitted to be "the Queen's monthly nurse." His portrait was painted by Ary Scheffer, the first to show him with hair on his face. Macready came, and some of the Lemon children seem to have stayed for a while in his house.

"The little Lemons," he told Collins while his friend was away for a little time, "depart tomorrow, under the charge of an unhappy Englishman whom we have inveigled into taking them. You will be glad to hear that on the day of your departure Lally began to transfer her Dinner Glares to Macready: and that Macready whenever he observed one of these terrible phenomena supposed it to mean that she wanted water, and instantly overwhelmed her with the largest decanter."

"Little Dorrit" was taking hold of him now, and he must have enjoyed "blowing off a little indignant steam which would otherwise blow me up," when he let himself go with the Circumlocution Office. On the other hand he may have had doubts about introducing Flora Finching; there is a suggestion of excuse in a letter he wrote to the Duke of Devonshire. It had come into his head one day, he said, "that we all had our Floras, and that it was a half serious, half ridiculous truth which had never been told." . . .

There were also frequent visits to London, mostly on Household Words business, but even with all this rushing about and Collins's companionship and the adulation he was receiving from French colleagues, he was not his old satisfactory self. "Sometimes," he told Mrs. Watson, "I fancy I have a digestion, or a head, or nerves, or some odd encumbrance of that kind, to which I am altogether unaccustomed," and in January, 1856, he was writing: "I am settling to work again, and my horrid restlessness immediately assails me. It belongs to such times. As I was writing the preceding page, it suddenly came into my head that I would get up and go to Calais. I don't know why; the moment I got there I should want to go somewhere else." But *did* it belong to such times? Never before had it been so necessary for him to be continually on the move.

In May he arrived in London, leaving his wife and family to follow. Another theatrical performance was in his mind, but beyond the fact that Stanfield "became immediately excited" at the prospect of painting more scenery, little was done at the time. In June he was at Boulogne again with Collins. They were working together on the Christmas number of Household Words; but it was, I suspect, the prospect of Collins's new drama "The Frozen Deep," that did most at this time to reconcile Dickens with life, and on his return to London he made preparations for its production, which were far more elaborate than any since the guild performances.

Indeed, it would seem as though only a complete disarrangement of his usual program would satisfy him. The whole house was turned upside down. He could joke about the general mess to Macready, but it must have held a kind of grim appeal for him. The carpenters in the back garden, the smell of boiling size, Stanfield "perpetually elevated on planks and splashing himself from head to foot," gasmen and mechanicians forever about him, and "foaming" rehearsals—all must have symbolized for him the disturbed state of his own mind. In some curious way the very fact that once again he was to turn himself for a while into somebody other than Charles Dickens was, I think, giving him a kind of security. With the footlights actually at his feet, he could forget. There was more in the business than some amateur theatricals: there was a possibility of escape.

Moreover, there was something about the play itself that had taken hold of him. He "derived a strange feeling out of it," he told a friend; "like writing a book in company; a satisfaction of a most singular kind, which has no exact parallel in my life; a something that I suppose to belong to a labourer in art alone, and which has to me a conviction of its being actual truth without its pain, that I never could adequately state if I were to try never so hard." Significant words. And it was because of this feeling that no pains must be spared to make the performance the high-water mark of amateur production.

Such, as a matter of fact, it proved to be. "All London" talked about it, and, as it happened, it was to be the indirect means of bringing matters to a head. The performance took place on January 6, and a hundred people somehow squeezed themselves in. Shortly afterwards, the Tavistock House Theatre was finally dismantled, but this did not mean that Dickens had finished his career as an actor. On the contrary he had only really begun it. In this year 1857 he not only repeated several times in public his performance of Richard Wardour in "The Frozen Deep," but came to a decision, which those who knew him best must long before have known to be inevitable: I mean his determination to become a professional reader.

[3]

If there was one event more than any other that can be said to have precipitated the crisis, it was, I think, the unexpected death, this spring, of Douglas Jerrold. He, poor man, had left his family with the slenderest means, and in his generous way Dickens immediately determined to do what he could to put matters right. He wrote to Forster, he sent for Edmund Yates, who was already making his mark. He found a good man of business in Arthur Smith, the brother of the well-known Albert, and formed a little committee.

A large sum, he said, must be raised. He himself would give a reading, Thackeray and W. H. Russell, just then at the height of his fame as a war correspondent, were to be asked to lecture, there should be a benefit performance of one of Jerrold's plays at the Adelphi, and "The Frozen Deep" should be given in some London hall. Everybody agreed to play his part, and at the end of it all a sum of £2,000 was raised for the Jerrolds. Dickens gave three public readings of the "Carol" in London, and they were huge successes.

In July "The Frozen Deep" was produced at a hall called the Gallery of Illustration. The queen had expressed a desire to see it, and as she could not break her rule of patronizing nothing that might be done for the benefit of private persons, an extra performance was given especially for her. She had suggested that Dickens should bring his company to Buckingham Palace. To this he had replied, as we learn from a letter of Georgina's, that "as neither he nor any of his fellow actors nor his family went to court, he would rather not go there, in the quality of actors and actresses, but that if the queen would come to a private performance at the gallery, to which she should invite her own party, he would be very happy to get it up for her alone.

This was accordingly done, and one is a little amused to find Dickens very firmly refusing to be "presented" in his farce dress, and this in spite of the queen's twice-repeated request that he should come to her.

The Jerrold fund, however, had not yet reached the sum aimed at, and when applications for more readings and more performances came from the provinces, they were not refused. It was just now that Dickens, wrapped up in the stage, mixing with "regular" actresses, for he had refused to allow his daughters to act outside London, forgot a little of his usual discretion. Even Forster could not be blind to the fact.

"Though it was part of his always generous devotion," he says, "in any friendly duty to organize the series of performances on his friend Jerrold's death, yet the eagerness with which he flung himself into them, so arranging them as to assume an amount of labour in acting and travelling that might have appalled an experienced comedian, and carrying them on week after week unceasingly in London and the provinces, expressed but the craving which still had possession of him to get by some means at some change that should make existence easier. What was highest in his nature had ceased for the time to be highest in his life, and he had put himself at the mercy of lower accidents and conditions. The mere effect of the strolling wandering ways into which this acting led him

Emigration

Mr Sidney says that for such an emigrant as I describe to him, Sydney is the place. That there, he will be able to learn the lesson he must learn, better than in any other place. That rent, clothes, and food, are cheaper there, than elsewhere; and that the emigrant and his family should be able to live there, for the first year, for about £100. I need suggest the addition of half as much more to this sum — say £150.

In saying this, Mr Sidney does not mean (he explains) that the emigrant should live, actually, in the town of Sydney. Any place along the coast, within a hundred miles of that town, is considered in the neighbourhood, and is rendered easy of access by the steamers which are always

The first page of an unpublished manuscript by Charles Dickens In the collection of Charles J. Sawyer

could not be other than unfavourable. But remonstrance as yet was unavailing."

Dickens, of course, was catching at straws. He was lapping up the adulation poured out to him equally in the theater and on the platform. Perhaps he was not too careful about the new friends he was making. In particular the young ladies of the stage—"little periwinkles," he called them—were mightily attractive. Perhaps, too, he knew that another book—"Little Dorrit," very fortunately, was now off his hands—would never be written while affairs remained as they were. And what of the new house in Kent upon which he was spending so much money? Was it to see a repetition of the unhappy scenes at Tavistock House? The idea must have been unbearable.

When "The Frozen Deep" had been played for the last time—it was also the last occasion, as it happened, when he was to take part in any theatricals—the reaction was dreadful. There was "grim despair," he wrote when the excitement had subsided. Once again he sought out Collins, and attempted to find peace with him on the Cumberland hills; but there was only one thing that would bring him peace, and as yet he could not make up his mind to take extreme measures. Instead he played with the idea of professional readings. Forster and his other friends tried to help, but they could do nothing.

"Too late to put the curb on," he wrote from the north, "and don't rush at the hills—the wrong man to say it to. I have now no relief but in action. I am become incapable of rest." The old days, he said, could never be brought back.

So the new year came round, and there was little blue in the skies. By this time all his particular friends were aware of what had happened, but what could they do?

"The domestic unhappiness," he was telling Collins in March, "remains so strong upon me that I can't write, and (waking) can't rest one minute. I have never known a moment's peace or content, since the last night of 'The Frozen Deep.' I do suppose that there never was a man so seized and rended by one spirit."

To Forster he wrote in more detail. "Poor Catherine and I are not made for each other, and there is no help for it. It is not only that she makes me uneasy and unhappy, but that I make her so too—and much more so. . . . God knows she would have been a thousand times happier if she had married another kind of man. . . . I am often cut to the heart by thinking what a pity it is, for her own sake, that I ever fell in her way; and if I were sick or disabled tomorrow, I know how sorry she would be, and how deeply grieved myself, to think how we had lost one another. But exactly the same incompatability would arise, the moment I was well again; and nothing on earth could make her understand me, or suit us to each other."

There was plenty of fault on his side, he admitted, but there was only one thing that would alter matters, "and that is, the end which alters everything." The end, indeed, was very near, and now it was not only poor stout Kate who annoyed him: he could not bear the sight of any of her family except Georgina. They, it seems, were staying at Tavistock House in April, and in explaining his absence, he wrote to Wills: "The Hogarth family don't leave Tavistock House till next Saturday, and I cannot in the meantime bear the contemplation of their imbecility any more. . . . The sight of Hogarth at breakfast!"

I cannot be sure, but I fancy that the Hogarths were now making veiled accusations against him. Kate may have believed them. At any rate, they left the house, and she went with them. In the following month a separation was jointly agreed on. Mrs. Dickens was to have £600 a year, and her eldest son was to live with her. The other children were to stay with their father and aunt.

"I am perfectly convinced," wrote Georgina to Mrs. Winter, who was still maintaining a fitful friendship with the family, "that this plan will be for the happiness of all. . . . My sister and Charles have lived unhappily for years. . . . Unhappily also, by some constitutional misfortune and incapacity, my sister always from their infancy threw her children upon other people." Catherine, she said, had "often expressed a desire to go and live away, but Charles never agreed to it on the girls' account."

One wonders what Maria thought of it all. . . .

[4]

It is at such times that the gossips really enjoy themselves. Dickens was not without his enemies. Time and again, I dare say, he had annoyed people by his rather imperious ways. To the public he had come to stand for the solid respectability upon which England had for so long been priding herself. The old ideas of his vulgarity and his "lowness" had been forgotten, and it was now very generally conceded that you could put every one of his books into the young person's hands without fear. He represented all that was safest and cleanest in literature, and was consequently considered wholly immune from scandal. And yet after all these years he had separated from his wife!

What a delicious morsel of news! Dickens of all people in the world! But—why? Well, it was a little difficult to explain. They had not been getting on very well for some time. Oh, but surely there must be another woman in the case? And at that question there must have come shrugging of shoulders and mysterious nods of the head. Yes, people *were* talking—about an actress. By name? Yes; a name had been mentioned; it was a girl who had been acting with Dickens in "The Frozen Deep." Really! Of course that would explain. And did Miss Hogarth propose to stay on in his house? Certainly she did, to look after the children. They were devoted to their aunt. Ah yes, but—surely that was a little unwise? . . .

You can imagine the things that were said. You can also imagine Dickens's fury when he learned, as he did, how the rumors were spreading and becoming ever more poisonous as they went. How far the scandal-mongers actually did go I do not know, but they went far enough to cause him to sit down at his desk and write out a statement which he asked Arthur Smith to show to "any one who wishes to do me right, or to any one who may have been misled into doing me wrong." This statement, I am convinced, was meant to be shown only to friends, but Arthur Smith allowed it to be seen by strangers. A copy reached America, and was printed in the New York Tribune. I give it in full:

> Mrs. Dickens and I lived unhappily together for many years. Hardly any one who has known us intimately can fail to have known that we are in all respects of character and temperament wonderfully unsuited to each other. I suppose that no two people, not vicious in themselves, ever were joined together who had a greater difficulty in understanding one another, or who had less in common. An attached woman servant (more friend to both of us than a servant), who lived with us sixteen

years, and is now married, and who was and still is in Mrs. Dickens's confidence and in mine, who had the closest familiar experience of this unhappiness, in London, in the country, in France, in Italy, wherever we have been, year after year, month after month, week after week, day after day, will bear testimony to this.

Nothing has, on many occasions, stood between us and a separation but Mrs. Dickens's sister, Georgina Hogarth. From the age of fifteen she has devoted herself to our house and our children. She has been their playmate, nurse, instructress, friend, protectress, advisor, and companion. In the manly consideration towards Mrs. Dickens which I owe to my wife, I will merely remark of her that the peculiarity of her character has thrown all the children on someone else. I do not know—I cannot by any stretch of fancy imagine—what would have become of them but for this aunt, who has grown up with them, to whom they are devoted, and who has sacrificed the best part of her youth and life to them. She has remonstrated, reasoned, suffered and toiled, again and again to prevent a separation between Mrs. Dickens and me. Mrs. Dickens has often expressed to her her sense of her affectionate care and devotion in the house—never more strongly than within the last twelve months.

For some years past, Mrs. Dickens has been in the habit of representing to me that it would be better for her to go away and live apart; that her always increasing estrangement made a mental disorder under which she sometimes labours—more, that she felt herself unfit for the life she had to lead as my wife, and that she would be better far away. I have uniformly replied that we must bear our misfortune, and fight the fight out to the end;

that the children were the first consideration, and that I feared they must bind us together "in appearance."

At length, within these three weeks, it was suggested to me by Forster that, even for their sakes, it would surely be better to reconstruct and rearrange their unhappy home. I empowered him to treat with Mrs. Dickens, as the friend of both of us for one-and-twenty years. Mrs. Dickens wished to add, on her part, Mark Lemon, and did so. On Saturday last, Lemon wrote to Forster that Mrs. Dickens "gratefully and thankfully accepted" the terms I proposed to her. Of the pecuniary part of them I will only say that I believe they are as generous as if Mrs. Dickens were a lady of distinction and I a man of fortune. The remaining parts of them are easily described—my eldest boy to live with Mrs. Dickens and take care of her; my eldest girl to keep my house; both my girls, and all my children but the eldest son, to live with me, in the continued companionship of their aunt Georgina, for whom they have all the tenderest affection that I have ever seen among young people, and who has a higher claim (as I have often declared for many years) upon my affection, respect, and gratitude than anybody in the world.

I hope that no one who may become acquainted with what I write here, can possibly be so cruel and unjust as to put any misconstruction on our separation so far. My eldest children all understand it perfectly, and all accept it as inevitable. There is not a shadow of doubt or concealment among us—my eldest son and I are as one as to it all.

Two wicked persons, who should have spoken very differently of me in consideration of earned respect and gratitude, have (as I am told, and indeed to my personal knowledge) coupled with this separation the name of a young lady for whom I have great attachment and regard. I will not repeat her name—I honour it too much. Upon my soul and honour, there is not on this earth a more virtuous and spotless creature than that young lady. I know her to be innocent and pure, and as good as my own dear daughters. Further, I am quite sure that Mrs. Dickens, having received this assurance from me, must now believe it, in the respect I know her to have for me, and in the perfect confidence I know her in her better moments to repose in my truthfulness.

On this head, again, there is not a shadow of doubt or concealment between my children and me. All is open and plain among us, as though we were brothers and sisters. They are perfectly certain that I would not deceive them, and the confidence among us is without a par.

C.D.

To this hurried statement was appended another signed by Mrs. Hogarth and her youngest daughter, Helen, wherein they pledged themselves to contradict "as entirely devoid of foundation" the statements that had been circulated which "deeply affected the moral character of Mr. Dickens."

It will be noticed that Dickens's statement contains a defense of Georgina Hogarth, and it is undoubtedly true that she was bitterly assailed for staying on in the Dickens household, but "the young lady for whom I have great attachment and regard" was not the children's aunt but a Miss Ellen Lawless Ternan, the daughter of a Manchester theater manager. One of the American papers mentioned her by name as one "well-known in Manchester, and latterly on the London boards, who had appeared with Dickens in the amateur theatricals. There was, said this paper, a "pure and very platonic affection" between them, and she was "now charged with being the cause of the separation."

Of this young lady I shall have very little to say. She had acted more than once with Dickens, but so had her mother and one of her sisters. It was another sister of hers, Frances Eleanor Ternan, who married Anthony Trollope's brother and became well-known as a novelist. Ellen Ternan did become a very great friend of Dickens's, and her own name is the first to be mentioned in his will: she received £1,000.

The point of importance lies in the fact that Arthur Smith showed the statement to so many people, including the New York Tribune's London correspondent. Rumors at home did not die down, and in a moment of something like madness Dickens issued another address to the public. Not content, moreover, to print it in his own paper, he took measures to see that it was printed in as many places as possible, and quarreled with one London paper—Punch—which, quite rightly, refused to take notice of it.

It was the stupidest thing that he ever did in his life. What did it matter that the "violated letter," as he called the statement given to Smith, had gone to America? The English papers would never have printed it. A hundred or a thousand people might chatter and gossip and lie about his affairs for a while, but in a month or two the thing would be forgotten. Why not treat them with the scorn they deserved?

Here again, however, Dickens was to show how incapable he was of treating his own affairs as he treated other people's. He could not bear to think that he was being involved in a misunderstanding; there must be an explanation. It was being said that he could not be practicing what he preached. It was probably being remembered that he had invented a creature called Pecksniff. And because a few people were doubting him, he must take instant measures to prevent the big public from doubting him as well. They must be taken into his confidence again, and asked not to lose their belief in him. He sought advice, it is true, before coming to a final decision, and Forster, Lemon, and Yates were amongst those who attempted to dissuade him, but he went further afield, and when Delane, the editor of the Times, astonishingly said, "Print!" he printed.

The statement that appeared in Household Words on June 12 was far less detailed, but far more pompous, than the "violated letter." It was, to be candid, a mass of conceit. He had now, he said, had relations with the public for nearly twenty-five years, and all that while he had tried to be faithful to them. It was his duty "never to trifle with them, or deceive them, or presume upon their favour." His "conspicuous position" had often made him "the subject of fabulous stories and unaccountable statements," but he had never "obtruded any . . . personal uneasiness" on his audiences. Now, however, that "some domestic trouble" had arisen, he would entreat all his brethren "to lend their aid to the dissemination" of what he desired to say. The trouble had been amicably composed, but "by some means, arising out of wickedness, or out of folly, or out of inconceivable wild chance, or out of all three, this trouble has been made the occasion of misrepresentations, most grossly false, most monstrous and most cruel —involving not only me, but innocent persons dear to my heart, and innocent persons of whom I have no knowledge, if, indeed, they have any existence—and so widely spread that I doubt if one reader in a thousand will peruse these lines, by whom some touch of the breath of these slanders will not have passed, like an unwholesome air."

"Those," he concluded, "who know me and my nature, need no assurance under my hand that such calumnies are as irreconcilable with me as they are in their frantic incoherence, with one another. But there is a great multitude who know me through my writings, and who do not know me otherwise; and I cannot bear that one of them should be left in doubt, or hazard of doubt, through my poorly shrinking from taking the unusual means to which I now resort of circulating the truth."

[5]

The public was bewildered and inclined to be angry. Editors, I fancy, were uncertain what exactly ought to be done. Some of them ignored the statement, others printed it without comment, a few indulged in a little plain speaking. "If an author is slandered," said the Liverpool Mercury, to take an example, "let him sue the slanderer, or live down the slander. If an author cannot live with his wife, let him separate from her. But in the name of common sense, and manliness, and self-respect, let him keep his private affairs to himself and his private friends, and not trouble the public with matters with which it has not the remotest concern."

In private, of course, the affair was widely discussed. People took sides, and it would seem as though the women were more often with Mrs. Dickens than with her husband. They considered, indeed, that she had been badly treated. If there had been a separation years ago, well and good, but after all these years the thing should happen, when, indeed, she had borne him ten children—no, they could not excuse him.

"What is this sad story of Dickens and his wife?" asked Elizabeth Barrett Browning. "Incompatability of temper, after twenty-three years of married life! What a plea! Worse than irregularity of the passions, it seems to me." In another letter she was even more uncompromising. She thought the statement was "dreadful," and considered it a crime "for a man to use his genius as a cudgel against his near kin, even against the woman he promised to protect tenderly with his life and heart, taking advantage of his hold with the public to turn public opinion against her."

Frith's daughter was another woman who did not hesitate to speak out her mind. Henceforth, she said, all Dickens's pathos would ring untrue, and all his bits of "goody-goody moralizing" would suggest to her that they had been written "with his tongue in his cheek."

On the other hand, most of Dickens's own friends rallied round him. Cerjat was only one of many to assure him that the unfortunate business had done nothing to lessen his regard and affection, and to him Dickens wrote gratefully in considerable detail. "I know very well," he said in the course of his reply, "that a man who has won a very conspicuous position, has incurred in the winning of it, a heavy debt to the knaves and fools, which he must be content to pay, over and over again, all through his life. Further, I know equally well that I can never hope that any one out of my house can ever comprehend my domestic story. I will not complain. I have been heavily wounded, but I have covered the wound up, and left it to heal."

Unfortunately the separation led to a very serious quarrel, not only, as I have said, with Mark Lemon, but also with B. and E. This meant a complete rupture with the publishers and was the direct cause of bringing Household Words to an end and inaugurating in its place All the Year Round.

It is almost incredible that Dickens could have allowed himself to act as he did, but in Punch's refusal to print his statement he saw an unforgivable insult. Immediately the absurdest orders were given. One can understand that the children were forbidden to utter "one word to their grandmother or to Helen Hogarth," for those two chatterboxes had undoubtedly helped to make mischief; but that they should be similarly forbidden "to see or speak to" their beloved Uncle Mark or ever to enter Mr. Evans's house, suggests that Dickens had come near to taking temporary leave of his senses.

It was not as if Lemon owned Punch: he was merely its editor. He had done nothing in the matter of the negotiations with Mrs. Dickens to which objection could properly be taken, and yet he too was to be treated like a pariah. Evans, indeed, seems to have protested at such treatment, which, to say the least of it, was ill deserved, for if there was one paper in the world which could legitimately ignore a private matter of this kind, it was Punch; but Dickens would not listen to reason.

"I have had stern occasion," he wrote, "to impress upon my children that their father's name is their best possession, and that it would indeed be trifled with and wasted by him if either through himself or through them he held any terms with those who had been false to it in the very greatest need and under the very greatest worry it has ever known."

Afterwards, it is true, both these quarrels were made up. Charley Dickens married Evans's daughter in 1861, and some years later Dickens and Mark Lemon were completely reconciled at the funeral of Stanfield. But at the time Dickens worked himself up into a state of sullen rage, and one is almost surprised to hear that Mrs. Dickens was to be allowed to see all her children "when, where and how" she pleased.

Chapter XIII

Professional Reader

[1]

"I SEND you a proof of what will begin tomorrow to be abundantly circulated, besides being printed in the Athenæum of next Saturday. It is a facetious facer—which I have given to those solemn impostors, *con amore.*"

In these words Dickens informed Wilkie Collins at the end of April, 1858, that he had come to yet another decision. The facetious facer was the first public announcement of his forthcoming professional readings, and the solemn impostors were, presumably, those of his friends who were endeavoring to turn him from his purpose. Forster had never disguised his dislike of the idea. Apart from the possibility of the sales of the novels decreasing, he considered that the novelist would not only be sacrificing his dignity and cheapening himself, but deserting his ideals. He knew well enough that it was not merely money that was attracting his friend, and feared the results of so much unhealthy excitement.

Dickens himself, years before, had taken much the same view. Now, however, with a new touch of worldliness about him, he wanted the applause and the excitement and had no objection to the money as well. Undoubtedly he had always taken his art seriously, but he had never pretended to be an esoterically minded poet with his eyes always turned to the stars. He had never pretended to be other than a plain man of the people. He had tasted the hectic joys of success on the stage, and he had found a novel outlet for his genius as a showman: what was the objection?

What, indeed, was it? Well, was it quite the *respectable* thing to do? Novelists, of course, gave lectures, but was that quite the same? Nobody objected to Thackeray appearing on a platform and delivering a written oration, but he was not reading from his novels, and there was not another novelist who had ever— I can imagine Dickens's scornful rejoinder. Was there another novelist in his position or with his histrionic ability? Was there another novelist who could have aroused the extraordinary enthusiasm that had greeted his readings for charity? There was not; he stood, in popular estimation, entirely by himself. And he was spending a great deal of money on Gad's Hill. The moment was opportune.

Even with the chance of his domestic troubles becoming known to the public? Yes, he would risk it. But did he realize that he would become a mere public entertainer? Certainly, he did. Had it occurred to those who were being so solicitous about his dignity that from the days of "Pickwick" he had never been anything else? Besides, at the moment, he was incapable of beginning a new book. Obviously the experiment was worth the making, and he was going to make it.

Little time was lost in preparation. For his man of business he chose Arthur Smith, whose good work for the Jerrold fund had not been forgotten. Wisely he decided not to confine himself to one type of reading. The "Carol" had always been popular, but he now proposed to read in addition from the trial in "Pickwick," a scene from "Dombey," a Gampish episode from "Chuzzlewit," and two or three excerpts from some of his Christmas stories.

The St. Martin's Hall was engaged, and barely a fortnight after he had read the "Carol" in aid of the Children's Hospital in Great Ormond Street, he made his first professional appearance. This was on April 29, 1858, and from the moment when he stepped onto the platform there was never the smallest doubt of his overwhelming success. Many people may have been present on that memorable occasion from motives of mere curiosity, but soon enough it became widely known that a reading by Dickens was an entertainment of the very first class. Undeniably it was delightful to be brought, as it were, into personal contact with the world's most famous writer, but it was thrilling to find yourself witnessing a new sort of play.

For these readings were plays—tragedies and comedies and farces in which every character was acted by Dickens. He had a splendid voice, and when he had learned how to conserve it, there was not a hall in the kingdom where every member of his audience could not hear the softest word that came from his lips; but it was not only his voice that was to help him. He may not have been a great actor, as Macready might understand the term, but the characters that he was now to assume were of his own making, and it was really a question of recreating them in public, as once he had created them for himself in his own study. Once again he would *become* his heroes and villains, and, remembering the old Chatham days spent in the disused room upstairs, you begin to see how inevitable it all was. You understand the enormous satisfaction that these readings gave to Dickens himself. At long last, it must have seemed to him, he had found the ideal stage. He was able to identify himself in a new way with his books: he was able to *show* his books as they had first appeared to himself.

As one reading followed another, and hours every day were spent at home in the most laborious rehearsals, the little plays became ever more polished. The book was always in front of him, but there was little need to consult it. Every word came to be learned by heart; every inflection and every gesture were studied until they were mechanically produced. He had his reward. The thousands who crowded themselves into the room or hall to listen to him roared with laughter when they heard Sam Weller or were introduced to Mr. Toots. They sobbed when they were told of little Paul's death, and their throats became tight when Scrooge turned himself into a human being again. Never before had there been such triumphs, and if there was no "dressing up," no paint on his face, there were for Dickens all the other enchantments of the stage he adored. He had his own arrangement of lights, his own "backcloth," his own "props."

As time went on, it is true, a few critics noticed with alarm that tricks were being played with the text— inexcusable enormity, they considered, even on the part of the author himself—but they distressed themselves without good cause. Dickens knew well enough what he was doing: there had been plenty of stage-pirates of his work in the past; now he had become his own adapter, and if he chose to "gag" now and then, as he undoubtedly did, why not? So, in place of a mere reading aloud, you had a vivid play with Protean effects.

Never before had such an unusual entertainment been offered. Never before had the chief actor been a man of such reputation. Hardly had the fifteen readings at the St. Martin's Hall been concluded before every town in the kingdom was beseeching him to pay it a visit. So far, too, from having a hurtful effect on the sales of his books, of which a new uniform edition was now in course of production, the readings were materially helping to increase them. Money poured in. It is no exaggeration to say that nearly all the time he was reading Dickens was receiving sums of from £200 to £500 a week—almost incredible sums, be it noted, for the time. Certainly the "clinking" that he had told his friend Cerjat would mitigate the hardships to which he expected to be put, was proving as "musical" as he could have wished.

The domestic crisis, as it happened, in no way interfered with his success. Once it was over, he prepared himself for his first provincial tour. A program of no less than eighty-seven readings was arranged, to be given between August and November. Arthur Smith was to accompany him, with two assistants, and a valet. There was no literary work to be done, except a story for the Christmas number of Household Words, and he was free to enjoy his new-found liberty. There were one or two public dinners to attend, and visits were paid to Gad's Hill, but most of his time was spent in further rehearsals.

One little matter perhaps deserves mention. Before he journeyed to Clifton, where the tour was to begin, there had come a serious quarrel with Thackeray. The two men had never really been on intimate terms— there may have been a little jealousy on Thackeray's part—but they had been friendly enough. Now, however, there was a clatter and rumpus which led to an estrangement that lasted to within a week of Thackeray's death.

Young Edmund Yates, a pioneer in that "personal" journalism which so many good folk deplore in public, but privately enjoy, today, had printed in Town Talk a fairly intimate sketch of Thackeray. It was a would-be smart vignette at which Thackeray took offense. He complained to the committee of the Garrick Club, of which they both happened to be members. The committee ordered Yates to apologize. He refused to do so, and was expelled. He had sought Dickens's advice, and it had not been refused. The dispute became public property, and it was freely said that Yates himself was merely playing shuttlecock in a struggle for supremacy between the two great writers. This, so far as Dickens is concerned, is quite absurd, though it seems to be a fact that the club split itself into two factions.

In the end Yates found himself unable to take legal action, and the matter dropped. It was not of great importance perhaps—Forster dismissed it in a short note—but it is to be noticed that Dickens resigned from the committee as a protest. (In a little while he also resigned from the club as a protest against the blackballing of his friend Wills.) Apart from this business, however, there was nothing to worry him, and when he left London for his "country work," he was probably in better spirits than he had been since "Copperfield" days.

And from that moment he was swept into a maelstrom. One triumph followed another, and for some time at any rate he was not conscious of fatigue. In Arthur Smith he had found the right man, an enthusiast who worked like the proverbial nigger day and night. Dickens always recognized what he owed to him. Arthur, he said, was "always corresponding like a Secretary of State," or being "transformed into a rout-furniture dealer of Rathbone Place," dragging forms about him "with the greatest violence, without his coat."

His letters in general had rarely been so cheerful. "You will be glad to hear," he wrote from Plymouth, "that at Clifton last night a torrent of five hundred shillings bore Arthur away, pounded him against the wall, flowed on to the seats over his body, scratched him, and damaged his best dress suit. All to his unspeakable joy."

Dickens had made it a rule to accept no private hospitality during the tour, but stayed at hotels, and soon he was confessing that he seemed "to be always either in a railway carriage, or reading, or going to bed." Collins warned him against doing too much, and suggested a break. Another little bachelor jaunt, he thought, was almost due, but Dickens laughingly refused.

"As to that furtive and Don Giovanni purpose at which you hint," he wrote, "that may be all very well for *your* violent vigor, or that of the companions with whom you may have travelled continentally, or the Caliph Haroun Alraschid with whom you have unbent metropolitanly; but anchorites who read themselves red hot every night are as chaste as Diana (I suppose she *was* by the bye, but I find I don't quite believe it when I write her name)." . . .

He crossed to Ireland, where Belfast gave him an uproarious welcome and Dublin told wicked lies about the size of his white tie. There were all kinds of quaint adventures, and every day large piles of silver were sent to the bank. At Newcastle his daughters joined him, and had the time of their young lives in Scotland. Incidentally he was nominated in November for the Lord Rectorship of Glasgow University, but it was against his wishes—Bulwer Lytton was the successful candidate—and, as a result of his feelings on the matter being published, he was placed at the bottom of the poll.

They gave him a dinner at Coventry during the Christmas holidays, and about the same time the first American offer for readings reached him. He played with the idea for a while, but decided that only a very large sum indeed should be allowed to tempt him. "It rather appeared to me," he told Felton a few months later, "that the agent who came over, was not prepared with details, and (perhaps) not prepared with money. Both were important; the last particularly so, as I could not enter on such a design in any reason, without having a large sum paid down here. However, I proposed terms to him, and gave him until the middle of July to consider them." Apparently they were unacceptable, for it was not until after the Civil War that he crossed the Atlantic again.

Meanwhile his daughter Katie had become engaged to Charles Collins, Wilkie's brother, and Dickens himself was preparing to write a new book.

[2]

The domestic crisis was over, but the quarrel with Bradbury & Evans was of too serious a nature to allow even the coldest business relations. It became clear that Household Words could not be carried on in the old way. Lawyers were consulted on both sides. Dickens launched a new weekly called All the Year Round, with Wills in his old position and owning a fourth share of it. For a few weeks both papers appeared, but Dickens was injudicious enough to announce in his new paper that Household Words was about to be discontinued. The publishers brought an action against him, and he was obliged to agree to qualify the statement by announcing that the old paper would be discontinued *by him*. Even so, there was no definite settlement until, under a decree of chancery, Household Words (with all the rights belonging to it) was put up to public auction.

Bidding for Dickens Arthur Smith purchased the property for £3,500—this was on May 16, 1859—and henceforth it was incorporated in All the Year Round. Bradbury & Evans ran Once a Week in opposition, but it was never a serious rival. The first number of Dickens's new paper contained the opening chapters of his own "A Tale of Two Cities," and from the first the sales were so large that in a very short while he had more than recouped himself for the enforced purchase of Household Words.

The new story had been in his mind on and off ever since the production of "The Frozen Deep." He had originally intended to call it "Buried Alive," and proposed to issue it at first in the usual monthly numbers. For this purpose he had reopened negotiations with the now forgiven Chapman & Hall, who were delighted to have him back with them, and as a matter of fact these monthly parts duly appeared; but it was considered necessary that All the Year Round should be given the strongest possible start, and so the story appeared in weekly instalments as well, a fact which says not a little for the extraordinary position its author now occupied.

Indeed, it seemed that, financially speaking, nothing could go wrong with him. True, there were two houses on his hands, there were his mother and his wife, at least one of his brothers, and his youngest brother's wife—all needing allowances, while his own younger children were receiving expensive educations; but the new editions of his books were selling, and, more important, money was now coming in large sums from

America. This year he was actually paid £1,000 for a short story, and a similar sum was forthcoming from an adventurous publishing firm for early proofs of his new novel.

"You will be glad to know," he was telling Felton in June, "that All the Year Round is an amazing success. It has left the circulation of old Household Words in remote distance. . . . My story, too, has taken great hold, and strikes deeper each week." It is a little curious, by the way, to find him once again trying his hand at an historical novel, but Carlyle's "French Revolution" had long been one of his favorite books. Carlyle himself was a warm admirer of the novel, though he objected to reading it, as he said, in "teaspoons," and on being asked to lend the novelist a few books of reference from his own library is supposed to have sent all he had: enough to fill two large vans.

In the summer Dickens worked at his story at Gad's Hill, though another of his sharp attacks interfered with its progress, and at Broadstairs, where both the Collins brothers were staying. It is interesting to find him at this time once again playing with the idea of writing his autobiography. With a number of other readings, however, arranged for the autumn, there was little time for anything but the novel. In July he definitely decided that all idea of going to America must be given up for the present. Felton was informed that he was suspicious of the "speculators without money" who had approached him.

But there was nothing to stop his provincial tour, and this began at Ipswich and ended at Cheltenham, by which time he had given 125 readings in all. There were the same scenes of enthusiasm, and the same steady streams of silver. Then for a while he rested. There were no readings in 1860. Instead he pondered over the suggested autobiography and finally wrote the series of personal papers called "The Uncommercial Traveller" which appeared in All the Year Round. It was now, too, that he gave up Tavistock House altogether, furnishing for himself two rooms in Wellington Street over the offices of his paper.

You find him suffering from insomnia at this time, and rather worried about his mother, whose paid companion had suddenly decided to relinquish her post. His brother Alfred died in Manchester, and he was sorely upset. But you also see him busying himself with alterations and improvements at Gad's Hill and settling down happily to play country gentleman. His eldest son had set up for himself as an Eastern merchant, and the third boy Frank was taken into his newspaper office. Katie was married to Charles Collins, and Sydney, now in the navy, was home on leave.

Now, indeed, you find a Dickens, not, it is true, in the best of health, but no longer the restless, tortured creature that he had been. Even when there was a temporary falling-off in the sales of his paper, due to a serial story by Charles Lever that was without any great popular appeal, and it became necessary that he should write its successor himself, there were few signs of the older worries and doubts usual on such occasions. He "prowled about," and took long walks at night when he could not sleep; but the new story "Great Expectations," which Forster (amongst others) was relieved to hear would not be lacking in humorous scenes, seems to have given him very little trouble, even though the painters drove him out of his study for a while.

He must have been convinced of a new security. The readings, the new editions of his books, All the Year Round, and America, were laying the foundations of that very considerable fortune which he was to leave at his death. He was a great public figure, preparing himself for a second series of readings, which would give him all the excitement he required and would certainly not be less remunerative than the last. Above all there was peace in his home.

The lines on his face had deepened, and a small beard did not make him look younger, but if he was not wholly free from troubles connected with his wife's departure, at least all signs of hysteria were gone. He was entering the last period of his life. There was still to come much rushing about, another American visit, and one long and elaborate novel, and he was to die, as he would have wished, in harness, but henceforth it is permissible to think of him as a happy man. With his "young men" about him, Sala and Yates and Percy Fitzgerald and the others, he could play amiable Mæcenas. And, as if to symbolize his break with the unhappy past, he piled up the accumulated correspondence of twenty-five years in a corner of the garden, and burned the lot.

An expensive bonfire. . . .

[3]

One of the most successful features of All the Year Round was the extra number that was issued each Christmas. The sales of these Christmas numbers ultimately reached a quarter of a million copies or more, and great care was taken in their preparation. So you find Dickens this autumn on a little tour in Devon and Cornwall, with Wilkie Collins, now making his name with "The Woman in White," and henceforth, with Lytton, whose "Strange Story" was about to appear, amongst his most valuable contributors. In the following February he rented a London house, chiefly for his unmarried daughter's sake, and the next month he began his second series of readings.

Unfortunately the invaluable Arthur Smith was ill— he died later on in the year—and Dickens engaged as his manager the far less satisfactory Mr. Headland who had been employed at the St. Martin's Hall at the time of the first readings. This hall, as it happened, had been burned down, and the 1861 readings took place at the St. James's Hall.

"Perfectly astounding audiences," he was able to record, and but for the claims of "Great Expectations," he would have continued his readings throughout the year. As it was, his six appearances in March brought him £500. He finished the book in June, in spite of "distressing pains in the face," and had the satisfaction of knowing that it was "universally liked." Marcus Stone had now become his illustrator, and undoubtedly his work was better suited than that of Phiz to the taste of the times, though whether modern readers will endorse the artistic views of the sixties is another matter. . . .

Then in the summer preparations were made at Gad's Hill for new adaptations, and scenes from "Nickleby," and "Copperfield" were added to his repertoire. Once again long hours were spent at rehearsals, and they were not wasted, for, although his autumn tour began rather dismally at Ipswich, where his audience, he thought, seemed afraid of him, the new scenes were enormously successful. Headland might make the most grievous mistakes, but there was no question now that all Britain was at Dickens's feet. He could do what he liked with the vast crowds who squeezed themselves into whatever hall he had engaged. Occasionally there were wildly tumultuous scenes, when his platform was stormed, and people lay within a few inches of his reading-desk. Once, in Berwick, a panic was averted only by his presence of mind.

"The room," he told Forster, "was tremendously crowded and my gas-apparatus fell down. There was a terrible wave among the people for an instant, and God knows what destruction of life a rush to the stairs would have caused. Fortunately a lady in the front of the stalls ran out towards me, exactly in a place where I knew that the whole hall could see her. So I addressed her, laughing, and half-asked and half-ordered her to sit down again; and, in a moment, it was all over. But the men in attendance had such a fearful sense of what might have happened (beside the real danger of fire) that they positively shook the boards I stood on, with their trembling, when they came up to put things right. I am proud to record that the gasman's sentiment, as delivered afterwards, was 'The more you want of the master, the more you'll find in him.'"

At Edinburgh there was "a blaze of triumph," and an equally splendid reception at Glasgow, in spite of an over-issue of tickets. "Such a pouring of hundreds into a place already full to the throat, such an indescribable confusion, such a rending and tearing of dresses and yet such a scene of good humour on the whole, I never saw the faintest approach to. . . . It was like some impossible tableau or gigantic pic-nic—one pretty girl in full dress lying on her side all night, holding on to one of the legs of my table!"

The sudden death of the prince consort in December caused him to break off the tour for a little while, and this allowed him a much-needed rest. Very naturally he was beginning to feel the effects of his exertions. The "Copperfield" reading in particular was taking a great deal out of him, and "my head," he confessed, "is dazed and worn by gas and heat."

Nevertheless before the end of January he was continuing the tour, and in March he was giving weekly readings in London, including a new one from "Pickwick," which brought him in almost £200 a night. These lasted until June. Australia now offered him £10,000 for a lengthy tour, and he was inclined to go, particularly when the Civil War came to close America to him, but it would have meant more than a year's absence from England, and he regretfully refused the offer. About the same time he was trying to plan out a new book, but was unable to do more than find a title: "Our Mutual Friend."

The summer he spent at Gad's Hill, where Georgina Hogarth was seriously ill, and in October he took her and his elder daughter to Paris, where in the following January he gave four readings for charity at the British Embassy and was lionized to an extent that must have reminded him of old Boston days. In the spring, while London was "going mad" over the arrival of Princess Alexandra, he gave Friday readings at the Hanover Square Rooms, and thought of including in his repertoire the murder scene from "Oliver Twist." This, however, proved "so horrible" that he was afraid to try it in public.

The year 1863 had its sorrows for him. In April his old friend Egg died. In September he lost his mother, who had been ailing for some time, and on the last day of the year his son Walter died at Calcutta. Much of the time he was able to rest quietly in the country, looking after his little estate, inventing Mrs. Lirriper for his Christmas number and paving the way towards the new novel. This, "a combination," as he told Collins, "of drollery and romance," was begun in the new year, and occupied his attention until the late summer of 1865. He found it a little strange, he said, to be working again with a full canvas, and, to say truth, he had now done his best work. It was not only that his readings had induced a new mood ill-adapted for the production of a sustained piece of work, but there were now signs of deep-rooted physical trouble. Before he had begun to write "Our Mutual Friend," there had been little warnings that all was not right, but he had been able to joke about them.

"Here am I," he told Collins, "with a swelling at the back of my head, and an itching—not palm, but neck. I cannot think the swelling was meant for me, and conceive that it *must* be a mistake." When, too, his left foot swelled up and became so bad as to lead to a permanent lameness and the adoption of a surgical boot, he believed that frost-bite was the cause; but in a little while, when his left eye was also attacked, and his heart became affected, he must have become aware that he was growing old.

Throughout these years he worked doggedly on, fighting against attacks that were becoming increasingly severe, and during a holiday in France managed to regain some of his old robustness; but on his return he was unlucky enough to be one of the passengers in the very serious railway accident at Staplehurst near Maidstone on June 9, 1865, and never wholly recovered from the shock. By some ghastly mistake the train from Folkestone was allowed to pass over a bridge where the line was under repair, "the rails being lifted and an opening of some width made in the soil. Into this gap the train dashed at full speed," and eight of the fourteen carriages were hurled into the muddy stream below. Ten passengers were killed, and double that number frightfully mutilated.

No account of the disaster is clearer than the one Dickens himself gave four days later to Mitton. "I was in the only carriage," he records, "that did not go over into the stream. It was caught upon the turn by some ruin of the bridge, and hung suspended and balanced in an apparently impossible manner. Two ladies were my fellow-passengers, an old one and a young one . . . Suddenly we were off the rail, and beating the ground as the car of a half-emptied balloon might. The old lady cried out, 'My God!' and the young one screamed. I caught hold of them both . . . and said: 'We can't help ourselves, but we can be quiet and composed. Pray don't cry out.' The old lady immediately answered: 'Thank you. Rely upon me. Upon my soul I will be quiet.' We were then all tilted down together in a corner of the carriage, and stopped. . . .

"I got out without the least notion of what had happened. Fortunately I got out with great caution and stood upon the step. Looking down I saw the bridge gone, and nothing below me but the line of rail. Some people in the two other compartments were madly trying to plunge out at windows, and had no idea that there was an open swampy field fifteen feet below them, and nothing else! The two guards (one with his face cut) were running up and down on the down side of the bridge (which was not torn up) quite wildly. I called out to them: 'Look at me. Do stop an instant and look at me, and tell me whether you don't know me.'

"One of them answered: 'We know you very well, Mr. Dickens.'

" 'Then,' I said, 'my good fellow, for God's sake give me your key, and send one of those labourers here, and I'll empty this carriage.' We did it quite safely, by means of a plank or two, and when it was done I saw the rest of the train, except the two baggage vans, down in the stream. I got into the carriage again for my brandy flask, took off my travelling hat for a basin, climbed down the brickwork, and filled my hat with water.

"Suddenly I came upon a staggering man covered with blood (I think he must have been flung clean out of his carriage), with such a frightful cut across the skull that I couldn't bear to look at him. I poured some water over his face and gave him some to drink, then gave him some brandy and laid him down on the grass, and he said, 'I am gone,' and died afterwards. Then I stumbled over a lady lying on her back against a little pollard-tree, with the blood streaming over her face (which was lead colour) in a number of distinct little streams from the head. I asked her if she could swallow a little brandy and she just nodded, and I gave her some and left her for somebody else. The next time I passed her she was dead.

"Then a man . . . came running up to me and implored me to help him find his wife, who was afterwards found dead. No imagination can conceive the ruin of the carriages, or the extraordinary weights under which people were lying, or the complications into which they were twisted up among iron and wood, and mud and water. . . . I have a—I don't know what to call it—constitutional (I suppose) presence of mind, and was not in the least fluttered at the time. I instantly remembered that I had the MS. of a number with me, and clambered back into the carriage for it. But in writing these scanty words of recollection I feel the shake and am obliged to stop."

His eldest son, rushing down to Gad's Hill, found him shocked and shaken. He tells us that while taking his father for a drive in the pony-trap he was constantly bidden to slacken speed. "Slower, slower," Dickens would murmur. . . . Yet in a little while he appeared to be himself again, working "like a dragon," eager to finish his book, delighted to have his friends about him.

What a good time these friends must have had at Gad's Hill! It is not very difficult to imagine yourself in their place.... You receive your invitation: written in very blue ink on very neat paper, with precise instructions about times and trains. A short run from Charing Cross brings you to Higham station, where you will certainly be met. It may be the basket-phaeton, or a smart brougham—a present, this carriage, from Wills—or Dickens himself may have driven over in the jaunting-car he purchased in Ireland during the first of the reading tours. Then away along country lanes, with hop-fields to be seen, to the village with its most respectable ale-house, and so through oak gates up a little semicircular drive to a porch really worthy of the name.

Immediately you are surrounded by dogs, huge beasts, who make a great deal of noise—tramps, you will be told, have always approved of the Kentish roads —but the dogs are well-behaved (all except one, poor Sultan, who has had to be shot) when once you have been formally introduced to them. You look about you, and at once decide that this would be a good place to work in: such a staid old house, you think, and so charmingly irregular. But, as your host will explain, he has been altering the place ever since he gave up Tavistock House, and his daughter is convinced that he will continue to do so as long as he lives.

After you have been shown to your room, you are taken to see everything else: the new drawing-room that has been built on at one side, the pictures, the study with those queer little figures (wrestling toads amongst others) arranged so neatly on the desk—never was there a tidier writer than Dickens—and the absurdly titled books hiding the door, which are no books at all, of course, but mere painted backs, brought, most of them, from Tavistock House.

Then, perhaps, there will be a walk through the gardens, and you will come to the new bricked passage which runs beneath the road and gives access to the shrubbery with its two magnificent cedars and the newly erected chalet, on the other side. A pleasant retreat? Your host is eager to know what you think of it all. But there is much more to be seen, and if you do not know the neighborhood, there must be a pilgrimage at once—on foot. Nothing like a good walk. . . . You find that Dickens certainly knows how to walk, in spite of the trouble with his foot. Indeed, were he not such a good companion, so interested in all that you have to tell him, so jolly and unaffected himself, you might feel inclined to forego any further explorations of the kind.

As it is, you are taken into Cobham Woods, where the dogs play wild games of their own, and to Rochester and Chatham, and perhaps to Gravesend and home by Chalk, where once on a time a chapter or two of "Pickwick" was written. But it may be that there is a cricket match or some festive sports in an adjoining field—Dickens will always be pleased to lend it to the village, though once or twice he has been pained to hear some unseemly language—and then you will be invited to assist and have the opportunity of seeing your host playing amiable tyrant and making sure that everybody is thoroughly enjoying himself. He is a very popular squire indeed.

Perhaps, too, the younger boys are at home, and then there may be croquet on the lawn, or you may be permitted to see the Gad's Hill Gazette being printed on a small hand-press by Master Henry Dickens, its accomplished editor. And later on, sitting at table, with Mamie and Georgina making sure of your comfort, you begin to understand what it is to be given a really good dinner. The host will have brought out his best wines for you, though he drinks very little himself. There will be the cheeriest chatter, and afterwards in the billiard room you may be kept up very late attempting to beat your host at that admirable game. He is not an expert, you find, but a doughty opponent, who fights on very sternly until the last point has been scored. There may be whist, too, and a glass of punch mixed by a master. The jolliest evening. . . .

And as the days pass, you will come to see what a well-ordered household it is. You may be the only guest or one of a fairly large party—it will make no difference: you are made to feel thoroughly at home. Incidentally, of course, you may meet all sorts of well-known people: Wills and his wife; the slightly alarming Forster; Wilkie Collins, rather fat these days, but very amusing; Bulwer Lytton; Charles Kent; Charles Fechter, an Anglo-French actor of little merit, but greatly admired by Dickens to whom he has presented the chalet; young men like Peter Cunningham or Fitzgerald or Yates. You may even have seen some small grandchildren who treat your host without any respect, and apparently believe that "Wenerables" is his only name.

And as the train bears you away, you find yourself in the best of good tempers, and wonder a little at things, for this kindly, boisterous man who has made the hours pass so quickly is not just a man who writes popular novels: he is Dickens, possibly the most famous man in the world. . . .

Charles Dickens reading to his daughters

[4]

"Our Mutual Friend" was finished, and "Doctor Marigold" was being written for the new Christmas number. What was to follow? Dickens began to think of more readings. It would be a strain, and he had had enough of Headland, but he was feeling the call. They tried to dissuade him, and this was all the more necessary because although this autumn he could begin to forget the horrors of Staplehurst his heart was now behaving in an alarming way. But the readings were extraordinarily remunerative, and he wanted to make as much money as he could in the shortest time. He was financially secure, but there were still many calls on his purse. The elder boys were not doing so well as he had hoped.

"This is a pretty state of things!" he wrote at the time to Collins. "That I should be in Christmas Labour, while you are cruising about the world. . . . But I am so undoubtedly one of the sons of Toil—and fathers of children—that I expect to be presently presented with a smock frock, a pair of leather breeches, and a pewter watch, for having brought up the largest family ever known, with the smallest disposition to do anything for themselves."

So, towards the end of the year he allowed it to be known that he would continue his readings, could arrangements be made whereby he would be wholly relieved from business responsibilities. Messrs. Chappell of Bond Street became interested, and made a definite offer. Negotiations took place, and by the end of February, 1866, Dickens had agreed to give thirty readings for a fee of £50 a night, Chappells to find a manager and pay all the expenses, traveling and personal, of

Dickens, his valet, and the very necessary gasman. It was a good offer, and against medical advice—the heart was still misbehaving and specialists had been consulted—it was accepted.

The choice of George Dolby as manager was an excellent one. Dolby had his faults—he died in poverty brought on by overindulgence in drink—but at this time he was not only a good man of business and well accustomed to handle crowds, but knew how to make himself very generally liked. Dickens speedily made friends with him, and in a little while was able to leave everything in his hands. And the new scheme worked well. Before a dozen readings had been given, Chappells had received sufficient money to pay Dickens his £1,500 and all their expenses.

It had been arranged that there should be eight London readings and thirty-two in the provinces, and "Doctor Marigold" was to be the new attraction. There had been no less than two hundred rehearsals in private, and it was deservedly popular. The series began in April in London, and when the time came for the provincial tour, Wills accompanied his chief.

Dickens soon found that he would have to take very good care of himself. We may consider him fortunate in discovering "the best restorative" in "a dozen oysters and a little champagne." In May, however, his eye was paining him again, and Forster and Wills were not the only ones to be relieved when he told them towards the end of the month that he had no idea now of going to America. But he retained his high spirits, and amongst the stories that Dolby tells of the tour is one of Dickens playing clown in Portsmouth. He saw a row of houses that reminded him of a harlequinade scene, and impishly knocked half a dozen times on one of the doors. He was about to lie down on the top step in true pantomime style, when a stout woman opened the door. Whereupon a shocked Wills, an amused Dolby, and Dickens himself took to their heels. A pleasantly unusual affair. . . .

By June all the readings had been given and Dickens went to "Gad's," but they had been so successful that Chappells were eager for more. Dolby went down into Kent to discuss matters, and as a result it was agreed that in 1867 there should be forty-two further readings at £60 a night. There followed a quiet autumn, during which Dickens wrote "Mugby Junction" for his new Christmas number, rehearsed parts of it for a new reading, and helped Fechter to stage a melodrama at the Lyceum Theatre; and in January he once again mounted the platform in London.

The new reading was not a success and was soon omitted from his program, but in all other respects the tour was but a continuation of his triumph. Now, however, there came new and graver symptoms which could not be ignored. There was a fainting fit one evening, and in February he was complaining of "a curious feeling of soreness all round the body." Also he was finding himself uneasy in express trains. Staplehurst was constantly on his lips, Dolby tells us, and for his peace of mind it became necessary for them to travel, when possible, by slow trains.

Wills was no longer his regular companion, but rejoined him for a while at Newcastle, and it must have been then that he became fully aware of the very serious effects that these readings were having on Dickens. The readings themselves may not have been as great a tax on his strength as is sometimes supposed, for every one of them had now been committed to memory, but the incessant traveling, the continual stimulants, the heat and the general excitement—all might well have been hurtful to a far stronger man than was Dickens these days.

But he went on, to Scotland and Ireland (in spite of Fenian scares), and when new offers reached him from America, he did not dismiss them. He knew Forster's views well enough. Forster considered any such venture suicidal; he was extremely doubtful about any large financial profit; and he feared a repetition of the old newspaper attacks. Wills was of much the same opinion. On the other hand, there was Dolby to take all the responsibility on to his own shoulders, and the new offer came from a man, James T. Fields, of most excellent reputation. If only he could be sure of really great sums, he would go.

But could he be sure, in spite of Fields's guarantee? Would there be suitable halls? Did America really want him again? He was obliged to make up his mind without delay, for there was to be a presidential election the next year, and in the end Dolby agreed to spy out the land for him.

At the beginning of August his manager left England (taking with him the manuscript of Dickens's delightful short story "Holiday Romance," which had been sold to Fields for £1,000), and after visiting Boston, New York, and Washington, and meeting a number of influential men, he convinced himself that a tour through the States would not only mean a large fortune but a personal triumph overshadowing even that of 1842. "American Notes" might have led to high words, but that had been twenty-five years ago. He returned to England with glowing accounts of what he had seen. A profit of more than £15,000, he thought, might be forthcoming. There was the greatest enthusiasm at the prospect of seeing the novelist, and he must certainly go.

At the time Dickens was far from well. His foot was rather worse than usual, and the old internal pains, wrongly attributed by himself to gout, had sent him again to the specialist. Sir Henry Thompson was not too happy about his patient. Wills implored him not to endanger his life by crossing the Atlantic at such a time. Forster raged, and swore that the thing must not be. But Dickens had implicit faith in his manager, and on September 29 definitely made up his mind.

"Decide to go," he wrote that day in a brief diary he was keeping at the time, and when Dolby had returned to America for the final arrangements, quietly made his own preparations. He completed his share of "No Thoroughfare," the new Christmas number (and incidentally the last of the series) which he had arranged to write in conjunction with Wilkie Collins, and helped in its dramatization for Fechter. Rumors arose about the critical state of his health, but he would not admit that anything was wrong. "I am perfectly well," he informed the newspapers, "and I have not been ill." A power of attorney was given to Forster, who had now resigned himself to the worst, and Wills was asked to attend to his correspondence. On November 2, there was a great farewell banquet at the Freemason's Tavern, newly decorated for the occasion, and a week later Dickens embarked on the SS. Cuba, once again to meet "a kind, large-hearted, generous and great people" in their own country.

Chapter XIV

THE SECOND AMERICAN VISIT

[1]

THE admirable Dolby, that "gladsome gorilla," as Mark Twain was to call him, rather unkindly, in later years, had made no mistake. There was never the least doubt that America was ready to pay royally for the privilege of listening to Dickens. There was to be no anti-Dickens feeling, no ill-mannered mobbing, and only one serious newspaper attack. The five months spent in the States brought in a net profit of nearly £20,000; and this sum would have been considerably larger had not President Johnson been impeached during the visit, and had not Dickens himself been so shy of American investments and always insisted on gold.

This time, moreover, the visitor was determined that the Americans should have no cause whatever to take offense. At the farewell banquet in London he had chosen his words with care, knowing that they would be telegraphed to New York and so throughout the continent. He had no intention of saying one word in public about international copyright, and no sum on earth should induce him to write any sort of sequel to "American Notes."

He was coming as a showman, in search of a fortune, and no step was to be taken which might militate against his success. And, indeed, as far as he himself was concerned, no such step ever was taken, except in the case of his refusal, an understandable one, to visit

Chicago. Yet he had hardly landed in Boston and been smuggled into his hotel before a problem was presenting itself that even Dolby with all his experience was never able to solve.

It was one of those maddening problems, apparently quite simple, which can never be satisfactorily solved. On the previous day there had been the first of the public sales of tickets, in this case those for the four Boston readings with which the tour was to open in December. It had been widely announced that these tickets could be obtained only at the offices of Messrs. Ticknor & Fields, the publishers who had paid Dickens so handsomely for "early proofs," and throughout the night a queue of people had been steadily growing, until by eight o'clock in the morning it was nearly half a mile long. The sale itself had taken eleven hours, at the end of which time every single ticket had been sold and a sum of $14,000 taken: the greatest possible success.

Almost immediately, however, there had been widespread dissatisfaction: not at the moderate price charged—it had been decided to make a fixed charge of two dollars for every seat, no matter in what part of the hall it might be—but because so many of those who had stood in the queue and obtained the best seats were the agents of cunning speculators, who had bought every ticket they could and were already offering them at a big premium.

The possibility of trouble over the tickets had not been overlooked. Care had been taken to prevent the circulation of forged issues, and it had been arranged that only a limited number of tickets should be sold to any one buyer. But what Dolby had not foreseen was the numbers and enterprise of these speculators, any one of whom might be employing as many as fifty agents. There were enthusiasts, of course, well-used to such dealings, who did not mind what they paid for their tickets, but the general public became angry, and blamed Dolby. What, then, was to be done? The New York sale was almost due, and the same trouble might be expected, probably in a more acute form.

A public auction of all tickets was suggested, but to this Dickens would not agree, though he might have doubled his profits if he had. Dolby went to New York, fearing the worst, and soon found himself "the best-abused man in America." He was attacked and libeled in the press; somebody called him "pudding-headed"; somebody else took the name of "Buz" and published a bellicose pamphlet called "Dolby and Father." Yet he could hardly have done more than he did.

In New York there were extraordinary scenes. All night long an immense queue stood, or sat down, or lay in blankets spread on the pavements. There were songs and dances and an occasional fight. The sale was due to begin at nine o'clock in the morning. Dolby scrutinizing those in the front ranks noted the large number who wore caps. One of his American assistants deduced speculators' representatives. The police were asked to announce that "four tickets only for each reading would be sold to each person, and those only to people in hats."

It was a bright idea, but the "caps" were not to be beaten. Within a few minutes enough hats had been begged, borrowed, or stolen from neighboring hotels and restaurants, and once again the best seats were in the speculators' hands. And from that moment Dolby was followed by the "caps" wherever he went. Dickens himself wrote home in detail of the "amazing scene" in Brooklyn.

"The noble army of speculators are now furnished

(this is literally true, and I am quite serious) each man with a straw mattress, a little bag of bread and meat, two blankets, and a bottle of whisky. With this outfit *they lie down in line on the pavement* the whole of the night before the tickets are sold; generally taking up their position about 10. It being severely cold at Brooklyn, they made an immense bonfire in the street—a narrow street of wooden houses—which the police turned out to extinguish. A general fight then took place; from which the people furthest off in the line rushed bleeding when they saw any chance of ousting others nearer the door, put their mattresses in the spot so gained, and held on by the iron rails.

"At 8 in the morning Dolby appeared with the tickets in a portmanteau. He was immediately saluted with a roar of Halloa! Dolby! So Charley has let you have the carriage, has he, Dolby? How is he, Dolby? Don't drop the tickets, Dolby! Look alive, Dolby! etc. etc. etc., in the midst of which he proceeded to business, and concluded (as usual) by giving universal dissatisfaction."

But it was in New Haven that the worst scenes took place. Dolby had sent an assistant—one of the men who had come out with Dickens from England, and for whom, as it happened, the novelist had conceived a dislike—to conduct the sale there. Without warning came the news not only that there had been serious rioting in the town, but that a meeting of protest had been held with the mayor in the chair, a mayor, too, who had not hesitated to inform his mayoral colleague at Hartford that "the whole thing was a swindle." This gentleman, indeed, bluntly accused Dickens's agent of selling several rows of the best seats privately to the speculators before the sale proper had begun. He admitted that he hated all forms of entertainment, but explained that as he had never even heard the name of Charles Dickens before that day he must be considered to be without personal feeling in the matter.

What, then, had the agent to say? The agent denied any such charge, and affairs were at a deadlock. Dolby was forced to rush off to New Haven, where to his own great chagrin he discovered that the charges were true. His man had been bullied and cajoled and finally bribed into a premature sale, and as a result of the subsequent brawling many arrests had been made.

Dolby attended a second meeting, admitted his agent's guilt—the man was forthwith packed off to England—and, acting under Dickens's instructions, announced that the New Haven readings would be canceled and all money taken returned. This by no means suited some of the protesters, who seem to have done a little speculating themselves, and in the end it was decided not to leave the city entirely "in the cold," and two readings were arranged for a date in March.

These, however, were the troubles of Dolby, not those of his chief, and his ten percent commission on the profits of the tour was good recompense. But they were by no means his only troubles. In England he had promised Forster to take good care of Dickens, and he kept his word, but there came anxious times. The chief might be maintaining his high spirits, he might be enjoying his usual long walks, but there were warning signs. A severe cold would not be banished. There were fainting fits, and further trouble in the foot.

So in addition to being secretary and manager, the "pudding-headed" man was obliged to play nurse as well. (How devotedly he played it Dickens always acknowledged.) On many occasions it seemed impossible that the sick man on the sofa could be reading with his accustomed vigor within two or three hours.

*A photograph of Dickens taken in
1869 and hitherto unpublished
From the collection of Charles J. Sawyer*

There came moments when Dolby would not have been surprised to see the chief collapse on his platform. In the States there never was such a collapse, and no reading there was ever postponed on account of illness, but the manager knew well enough the risks that were being run. America might be producing a fortune, but she was also exacting her price, and it was the price that both Forster and Wills had feared.

[2]

"These winter crossings," Dickens had written on his arrival in Boston, "are very trying and startling." He had, it is true, suffered from headaches on board, and his foot was giving him trouble, but, unlike his machinist, Kelly, he had not been sick, and during the ten days' voyage was fairly comfortable. Scott, his valet, or "dresser" as he preferred to call him, "was always cheerful and ready," and even the captain, rather a morose fellow, it would seem, responded to his banter.

The Cuba reached Boston on November 19, a fortnight before the date fixed for the first reading. A short time for acclimatization had been considered advisable, but once in his hotel, the Parker House, Dickens would have preferred to "open" without delay. He disliked the long wait. But at least there were no misgivings now. The tickets were selling, he was the "sensation" of the day; and when America came to understand that he was not proposing merely to read out of a book but to provide such an entertainment as had never been given in the country before, she, like England, would be at his feet.

The fortnight's vacation was not without its compensations. There were old friendships to be renewed, new ones to be made. James Fields and his wife, in particular, saw to it that the quiet program arranged for him was sufficiently varied. A number of his old friends were gone—Felton and Irving and Prescott among them—but there was Longfellow to see, and Holmes and Dana and Emerson were all alive.

He met Agassiz, the naturalist, who had married a sister of Felton, and liked him. He was delighted when Putnam, his old secretary, called to see him. There were little dinners out at Cambridge, and incognito visits to the theaters.

Fortunately, too, his desire for privacy was respected. His own men kept watch all the time outside the door of his suite, but their services were seldom required. He could walk out of the hotel by a private door, and though people might stare at him in the streets, he was never molested. So there came explorations of the city, which had grown so large since 1842—it was "like Leeds," he thought, "mixed with Preston, and flavoured with New Brighton"—and inspections of the Tremont Temple where he was to read, and final rehearsals.

And on that Monday night when all Boston drove to the not very fashionable hall Dolby had chosen, he had what was possibly the most magnificent reception yet accorded him. He read the "Carol" and the Trial from "Pickwick," and the cheering at the end of the first piece was so prolonged that he was obliged to break a rule and "take his call."

One little incident may be recorded. While dressing in his hotel before the reading he had been touched to find laid out with his clothes a buttonhole such as he had been accustomed to wear in England. This was the gift of his old friend Mary Boyle, who had arranged with a Boston florist for its regular appearance. It was a thoughtful act which was very far from deserving the ill-natured jibe which appeared in the Boston Post a month later. A local lady, it seems, had also sent the novelist a small bouquet which had been "returned with the thanks of the recipient and the announcement that a lady of London supplied him with flowers not only in England but America."

The Boston Post printed this item of news, but also took occasion to see more in the little attention than was there. "Oh, Charles," it cried out, "at your age, and with that bald head and that gray goatee!" Dickens, however, could afford to laugh at such "smartness," for he was soon earning for himself considerably more than £1,000 a week, and knew that nothing except a political upheaval or the loss of his strength could interfere with his success.

Until the end of the year he was either in Boston or New York, reading on the average four times a week and refusing all purely social invitations. One day, indeed, was much like another. Occasionally, of course, there came something droll or unexpected. A fire in his New York hotel alarmed his valet but nobody else: they were used to fires. A dissatisfied Pickwickian after listening to Dickens one evening considered that Sam Weller's inventor knew nothing about Sam Weller, and said so: but he was in a minority of one. Would-be pirates made their appearance, but were forestalled by Fields arranging to issue printed versions of the readings at a price which could hardly be rivaled. There was a night visit to a New York police station, where an album of thieves' portraits fascinated Dickens so much that he could hardly bring himself to close it.

There was also an amusing conflict with the law. A man who considered himself injured in the matter of tickets brought an action against the reader; but the marshal who presented the writ, or whatever it was, was not proof against the novelist's courtesy or, indeed, against his champagne, and the affair ended in a general jollification. Once, too, there was trouble with the ushers at Steinway Hall, New York—Dolby could be high-handed on occasion—and they walked out in a body before one of the readings; but an American audience has small need of ushers, and there was no disorder. The autograph-hunters, as before, were a nuisance, and it was necessary to engage three clerks to post off polite but printed refusals to comply with "even so modest a request."

For his own convenience Dickens hired a carriage and pair in New York, though when the snow came, he changed it for a sleigh. Already, however, he was beginning to feel the effects of the American climate. It was bitterly cold, and he was not used to hot rooms with all the windows shut. He caught a cold which refused to leave him. It turned itself into a "true American catarrh": some sort of influenza, I suppose. He tried various remedies, including a "Rocky Mountain Sneezer" prescribed by a solicitous hotel manager. Finally he was obliged to consult a doctor, Fordyce Barker by name, who happened to be a friend of his own friends the Oliffes. Whole days were spent on a couch, yet when the evening came he would make the required effort, and not a member of his audience would know how anxiously Dolby was watching at the side of the platform for the least sign of distress. . . .

He spent an old-fashioned Christmas in Boston with Fields and his wife, but was back in New York for the New Year, eager to have his future plans definitely fixed, but well content to watch Dolby "going about with an immense bundle that looks like a soft-cushion, but is in reality paper-money"—a cushion, he was pleased to report, which "had risen to the proportions of a sofa," on the day when the manager left him to play advance agent in Philadelphia.

And at the readings themselves one triumph followed another. In New York the "Carol" and the Trial from "Pickwick" were hardly more popular than "Doctor Marigold." "The people doubted at first," he wrote home, "having evidently not the least idea what could be done with it, and broke out at last into a perfect chorus of delight." He came to Philadelphia, and after that staid city had recovered from its surprise at "Mr. Dickens's extraordinary composure"—it had apparently expected a brass band at least to introduce him —it was no less appreciative than Boston or New York. His personal appearance had given many a reporter a chance to display considerable skill, and he had been variously likened to Louis Napoleon, the Emperor of China, and several local celebrities; but in Philadelphia he was paid the signal compliment of being likened to "a well-to-do Philadelphian gentleman."

He returned to New York to read over in Brooklyn, where the only available hall was a huge chapel: a celebrated meeting-house, however, for its pastor was Henry Ward Beecher. "We let the seats by pews," Dickens gleefully recorded. "The pulpit is taken down for my screen and gas! and I appear out of the vestry in canonical form!" But the "ecclesiastical entertainments" were no less successful than the others, in spite of a little misunderstanding on the first night over a gallery that was usually reserved for colored people.

By this time £10,000 had been remitted to London, as the result of thirty-four readings, and it became necessary to make final plans for the rest of the tour. There were to be farewell series of readings in both New York and Boston in April, but how much work could he undertake in the interval? The catarrh showed no signs of going, and the exhaustion after the readings was not becoming less. It was decided that all idea of a tour in Canada and the West must be abandoned. Small towns, moreover, could not be considered. Horace Greeley, the editor of the Tribune, even advised against Washington, which, he thought, would be found full of rowdies, but Dolby had reconnoitered and brought in a favorable report, and Washington was included in the program.

On the other hand, Chicago was deliberately omitted, not on account of its geographical position, but for a painful family reason. Once upon a time Augustus Dickens had been the favorite brother. It was he, you remember, who had been nicknamed Moses, and called himself Boses, and so given rise to "Boz." But for long years his name had rarely been mentioned in the family. Like his brother Frederick he had made a mess of things, and Dickens had lost all patience with him. For some time he had been living very humbly in Chicago. I fancy that he had only recently died.

The local newspapers "discovered" that his widow was living in the greatest poverty, and raised a howl of indignation. Here in their city was the great novelist's sister-in-law practically starving, and the great novelist refused to help her! What were they to say of a man who was taking large sums of money out of the country and yet could not spare a dollar for his own kith and kin? It certainly seemed rather odd. The comments became more bitter in tone, and once again Dickens issued a personal statement. It was short enough. It merely announced the fact that for some time past he had been helping to support the only genuine Mrs. Augustus Dickens, who was living in England. Whereat the indignation died down. But there were no readings in Chicago. . . .

The tour continued. In Brooklyn he had read in a chapel; in Baltimore he was in more congenial surroundings on the stage of the opera-house. This was the first of the Southern cities to be visited, and he fancied that it was still wearing "a look of sullen remembrance" of the war. He was naturally interested in the recently freed slaves, but was not optimistic about their future. The race, he thought, "must fade out of the States very fast."

At the beginning of February he was in Washington. Here on the advice of a resident Englishman who could find no good word to say of the hotels, he hid himself in rooms over a small German restaurant for his few days' stay. The hall where he read was small, and the price of a seat had been raised to three dollars. There were brilliant gatherings, with President Johnson reserving an entire row for each reading and all the ambassadorial staffs.

The President himself came to every reading, and a small dog endeavored to follow his good example: a literary-minded beast, it would seem, who on the first night took up a position in the center of the hall and gazed intently at the reader. Exercising the usual canine privilege he moved about once or twice, but continued to stare at the chief figure. Dickens saw him, and was not surprised when at a moment of extreme comicality the intruder barked out his appreciation. Dickens could not restrain his laughter, and his audience laughed with him, but when the small beast arrived on the following evening and ventured nearer to the platform, he was unceremoniously thrown out. He made a third attempt at the next reading, and this time brought another dog with him, presumably for protection; but the staff was on the lookout, and he "didn't get in." . . .

On his birthday Dickens went to the White House—

the President had bidden him choose his own time—
and he broke a rule by dining with his old friend
Charles Sumner. The catarrh, however, had become
worse, he was now suffering from insomnia, and he
could no longer take proper food. Calling at the little
restaurant one day, Sumner was shocked to find him
"covered with mustard poultice, and apparently voice-
less," and wondered that Dolby could possibly be
allowing him to read the same evening. But, as the
manager pointed out, it was hardly a question of permission.

The same thing would happen day after day: long
painful hours on a sofa, a very sick man, and then,
on the platform, miraculously, a robust and tireless
figure, yet there were times when he was considerably
better, and Dolby and James Osgood, a member of the
Fields publishing house who was acting as general
treasurer on the tour, would go to great lengths to amuse
him. It was for this reason that the great walking-
match between them at Boston—it must have considerably startled the natives—was arranged.

It was while the two men were training for this
mock-heroic affair, news of which, of course, had fil-
tered through to the newspaper offices, that all America's attention was directed to President Johnson. A
motion for his impeachment on account of his dismissal
of the Secretary of War without the consent of the
Senate had been passed by the House of Representatives, and nobody could think of anything else. Dickens
was immediately made aware of the effect on his audiences, and decided to cancel all readings for the following week.

But before this unexpected and not unwelcome holiday came he was busying himself with the preparations
for the great match. He and Fields examined the

course—thirteen miles of terrible, snow-covered roads. The stakes were to be four hats, which were to be presented to the winner at a banquet that Dickens proposed to give immediately afterwards.

An amusing business, but also a very wise move on Dolby's part. By this time he knew the sort of man Dickens was. He knew well enough the kind of diversion most likely to remove his growing depression. So, indeed, it was. The match took Dickens out of himself. He must have enjoyed drawing up the absurd Articles of Agreement between the Man of Ross and the Boston Bantam. He must have relished the sight of Dolby pounding on through the slush. He must have delighted in the very serious debate, which took place after Dolby had been beaten by a good half-mile, as to whether the winner ought not to be disqualified for having allowed Mrs. Fields to put bread soaked in brandy into his mouth during the contest. And he certainly enjoyed himself at the banquet that followed, when the wine seems to have flowed very freely indeed.

The walking-match took place on February 29, and it undoubtedly achieved its purpose. It allowed Dickens to enjoy his week's holiday. There was a little round of gaiety. He dined with Mrs. Fields. He gave a dinner party at his own hotel—a hilarious evening, Fields tells us, when a mock political election was held, with Dolby as Dickens's candidate and the novelist shouting his merits in the most professional manner. He gave an audience to an eleven-year-old schoolboy who knew and loved all his books. Samuel Howe, whose splendid work for the blind he had first heard of during the 1842 visit, invited him to present a copy of one of his books printed in raised type to his institution; he put at the good doctor's disposal a sum sufficient to have 250 copies of "The Old Curiosity Shop" so printed.

He dined out at Cambridge with Longfellow, and was shown the University Press and indeed so many other things that on his last visit to Mrs. Fields's house he threatened to hate anybody who showed him anything else. It was fitting that at that moment his host should walk in and invite him to inspect his new fruit-house. . . . But that jolly week was the last of its kind, and in a very short while, even with the best will in the world, Dickens was finding it impossible to continue without the aid of the strongest stimulants, not excluding drugs.

[3]

Longfellow had seen what was happening, and urged him to give in. Already a small fortune had been sent home; why run further risk? But your good showman does not disappoint his public, and, braving the long railway journeys which were now so "alarming" to him, Dickens went on.

During the first half of March he read in Syracuse, Rochester, and Buffalo. He saw Niagara again, and in spite of the suspension bridge found new glories in it. Then with considerable relief he turned eastwards to read in Albany, Worcester, Hartford, and New Bedford. Yet, although his letters remained cheery and although he could bring himself to sign a contract with Chappells for yet another series of readings at home, he was very seriously ill most of the time: worse, perhaps, than ever his own staff realized.

"However sympathetic and devoted the people are about me," he told his daughter, "they *can not* be got to comprehend that one's being able to do the two hours with spirit when the time comes round, may be coexistent with the consciousness of great depression and fatigue. I don't mind saying this, now that the labour is so nearly over."

When he wrote in this way continual insomnia had affected his nerves, his foot was painful, the catarrh was worse, and he could hardly bring himself to touch solid food. An examination of his daily menu illustrates well enough his condition. At an early hour a tumbler of new cream with two tablespoonfuls of rum would be brought to him in bed. At noon there would be a sherry-cobbler and a biscuit or two. His dinner at three would generally consist of little more than a pint of champagne. An egg beaten in sherry enabled him to reach the hall, and a cup of the strongest beef-tea helped him to revive after the first part of his entertainment. Finally for supper there would be a little soup and any drink that he fancied. What a menu for a man who had long been accustomed to do himself well—too well, some people had said! But the day came when even "spirits and spirit" would not bring him to the mark, and you are not altogether surprised to find him taking laudanum in Portland. . . .

Fortunately there were only the farewell readings to follow, and somehow he managed to give them. The political crisis interfered to some extent with their success, but not nearly so greatly as some of his friends had feared. On his return to Boston he was seen to be very lame, and Dolby was obliged to assist him onto the platform; but once there he read as well as ever he had in his life, and, knowing that Mrs. Fields and her husband were present, "gagged" freely for their benefit.

In the days that followed it became generally known how ill he was, and as a mark of sympathy his reading-table was decorated with flowers. Then came the last of the Boston readings, and after it was finished and during the tumultuous applause he returned to the platform to make a little speech of farewell. Reading it today one sees how exactly right it was.

They had wanted to give him a farewell banquet in Boston, but he was too unwell to attend any such function. Some time before, however, he had accepted an invitation to dine with the press in New York, and this engagement he was determined to keep. At this banquet, held at Delmonico's on April 18, two hundred newspaper men were present, and it was possibly the most magnificent gathering of the kind ever seen in the city. But it was only with great difficulty that he was able to reach the banqueting-hall. Three times that week he had read, and he was almost unable to move.

The dinner was to have begun at five o'clock, but at that hour no Dickens had appeared. They knew that he was ill, but patiently waited on, and at six o'clock their guest limped painfully in on Horace Greeley's arm. These were colleagues of his, and he was not going to disappoint them. So he sat there, on Greeley's right, and listened to the toast of the evening, and prepared himself to make some sort of reply.

And even he must have been affected by the warmth of his reception when he rose from his chair. They cheered him again and again, and as always happened on such occasions the foot and the cough and the nervous depression straightway disappeared. He stood erect before them, and there was the old light in his eye and the old robust note in his voice. Taking his cue from some words of the chairman, he spoke of the old Fleet Street days.

"To the wholesome training of severe newspaper work," he told them, "when I was a very young man, I constantly refer my first successes, and my sons will hereafter testify of their father that he was always

Charles Dickens's last reading, 1870
From an old print

steadily proud of that ladder by which he rose. If it were otherwise," he added slyly after the applause had died down, "I should have but a very poor opinion of their father, which, perhaps, on the whole I have not." He spoke, of course, of that "true American catarrh," about which he was always ready to joke. He had highly appreciated it, but would have "preferred to be naturalized by any other outward and visible signs."

After mentioning the great changes in the country since his former visit, he spoke of his own reception. They had welcomed him, he said, "with unsurpassable politeness, delicacy, sweet temper, hospitality, consideration, and with unsurpassed respect for the privacy daily enforced upon me by the nature of my avocation here and the state of my health." And there followed the well-known passage which is always quoted when Dickens's relations with America are being discussed.

"This testimony, so long as I live, and so long as my descendants have any right in my books, I shall cause to be republished as an appendix to every copy of those two books of mine in which I have referred to America. And this I will do and cause to be done, not in mere love and thankfulness, but because I regard it as an act of plain justice and honour."

They cheered him for his promise, which was faithfully kept, and they cheered him again for a peroration on Anglo-American relations which probably had more effect than a dozen ministerial speeches. "Points of difference there have been, points of difference there are. Points of difference there probably will be between the two great peoples. But broadcast in England is sown the sentiment that these two peoples are essentially one, and that it rests with them jointly to uphold the great Anglo-Saxon race. . . . If I know anything of my countrymen—and they give me credit of knowing something ... the English heart is stirred by the fluttering of those stars and stripes as it is stirred by no other flag that flies except their own."

He sat down, and listened to a few of the speeches that followed, but now that he had delivered his message and given America his thanks, he was a sick man again. The pain had returned. He begged to be allowed to slip out unnoticed. Greeley rose to explain. They gave their guest a last three cheers, and he was helped into his carriage. On the 20th he gave his last reading in a final blaze of triumph, and two days later stepped on board the Russia, having done what he said he would do: an exhausted, but wealthy, old man.

It should be added that Dolby's troubles pursued him to the end. Some bumptious official in the New York branch of the Inland Revenue Department was making trouble about the non-payment of income-tax. According to law, Dickens was quite distinctly immune from such tax, and had papers from the head of the department to say so; but the New York official, for very good reasons of his own, preferred to act on his own authority, and finding that no money was forthcoming, threatened to arrest Dolby as a hostage. This led to the unfortunate man being smuggled on board, and, absurdly enough, being guarded by detectives under orders from the superior authorities against those who were obeying the New York official.

The superior authorities carried the day. Dickens, I fancy, must have enjoyed the joke.

Chapter XV

"From These Garish Lights...."

[1]

THE Russia, according to Dickens, was "a magnificent ship," and the weather was kind. The sun shone down. In a day or two the tired man was experiencing the good effects of a sea voyage under ideal conditions. Once again he could take an interest in the menu and enjoy his meals. He was able to put on his boots. The "true American catarrh" showed a welcome unwillingness to stray too far from its native shores. Rapidly he began to mend.

Some misguided idiot came to his cabin to ask for a reading on board, and was very properly snubbed. Readings, forsooth, when he was able to enjoy the breeze and eat and sleep and "laze" when the inclination came! It was quite enough that he had pledged himself to read again in the autumn. No, he was going to make the most of his holiday, more especially as it would probably not be a long one. Wills had met with a hunting accident, and although few details as yet had been forthcoming about it, there seemed little doubt that most of the work in Wellington Street would devolve on his chief.

Then there was the dramatic version of "No Thoroughfare" at the Adelphi. Apparently it was enjoying a success, but there were points about the production that did not meet with Dickens's whole-hearted approval, and he would have to attend to them himself. In addition, Fechter was talking about a French version for Paris, and it might be well to supervise matters there. Also there would be the unexpected work to be done for Chauncey Hare Townshend, a very old and rather odd friend of his who had died during the American visit. Townshend had left him £1,000, appointed him his literary executor, and begged him to publish a mass of notes he had left, representing his "Religious Opinions." . . . And so he rested, and allowed the sun to tan him, and when he parted from Dolby at Euston—as though, he said, they had been away together for no more than a night or two—he was for the time being a new man.

There had been nobody to meet him in Liverpool or at Euston, but his daughter had warned him that the Higham villagers were making all manner of preparations, and to avoid their attentions he returned home by Gravesend. Once there he found that he had not been mistaken. Wills was suffering from concussion, and quite conceivably would be obliged to retire altogether from All the Year Round. The Townshend papers were as bulky as they were uninteresting, and Fechter had chosen this moment to be ill.

All of these meant fairly strenuous days. But there was no rushing about from town to town every twenty-four hours, and there was no terrific strain in the evenings. He divided his week between London and Gad's Hill, generally returning to the country for the week-end. He settled the details of his farewell readings—there were to be a hundred of them at £80 a night—and he went to Paris for the French production; but he was soon back, busily endeavoring to master the financial as well as the literary side of his paper, of entertaining his friends, Longfellow among them, at Gad's Hill.

It was now that those who knew him best became anxious again, for there was trouble in both his feet, and for the first time his vision was affected in an ominous way. Forster had been shocked at the change that America had produced, and made yet another attempt to dissuade him from reading. So far, however, from being able to turn him from his purpose, he was mortified to learn that Dickens was still playing with the idea of making a new and "passionate" reading from the murder in "Oliver Twist"—a novelty he opposed both for its "unsuitable" nature and for the enormous strain to which it must subject the reader.

There followed "a painful correspondence" between the two men, and there is no question that in the last two years of Dickens's life, Forster was no longer the first amongst his friends. He was still consulted on all business matters, his good qualities were still freely acknowledged, but more than a little of the old intimacy was gone. In a letter written in the following year to his sister-in-law Dickens showed clearly his resentment.

"God forgive me," he wrote, "but I cannot get over the mania for proprietorship which is rampant in Palace Gate House," where Forster was then living. And, indeed, his attitude is not difficult to understand. For so long a time had Forster found his advice being taken as a matter of course that when this was no longer so, there was bound to come a coolness if no actual rupture. . . .

Meanwhile there were family matters, not very happy, to occupy Dickens's attention. The "noble Plorn" of a few years ago seemed unable to find anything to do in England. It was thought advisable that

he should join his brother Alfred, who was sheep
farming in Australia, and in September he sailed, much
to his father's regret. In the following month Frederick Dickens died in Darlington, and in spite of all
the trouble he had caused—like his brother Augustus
he had had matrimonial as well as financial worries—
Dickens felt his loss. "A wasted life," he told Forster,
"but God forbid that one should be hard upon it, or
upon anything in this world that is not deliberately
and coldly wrong."

At this time, too, it seems, his son Sydney showed
signs of following in his grandfather's financial footsteps. Apparently he was doing well in the navy, but
there are letters in existence to show that he was no
longer welcome at home. On the other hand, Henry
was doing exceedingly well at Cambridge, and it was
hoped that the future common sergeant would add a
fellowship to the honors he had already obtained.

Then, at the beginning of October, 1868, the fatal
farewell readings began.

[2]

Undoubtedly Dickens was excited at the prospect.
For all his American hardships, the platform had lost
little of its fascination for him. Once again the faithful Scott became his dresser; once again Dolby, now
free of all ticket troubles, arranged matters so that the
chief should be as comfortable as possible. And both
London and the provinces showed that the name of
Dickens had lost none of its magic. The halls were
crowded, the audiences enthusiastic.

In November there was a general election, and no
readings, except one or two in London, were given,
but Dickens utilized the occasion to give a trial read-

ing of the Nancy murder before a select audience of his own friends, a few well-known critics and a small number of pressmen. This took place at the St. James's Hall on November 14. Forster was not alone in opposing the new "sensation," for Dolby was also afraid lest the exertions it entailed might be too great; and after the reading had been given, and Dickens came down into the body of the hall to hear what people had to say, there was no unanimity.

Some of the ladies considered it too horrible. One well-known man confessed that he had had an almost irresistible desire to scream. A physician prophesied unfortunate scenes if even one woman in the audience were to cry out at the moment of the actual murder. On the other hand, a distinguished actress was convinced that it would be immensely successful, and the Chappells themselves agreed with her. Dickens listened to the various verdicts, and promised to consider them, but during the champagne and oyster supper that he had provided for his guests at the back of the platform, I fancy that he must have made up his mind not to give up the new reading without a struggle. It was finally agreed that two trial readings should be given in public at the New Year, and in the event of their being a success, the murder was to become a regular feature of his program.

The murder was duly read in London on January 5, and its success was never in doubt. "The crime being completely off my mind," he told Mary Boyle the next morning, "and the blood spilled, I am (like many of my fellow criminals) in a highly edifying state today." But those who had feared hysterical scenes were not disappointed. At Clifton later on in the month people screamed and fainted in the most satisfactory way. "I should think we had a dozen or twenty ladies taken out stiff and rigid, at various times. It became quite ridiculous."

Dickens could write in this way, but the new reading was far from being ridiculous in its effect on himself. It was essential that he should be worked up into something like an hysterical state himself. This happened, and, as Dolby had feared, he suffered for it. The murder of Nancy, indeed, did more than anything else to sap his waning powers of resistance. Moreover, seeing the effect it was having upon his audiences, he deliberately set out to increase its horrors, and, closing his eyes to the additional risks he was running, persisted in reading it night after night.

Dolby could do nothing to stop him, and became exceedingly anxious. Five readings had been given in Ireland, and they had been hugely successful, but there had been an alarming, though luckily harmless, mishap in a train, and Dickens's fears had in part returned. A jolly evening in Cheltenham with Macready, now old and enfeebled and choosing to think himself entirely forgotten, and a day or two spent at Ross as Dolby's guest, had considerably cheered him; but barely a fortnight after their return to London there came the first ominous check.

This was on February 16, 1869. Dickens was to have read that night in the St. James's Hall, but in the morning he was in great agony with his foot. His own doctor, Carr Beard, summoned Sir Henry Thompson. They forbade him to read and would not even consider the possibility of his traveling to Scotland, as he had intended to do, the next morning. Dickens was greatly upset, not least on Chappells' account, but he could not disobey such positive orders as the doctors had given.

Dolby rushed north to postpone the Glasgow readings, which had been arranged for the following week, and found the greatest excitement both there and in Edinburgh. By this time most people had heard of the extraordinary nature of the Sikes impersonation, and were eager to see it; and when it was known that the novelist was ill the excitement increased. Fortunately better reports were soon forthcoming, and on the 20th Dickens was well enough to travel with one of the Chappells to Edinburg, where he managed to read. But after the "Murder" had been given, he was utterly prostrate, and the next morning sent for James Syme, one of the most famous surgeons of his day.

Syme told him bluntly that only a complete rest could restore him to health. Dickens, however, was determined to go on. Dolby implored him at least to omit the "Murder"—he was now proposing to read it three times a week—at all towns except the largest: he met with an angry refusal. In a little while, however, Dickens was forced to see that the manager's advice was good. He apologized for his burst of temper, excusable enough in his present state, and amended his program. But even so it seemed that everything was conspiring to tax his strength.

In Manchester he heard of the death of another old friend, Sir James Tennent, and was urged to attend the funeral in London. He hated funerals, but could not bring himself to refuse the request. Yet it was only with the greatest difficulty that he managed to be present. On the evening before the funeral he was reading in York. He was obliged to rush straight from the platform to the train. Dolby and the stationmaster between them had done all that was possible for his comfort. In a special carriage Scott was waiting to give him the usual "rubdown," and his traveling clothes were laid out. A supper was waiting for him, and he slept for several hours, but he was unnerved again, and at the funeral next morning Forster found him "dazed and worn."

There was also the strain of his Liverpool visit. He was delighted to read in a theater, old and disused though it was, but there was also to be a great banquet in his honor at the conclusion of his readings in the town, and it was not too satisfactorily arranged. Six hundred people were to attend, and the only hall capable of seating that number was singularly ill-suited for the purpose. Dickens interested himself in the preparations, and made suggestions for their betterment, but for some reason they were not adopted.

The evening itself was a splendid success, but the proceedings were far too long. One speech followed another: Dickens himself being called on to speak three times. One wonders, by the way, whether Sala, who was also amongst the speakers that night, was sober for the occasion.

"I hear," Dickens had written earlier in the week, "that Anthony Trollope, Dixon, Lord Houghton, Lemon, and Sala are to be called on to speak, the last for the newspaper press. As he is certain to be drunk, I am in great hesitation whether or no I should warn the innocent committee."

And then, a week later, the dreadful suspicion which for some time now had been distressing his closest friends became a certainty. There had been the usual four readings in smoky Lancashire towns, and Dolby suggested Chester as an agreeable place for a quiet week-end. They went to Chester, and that night a new symptom made its appearance of such a character that even Dickens was alarmed.

On the Sunday they drove out to Mold for the sake of the air. The chief, Dolby tells us, seemed greatly depressed. He talked of this new trouble, and for the first time appeared to be doubtful of the future. Were it not for Chappells, he said, he could almost persuade himself to give in at once. Dolby, hardly disguising his relief, was in favor of an immediate abandonment. Chappells, he declared, would understand. Dickens, still perhaps trying not to believe, still fighting hard, resolved to leave the final decision to Carr Beard. He fell asleep on the homeward drive, and that evening wrote in detail to his doctor.

Two or three days later they were in Preston. They had arrived from Blackpool at midday. There had been no reply from Beard, but it came that afternoon. The doctor was already on his way north. His train was late, and it was not until five o'clock that Dolby heard his report. If Dickens were to read that night he would probably go through life "dragging a foot after him."

Paralysis; the left side in danger; apoplexy likely to occur at any moment. There was only one mode of treatment: immediate and absolute rest.

"My weakness and deadness," wrote a tearful Dickens that day, "are all in the left side; and if I don't look at anything I try to touch with my left hand, I don't know where it is." He told his daughter not to be alarmed, but, indeed, there was good cause for alarm. As usual, however, Dolby took instant command. There were only two hours before the doors of the hall where the reading was to have taken place would be open: no matter. If the doctor would take Dickens to Liverpool at once, he would be able to deal with the situation, and deal with it he did like the good man he was. There was no reading that night, or ever again in Preston, but there was no disturbance. . . .

In London Sir Thomas Watson was called into consultation. He confirmed Beard's opinion. A medical certificate was issued. There were to be no more readings for several months.

So Dickens returned, for the last time, from "the road."

[3]

He went to Gad's Hill, and in a little while seemed, to those who did not know him well, to have wholly recovered. It had been dreadful to him that he should be "owing" Chappells twenty-five readings, but a letter from the head of the firm, graciously sympathetic and insisting on his freeing himself from all worry on their account, allowed him to take full advantage of the rest. He was delighted, too, when in a few weeks' time Sir Thomas Watson saw no reason why he should not give a final series of twelve readings at the end of the year in London.

And so in a brighter mood he turned his attention to his other, less nerve-racking work. He took rooms in the St. James's Hotel, Piccadilly, in May, to keep in touch at once with his doctors and All the Year Round, and when it became clear that Wills would never be coming back to the paper, he put his eldest son into the vacant post. At the same time he began to think about a new book, though for a month or two he refused to worry too much about it. Instead, he enjoyed the unaccustomed leisure, going to the theaters, entertaining his friends, waiting patiently for the day when Watson would permit Dolby to make arrangement for the last readings.

In the summer, too, James Fields and his wife arrived in London, and he busied himself arranging for them a most elaborate program. The Boston publisher was shown London by the man who of all others probably knew it best. Together they carried out a series of explorations such as had always appealed to Dickens. An excited Fields was shown the room in Furnival's Inn where much of "Pickwick" had been written; he was taken to the docks; he was smuggled into an opium den which in a few months' time he was to see described in print. And then, when he and his wife and a few American friends were taken down into Kent, they were shown a bit of old England by a guide who stood in a class by himself. Dickens, indeed, could not do too much for his visitors. Like the good showman he was, he even found two post-carriages for them, complete with postillions in the red jackets and buckskin breeches of long ago. The merriest days . . .

Then in August came an idea for the new book. It was to be a new sort of crime-story, a mysterious business in which even Wilkie Collins, that master of plot, might find himself beaten at his own game. The idea grew. It became necessary to see Chapman & Hall. He was proposing, he told them, to write a new serial story, which would fill twelve monthly numbers. A title had already been found. And so that autumn a contract was signed for the publication of "The Mystery of Edwin Drood."

It is little wonder that Dolby was startled at the terms, for never before, I should think, had such an amount been paid for a work of fiction. The sum of £7,500 was to be paid for the copyright, and all profits after the first twenty-five thousand copies had been sold were to be equally divided. There were, of course, several clauses in the agreement. At the last moment Dickens himself suggested another. If he were to die during the composition of the work or be unable for any reason to complete it, part of the money already paid was to be returned to the publishers. An arbitrator must therefore be appointed to decide on the proper amount to be paid back. Chapman & Hall could not but agree, and Forster was invited to act in the matter.

So for the last time you see Dickens sitting down at his desk to write a novel. At the end of September he had gone to Birmingham to open a new session at the Midland Institute, but this was his only public engagement before the end of the year. Watson had now given permission for the readings to begin in January, and Dickens was naturally eager to have at least two or three numbers ready before Christmas.

He worked hard at the little chalet across the road, and by the third week in October had finished the first number. It was good work, he knew, but it had not been produced without effort, and he could not remain blind to the fact that hard work of any kind now meant a recurrence of his old ills. Once again his foot had become painful; once again there were giddy attacks. And as the time approached for the readings his pleasure at the idea of mounting the platform became mixed with a vague anxiety. Could he manage the series? There were to be no train journeys, and after January there was to be only one reading a week. Even so, the strain would be great. He said nothing to his friends, for they would do their best to dissuade him, and he was determined to make what reparation he could to Chappells. But he did consult Beard, who decided to be present at each of the readings in case his help should be wanted.

He spent a quiet Christmas at home. On January 6 he was at Birmingham again at a prize-giving. Then with a growing excitement he prepared himself for the 11th, when the first of the readings was to be given.

Dickens and Disraeli
From the Tailor and Cutter, 1870

He had taken a London house near the Marble Arch, and a few minutes' drive would bring him to the St. James's Hall. He knew now that he was to have a success no less than the others, for all the tickets had been sold, and thousands of people were clamoring for more.

There was a particular reason, moreover, for his excitement. A year ago some professional actors had written to him asking for a morning reading to which they could come. He had immediately arranged for three to be given in May, but they had had to be postponed. Now, these professionals were to be given the opportunity of seeing what he could do in their own art without the aid of make-up or scenery, and he was determined that they should have no cause for disappointment. . . .

The 11th came, and there was a repetition of the old tumultuous scenes. He read to "the profession," and their unstinted applause was a final tribute to his powers. But as the days passed, those about him became increasingly anxious. At the end of January his left arm was in a sling. His eldest son noticed that he was making mistakes with his words: even Mr. Pickwick's name was not right. And in his little room at the back of the hall there would be times when it seemed that he would have to break off after the first half of his program. This time, however, there was no postponement, though as that last Tuesday, March 15, came nearer "his feverish excitement and his bodily pain increased." And when he was driven to the St. James's Hall for the last time, you can well imagine his feelings.

On more than four hundred occasions he had given these professional readings, and now he had come to the end. He was dreading the ordeal—not of the readings themselves but of the painful scene at the end when they would expect him to make a farewell speech. But it would have to be done, and he braced himself for the effort.

Nobody who was present on that memorable occasion could ever forget it. There was the greatest excitement. Huge crowds were waiting in the streets to watch his arrival, and somehow or other two thousand people had squeezed themselves into the hall. The "Carol" and the Trial from "Pickwick" had been chosen, and when Dickens, extremely agitated, walked onto the platform all that huge audience rose to its feet and cheered him unceasingly for several minutes.

It was, as Dolby says, his crowning triumph. And that night he read as well as he had ever read in his life. At the end there was such a scene as even he had never experienced. They cheered him again and again. He took several "calls" before he could make up his mind to say the few words of farewell that he had prepared. To Dolby it seemed that he was endeavoring to postpone those few words to the last possible moment. Then, while the cheering was louder than ever, they saw that he had returned to his reading-table. Immediately there was silence, and looking up he bade them farewell.

"It would be worse than idle," he told them, "for it would be hypocritical and unfeeling, if I were to disguise that I close this episode in my life with feelings of very considerable pain. For some fifteen years, in this hall and in many kindred places, I have had the honor of presenting my own cherished ideas before you for your recognition, and, in closely observing your reception of them, have enjoyed an amount of artistic delight and instruction which, perhaps, is given to few men to know.

"In this task, and in every other I have ever undertaken, as a faithful servant of the public, always imbued with a sense of duty to them, and always striving to do his best, I have been uniformly cheered by the readiest response, the most generous sympathy, and the most stimulating support. Nevertheless, I have thought it well, at the full flood-tide of your favor, to retire upon those older associations between us, which date from much further back than these, and henceforth to devote myself exclusively to the art that first brought us together.

"Ladies and gentlemen, in but two short weeks from this time I hope that you may enter, in your own homes, on a new series of readings, at which my assistance will be indispensable; but from these garish lights I vanish now forevermore, with a heartfelt, grateful, respectful, and affectionate farewell."

He turned away to hide the tears that were running down his cheeks, and walked slowly off, but the cheers had returned and would not stop. He was obliged to show himself once again. There was a last frantic roar of applause. Dickens looked round the hall for the last time, kissed his hand to his audience, and was gone.

[4]

There is little more to be told.

He had given his readings, and they were to kill him. Yet there were still a few functions to attend, and still a little work to be done. The first number of "Edwin Drood" appeared at the end of the month, and in a little while fifty thousand copies had been sold. A few days before its appearance Dickens had met the queen. Arthur Helps had told her about some photographs of the American Civil War which Dickens possessed, and she had expressed a desire to see them. They were forwarded to her, and she invited their owner to receive her thanks in person. He went to the palace, and they talked for more than an hour. She gave him a copy of her Highland journal and begged for a complete set of his works. He promised to send her a set specially bound.

Then a day or two later he received her command to attend the next levee, and did so; and this fact, combined with the news that he had breakfasted with Gladstone, then prime minister, gave rise to rumors that he was about to receive some title. But it does not seem that he was offered any honor, and Forster was probably right in supposing that had any such title been suggested it would have been refused.

There were various little parties in his London house and a few public dinners. He spoke for the last time in public at the Royal Academy banquet, when he paid a tribute to his old friend Maclise, who had recently died; but three days later his foot was bad, and he was unable to move from his room. He had received an invitation for himself and his daughter to a ball at Buckingham Palace, but was unable to go, and it was only with the greatest difficulty that he managed to dine, a few nights later, at Lord Houghton's house to meet the Prince of Wales.

Yet even at this time he could not resist the temptation to conduct the rehearsals of some private theatricals in Kensington in which both his daughters were appearing. He went down to Gad's Hill at the end of the month, but returned for the performance on June 2, playing prompter and manager as he had long ago, lame and not free from pain, but thoroughly enjoying himself behind the scenes.

Then for the last time he returned to Gad's Hill, and set to work on his novel. On Monday, June 6, he was out with his dogs. The next day he was driven to Cobham Wood and sent the carriage home to take his favorite walk. In the evening he helped his sister-in-law to put up some Chinese lanterns in the new conservatory that had just been built. On the Wednesday he was working all day in the chalet.

There was only Georgina Hogarth in the house at the time. They lunched together, and, rather to her surprise, he returned to his work in the afternoon. Dinner had been ordered for six o'clock, and they had begun their meal when she noticed "a singular expression of trouble and pain" on his face. He confessed that he had been very ill for an hour, but wished the dinner to go on. A few moments later he was rambling on in a curious disconnected way. Finally, he announced his intention of going immediately to London, rose from his chair, swayed, and would have fallen heavily to the floor but for his sister-in-law. "On the ground," he muttered, as she tried to get him onto a sofa, and they were the last words he spoke.

It was ten minutes past six when he became unconscious, and for exactly twenty-four hours he continued to breathe. Beard arrived that night, but there was nothing to be done. The children were summoned, and the two daughters and Charley arrived in time to hear the dreadful stertorous breaths. They watched and waited, and on that Thursday afternoon, June 9, 1870, at ten minutes past six, they saw him shudder and give a deep sigh. A single tear rolled down his cheek, and all was over.

He had asked to be buried, privately and without trappings, in an old graveyard beneath the shadow of

Rochester Castle, but this could not be, for burials there were no longer permitted. It was therefore suggested that he might be laid to rest in the cathedral itself, and a position had actually been chosen, when the England who had loved him and been terribly shocked at his death raised her voice. There was only one place to which he must be taken.

A funeral in Westminster Abbey suggests great pomp and ceremony, and Dean Stanley was criticized for allowing Dickens to be "secretly" buried. But of course he was right. The dead man had left instructions that could not be disobeyed. And so early one morning three closed carriages drove into Dean's Yard. Thirteen people walked slowly into the empty abbey. Most of them were members of the family, but Beard was there and Wilkie Collins, and a burly man in a black frock coat fastened tightly about him, who could not trust himself to speak.

THE END

MIDNIGHT ALARM OF THE YOUNG LADIES SEMINARY
MR. GUPPY ENTERTAINS HIS FRIENDS
OLIVER TWIST ASKS FOR MORE
NICHOLAS NICKLEBY AS TUTOR IN THE KENWIGS FAMILY